The Resour

A Teacher's Tool Kit

**Developed by Bryan Strong
and
Barbara W. Sayad
California State University, Monterey Bay**

to Accompany

HUMAN SEXUALITY

**by Bryan Strong, Christine DeVault, and Barbara W. Sayad
Third Edition**

Mayfield Publishing Company
Mountain View, California
London • Toronto

International Standard Book Number 0-7674-1045-9

Manufactured in the United States of America

10 9 8 7 6 5 4 3 2 1

Mayfield Publishing Company
1280 Villa Street
Mountain View, California 94041
(415) 960-3222

PREFACE

Our teacher's tool kit for *Human Sexuality* consists of two separate volumes: *The Resource Book: A Teacher's Tool Kit to Accompany Human Sexuality* and an extensive book of examination questions. We developed the concept of *The Resource Book* as a result of our frustration in using instructor's manuals. We found that most of the material in instructor's manuals did not help us significantly in either developing a new course or teaching an ongoing one.

In developing *The Resource Book: A Teacher's Tool Kit,* we asked ourselves a basic question: What kind of teaching support material would we like to have? The answer we came up with was the metaphor of a tool kit. We think of *The Resource Book* as a "tool kit" that contains various tools that we, as teachers, can easily use to "build" or "remodel" a human sexuality course. We have carefully organized the tool kit to make it easy for you to find the right tool for whatever particular task is at hand. For example, you can find background material for a particular lecture, lead a discussion section, or enhance a lecture with transparency masters. We have cross-referenced material between the *Study Guide* and *The Resource Book,* both of which reinforce concepts from the textbook.

Part I of *The Resource Book* consists of several sections of general teaching materials, ideas, and resources. We believe you should review the material in this part before the course begins because it presents background information and essays on teaching, course preparation ideas, bibliographies, a semester-long assignment on gender identity, and essays that help to explain and support the rationale of the text.

Part II consists of support material for each individual chapter. A chapter outline, learning objectives, general discussion questions and activities, and specific discussion questions relating to popular culture and to health concerns are provided for each chapter. In addition, each chapter contains student handouts and/or worksheets, transparency masters, and a list of films or videos. Finally, each chapter contains a short bibliography that may be useful in preparing lectures on topics covered in the chapter.

For ease of use, the test bank, by Roy O. Darby III, University of South Carolina-Beaufort, has been produced in a separate volume. The questions in the printed test bank are identical to those found in the Microtest III computerized test bank from Chariot Software Group. Test questions can be edited and new questions added; the test bank is available in Windows and Macintosh versions.

We want to remind adopters that in addition to *The Resource Book* and the printed and computerized test bank, adopters can also receive videos, including the *Mayfield Relationships and Intimacy Videotape.* This video comprises thirteen 10- to 15-minute video segments on subjects such as gender roles, the effect of AIDS on women, and date rape (see page 20 of this book for recommendations of video segments that apply to chapters in the text). You may also choose to make the *Study Guide,* which is cross-referenced in this edition, available to students. A new resource for students is the *Mayfield Quick View Guide to the Internet for Students of Intimate Relationships, Sexuality, and Marriage and the Family.* This short text introduces students to the Internet and provides them with extensive resources for using the Internet in the study of human sexuality. The guide can be shrinkwrapped with *Human Sexuality* at no additional cost to the student.

We thank Julie Rogers for assisting us with this resource guide. Special thanks go to James Barbour for allowing us to reprint his essay on human sexuality discussion groups and to Mark Temple for his thoughts and input on ethics.

Mayfield Publishing will be happy to assist you in any way possible. If you have any questions or need teaching support material, do not hesitate to call your Mayfield representative, or call the publisher at 800-433-1279. You can also contact Mayfield at http://www.mayfieldpub.com.

CONTENTS

PART II • INDIVIDUAL CHAPTER RESOURCES FOR HUMAN SEXUALITY

Note: For each chapter of the textbook, the following materials are included:
    Chapter Outline
    Learning Objectives
    Discussion Questions
    Activities
    Sex and Popular Culture Discussion and Activities
    Health Considerations Discussion and Activities
    Support Material: Films and videos, bibliography,
    student worksheets, student handouts, and
    transparency masters

PART I

CONCEPTS AND STRATEGIES FOR TEACHING HUMAN SEXUALITY

CONCEPTS AND STRATEGIES FOR TEACHING

Who Your Students Are

Both our own experience and research indicate that students who take a human sexuality course tend to be slightly more liberal in their sexual attitudes than the general student population. Women generally outnumber men, sometimes as much as a 2:1 ratio. This gender imbalance may reflect women's greater willingness to acknowledge that they "don't know it all" about sexuality; it may also reflect gender imbalances in majors, especially in health and psychology, which tend to enroll more women than men. Members of different ethnic groups are often underrepresented.

The age mix of students enrolled in the class may differ from college to college, but the majority of students tend to be in young adulthood, reflecting their concern with developmental issues revolving around sexuality.

Students come to the class with different levels of sexual experience; many are sexually inexperienced, especially younger students. They also have their own unique sexual histories; sometimes these histories include sexual abuse or aggression. They are often dealing with sexual issues in their dating or cohabiting relationships.

Unlearning Myths and Stereotypes

More than in other classes, your students enter the course with an enormous amount of pre-learning. If this were a basic accounting, astrophysics, or foreign language class, your students would come to the first class with few opinions, preconceptions, myths, stereotypes, and taboos. But when they enter a human sexuality class, they bring with them a lifetime of learning, a mixture of genuine knowledge, values, prejudice, beliefs, and stereotypes.

In order to "unlearn," students must become aware of what they have unconsciously learned throughout their lives. One of the most important sources of their learning is popular culture. To make them aware of the influence of popular culture, we begin the textbook in the first chapter with a section on the media, especially TV and movies. In Chapter 2, we introduce the study of sexuality with a discussion of so-called "sex experts," the media, and how to evaluate pop psychology. We then move into critical thinking skills, which give students the tools for evaluating what they read and hear about sexuality.

Your Role as a Teacher

Teaching Goals. If this is the first time you've taught human sexuality—or even if you're a veteran—it is valuable to set aside time to think about what you want your students to learn from your course. If you have your teaching goals clearly in mind, you will be able to give your course a clear and consistent structure that will facilitate student learning.

Some of the questions to ask include: What is the core knowledge you wish to transmit? Do you want to encourage attitudinal and behavioral changes? If so, what are they? Are decision-making skills important to you? Interpersonal skills, such as communication? Sexual and relationship satisfaction? What about changing health behaviors, such as unsafe sex practices?

Modeling. One of the most important teaching tools is yourself—you act as a model for students in dealing with human sexuality. How comfortable you feel with the material, your ability to be open, the respect and empathy you show your students are all important to setting your classroom environment. Let students know about your areas of expertise. And don't be afraid to admit gaps in knowledge. Your own willingness to learn is a valuable lesson for students.

Creating a Supportive Classroom Atmosphere

Because student learning is multidimensional—cognitive, attitudinal, and behavioral—creating a supportive class atmosphere that encourages the exchange of experiences, ideas, and viewpoints is especially important. It is important to encourage diverse ideas and to show empathy and respect. You can help create a supportive environment by your style of teaching and how you respond to your students' emotional reactions to the course material. The Self-Assessment features in the Study Guide and many of the discussion questions and exercises in *The Resource Book* will help facilitate classroom interactions.

In creating a liberating environment in which diversity is embraced and contradictions are explored, it is important that students feel safe, respected, and free to address the many complex subjects and feelings that may arise as a result of their readings and discussions. In order to facilitate this, you may introduce the following ground rules (thanks to Mark Temple for their use):

- Any question is appropriate.

- People should respect diversity in opinions and ideas.

- Speak from personal experience; however, avoid generalizations.

- Take turns speaking and listening (especially the latter).

- Be open to growth and change.

- Sincerely attempt to understand other attitudes, beliefs, opinions, and behaviors.

In the early class sessions, it is important for students to feel at ease in using a sexual vocabulary. Many have probably never used such words as "sexual intercourse," "masturbation," "cunnilingus," and so on in a class or other public setting. In Chapter 1 activities, we suggest ways to raise student comfort level. You may want to address the issue of vocabulary in an ongoing manner in your first few class sessions and periodically throughout the course.

Keep an ongoing assessment of class dynamics. What teaching techniques seem to be especially effective? Attention span often diminishes after 10–15 minutes, so alternate your teaching techniques several times. After 15 minutes of lecturing, open up the subject for discussion, then return to lecturing, then break the lecture with writing, self-assessments, video excerpts, slides, or transparencies, and so on. If the class is long, students may need a break to get up and stretch.

Periodically you might ask students for feedback about what they are learning, what they would like to learn, the classroom environment, and so on. One way of doing this is asking students to anonymously write feedback and suggestions on 4x6 cards at the end of class.

The larger the class, the greater the challenge in creating a supportive atmosphere. In large classes, small discussion groups can foster an open learning environment. Teaching assistants or undergraduates can lead discussion groups. We have found that students generally prefer groups led by undergraduates because they perceive such groups as less hierarchical and more personal. (For articles on undergraduate-led discussion groups, see Barbour 1989a & 1989b and Sprecher & Pocs, 1987).

Teaching Controversial Material

By its very nature, human sexuality is controversial. Homosexuality, abortion, and sexually oriented material tend to be the most controversial because they touch on deep personal feelings and religious beliefs.

We believe that the most effective way of teaching such controversial subjects is by (1) presenting objective, scientific data and (2) utilizing critical thinking skills, and (3) especially in public institutions, limiting the time spent in discussions relating to religion and politics.

We have tried to present empirical evidence when dealing with issues of homosexuality, abortion, and sexually oriented material. Within the textbook, students will find solid research on these topics. Some may nevertheless be disturbed by these findings. You may find it valuable to discuss the distinction between social science and religion. Social science seeks to describe behavior; religion seeks to morally evaluate behavior. Social science is based on reason and empiricism; religion is based on revelation and authority. The two have different goals and ways of knowing. As a social science or health instructor, your goal is to describe behavior based on empirical research.

Controversial topics also offer the instructor an opportunity to reinforce critical thinking skills (discussed in Chapter 2). Discussions in this area can become heated; encourage students to step back and critically examine their statements and beliefs. Are they making objective statements or value judgments? What are their sources? Are they expressing opinions or facts? What evidence do they have to support their assertions?

It is also important to encourage students to respect diversity of beliefs and opinions. Controversial questions are rarely resolved in class.

GETTING STARTED WITH THE COURSE

Setting the Learning Environment. A key element in the early class meetings is to set a positive learning environment. Some considerations include: What are the parameters of legitimate discussion? How are moral/ethical disagreements to be handled? What is acceptable classroom vocabulary? Periodically you might want to monitor the class environment by asking students to anonymously write about class dynamics and to make suggestions for improvement.

Respect and Confidentiality. Because much class and group discussion may revolve around sensitive issues and events, it is important to discuss the issue of respecting individuals and maintaining confidentiality. Ask students how they would define "respect" and "confidentiality." Some possible guidelines might include: (1) Respect differences; (2) Ideas and opinions may be challenged, but individuals are to be respected; (3) What individuals reveal in class is confidential; (4) All students have the right not to participate; (5) The goal of the class is to understand, not to judge.

Discussion Groups. If you plan to have class discussion groups or sections, discuss how to run and participate in such groups. Ask students what makes a good discussion group, what kind of ground rules they would like, the type of questions they would like to discuss. James Barbour's essay "Group Discussions in Human Sexuality" later in *The Resource Book* offers useful guidelines and suggestions.

Computer Networking. The *Mayfield Quick View Guide to the Internet for Students of Intimate Relationships, Sexuality, and Marriage and the Family* will be available as an accompaniment to the text and *Study Guide*. This guide serves as both an introduction to the Internet for beginners as well as a listing of Internet resources on topics relevant to this course. If your campus has a computer network, you may be able to form a discussion group for your class. This can be a very valuable forum for students to discuss class issues. The group can be moderated or unmoderated. (The disadvantage of an unmoderated group is that occasionally discussions can become offensive or sexually explicit. If this is a concern, you may want to moderate the group.) Check with your computer center about how to set up such a discussion group.

Using the Textbook: The more familiar students become with the structure of their textbook, the better equipped they will be to fully utilize it. Briefly discuss the components of the textbook. The handout "Getting to Know Your Textbook: A Self-Guided Tour," found in the *Study Guide,* will give students a quick tour of the textbook and tips for studying.

GETTING TO KNOW YOUR STUDENTS: EXPLORING SEXUAL IDENTITY

Students are willing to reveal only so much about themselves and the issues with which they are dealing. Even the safest classroom environment leaves many critical issues, feelings, and problems unexpressed. This is particularly true for shy students.

An effective tool for letting students express these personal aspects, as well as allowing them to recognize and begin to deal with any confusion they may feel regarding mixed and conflicting messages about sexuality, is a writing assignment that explores the issues that have influenced their sexual identity and development. For many, this is the first attempt to understand the dynamics and complex situations that formed the foundation of their sexuality.

The assignment asks students to select four of seven factors—religion, family, education, peers, media, culture or ethnicity, or another area of their choice—and write about how these factors have influenced the development of their sexual and gender identity. They are also asked to examine the positive and negative impact of each factor and to describe constructive means by which they can help themselves develop a healthier sexual identity.

To provide students with a solid theoretical foundation, integrate major influential factors that shape sexuality into the course via the text, discussions, speakers, audiovisual presentations, the student workbook, and lectures. This enables students to see that others often share their histories, secrets, and concerns. We emphasize healthy and constructive methods for dealing with sexual issues so that students can begin to understand themselves and feel empowered to change what they wish. Often, it is not until students take the time to examine their behaviors that they begin to realize the connection of past traumas and events to current sexual behaviors, attitudes, and problems.

The sensitive and sometimes traumatic nature of this assignment creates challenges for the professor. It is important to explain to your students that dealing with past experiences may cause turmoil in their lives, and to give them the option of not doing this assignment. (An alternative such as a weekly response paper, book reviews, or a research paper may replace this assignment.) For students who choose this option, you must be prepared to offer feedback, confidentiality, support, and respect, and be able to refer students who are dealing with unresolved issues to counseling. Locating and assessing low-cost, professional resources before assigning this paper is helpful.

Grading the assignment is, at best, a difficult and time-consuming process. Unlike other written assignments, students are not penalized for incorrect spelling or grammar. Instead, we look for the ability of the student to meet the criteria of the assignment, the breadth of discussion given to each contributing factor, and the quality of insight they demonstrate in articulating ways they can deal with or change the quality of their lives. Overall, the high grades given to those who complete this assignment are a reflection of the amount of time and effort students give to fulfilling this assignment, as well as the level of success they achieve.

We suggest a five- to seven-page paper in which students are asked to address the impact of at least four contributing factors on their experiences and observations as a sexual being. Their essay should include their age, culture, the number and sex of children in their family, where they are in the birth order (oldest, youngest, etc.), and their parents' marital status. The conclusion should summarize key positive and negative experiences, and possible ways they could, should, or do cope with negative experiences to help themselves shape a more positive sexual identity. They should also be encouraged to give their essay an interesting title that reflects their key issues, challenges, or successes.

From the papers emerge insights about how the past has affected students' lives. Many students have discovered that it is no small task to break the patterns of silence and negativity, and to consciously work toward improving their attitudes and behaviors. We find that this personal exploration adds an important and meaningful dimension to the course.

A description of the assignment is on the next page, as well as in the *Study Guide*.

FORMATION OF YOUR SEXUAL
AND GENDER IDENTITY

This exercise is designed to help you explore the formation of your sexual and gender identity and your sexual personality, using your personal experiences to describe the psychological, emotional, cultural, religious, and social aspects of sexual identity formation. This will give you a chance to look at both conscious and subconscious behaviors and beliefs, and both the positive and negative experiences which have directly or indirectly influenced your personal sexual identity.

Please select and describe a minimum of four of the following areas:

- religious upbringing

- social/educational experiences and/or teachers

- peers or friends

- the media (music, TV, magazines, movies, etc.)

- parents and family (involvement, education, family life)

- cultural or ethnic background (including travel)

- other (see the instructor if there is another aspect you feel is important, such as past relationships)

Depending on how much exposure you have had to psychology, you may find it helpful to relate the following core issues in human beings' lives to the above areas:

- control/power and boundaries

- self-esteem

- feelings about rejection and abandonment

- grieving ungrieved losses

- resolving conflicts

- giving and receiving love or being intimate

Your essay should be five to seven pages in length, and should address the impact each of these factors has had on your experiences and observations. The essay should include your age, culture, the number and sex of children in your family, where you are in the birth order (oldest, youngest, etc.), and your parents' marital status. The conclusion should summarize key positive and negative experiences and possible constructive ways you can, should, or do cope with negative experiences to help shape a more positive sexual identity. Give your essay an interesting title that reflects your key issues, challenges, or successes.

ADDITIONAL TEACHING STRATEGIES

Anonymous Papers

If you feel as though your students are hesitant to reveal themselves and the issues with which they are dealing, an anonymous paper may be appropriate. Even the safest classroom environment sometimes leaves many critical issues, feelings, and problems unexpressed. This is particularly true for shy students.

An effective tool for letting students express these personal aspects is through the use of ungraded anonymous papers. These papers also permit you a glimpse inside student lives that are not otherwise accessible. (We often have found such papers moving as well as a reminder of how important sexuality is in students' lives.)

The method we use to preserve student anonymity is quite simple: Students turn in their papers with a cover page with their name on it. When they hand in their papers, we separate the cover page and paper and place the two in separate piles. We then record the student's name from the cover page.

There are several types of anonymous papers you can have your students write. We use both a weekly response paper and an end-of-course sexual autobiography. The weekly response paper can take several forms: It can be a specific assignment, such as their response to a particular topic, guest lecturer, film, and so on. Or the paper can be on any topic the student wishes, including his or her past experiences, relationships, family, the textbook, lectures, and so on.

The Student Journal

Student journals may be used for cognitive or affective goals. A student journal can either focus on (1) the process of critical inquiry or (2) increasing self-knowledge. These journals should be in separate spiral-bound notebooks or bound blank books. To assure confidentiality, we ask our students to identify themselves only by their student ID. (We record their grade or note they completed the assignment on a class list arranged by ID numbers only; later we transfer the grades to our alphabetical class list.)

Student journals focusing on critical inquiry involve the student in thinking about and applying the information and concepts to his or her personal life. The student keeps a journal in which she or he reflects upon and analyzes what is learned in the course. It should incorporate the student's own observations and experiences.

Student journals focusing on increasing self-knowledge involve students in reflecting upon their psychosexual development. Although the journal is personal, it is not a diary; it is more structured and depth-oriented. The instructor can give students a list of 10–15 topics to be explored, one topic per week. These topics can be tied to lecture topics or chapters in the textbook. A topical approach can ask the student to identify turning points in his or her sexuality, the status of current relationships, what he or she requires for good sex, communication issues, and so on.

Using Speakers, Films, Videos, and Transparencies

Guest speakers or panels are valuable resources that provide students with expert or firsthand knowledge. Some of the most powerful speakers in our human sexuality class include a student panel of gay men, lesbians, and bisexuals; a person (or group of people) with AIDS; a sex therapist; and the campus rape educator.

Well-chosen films and videos can provide information and insight for students. We have included an annotated list of films/videos and distributors. The videos we use in our course to discuss popular culture include "What Sex Am I?" on transsexuality and cross-dressing; "The Miracle of Life," Lennart Nilsson's film on conception; and excerpts from Woody Allen's "Everything You Ever Wanted to Know About Sex," "Thelma and Louise," Madonna's music video "Justify Your Love," and "Donahue" and "Geraldo."

Some instructors use sexually explicit films—either educational or erotic films—as a means of expanding students' knowledge. Students have a wide range of reactions to them, but if the films are well chosen, their response is generally positive. When explicit films are used, it is customary to advise students in advance and to give them the option of not viewing them. Students should not be penalized in any way if they choose not to view such films. It may also be advisable to check with your department chair before showing an explicit film to make sure that doing so does not violate any university policy and that you have his or her support.

Transparencies visually enable students to better comprehend material. We have included transparency masters within this *Resource Book* for use in a lecture format.

GROUP DISCUSSIONS IN HUMAN SEXUALITY

by James Barbour

An Introduction to Group Discussions

One of the most valuable and enjoyable components of our course is the weekly discussion group. I want to provide a more detailed description of what these groups are all about, with the hope that you will be able to increase the benefit you derive from this experience.

Let's begin by considering some of the things our students have said about groups.

- Groups are a great way to get to know other students, especially in a big class like this one.

- It's important to be able to talk about these topics in a less formal atmosphere.

- It was fun when we compared our childhood experiences. I never realized how much our parents didn't tell us!

- I discovered that there are a lot of other people who feel the same way I do about relationships.

- I learned a lot about myself.

- Our leader didn't have much planned, so our group was really a waste of time.

- My discussion group took up a lot of time that I really didn't have.

- Some sessions were good; other times I didn't feel I got anything out of it at all.

- I gained a lot of respect for other people's ideas and attitudes.

- Sometimes when I was tired, I just didn't feel like getting involved at all.

It should be clear from this brief sample of reactions that feelings about discussion groups vary widely. Our class surveys, however, indicate that groups are seen to be highly beneficial by most students. What factors seem to contribute to a valuable group experience?

GOOD GROUPS—WHY THEY WORK

Groups that function smoothly and effectively carry on three key activities: they have goals and they accomplish them; they maintain themselves; and they develop and change to become more effective. To be an effective group member, it is important that you recognize from the beginning that each participant bears an equal responsibility for the group's success. Good groups aren't good because one person makes them that way, but rather because everyone makes them that way. Let's expand on each of these core group functions in more detail.

Group Goals

A group goal is simply a condition that the group wants to attain that is sufficiently important to motivate the group to achieve it. Our groups have two very broad goals: first, for each group member to try to establish and develop a relationship of some closeness with each of the other group members; and second, to allow participants to develop and practice skills essential to improved human relationships. These two goals seem very basic to me. They serve to provide the underlying foundation for anything that the group decides to do.

Effective Communication

Members of effective groups are able to communicate their ideas and feelings clearly. This sounds easy, but many students haven't had a lot of experience with groups, and they sometimes find it difficult to put their ideas into words. This is especially true when they want to express a feeling. There is often some distance between the act of identifying a feeling and being able to express this feeling to others. But not to try means that the others in the group will not be able to benefit from the resource that is you.

Participation and Leadership

In effective groups, everyone participates. This means that everyone talks, and that everyone is listened to. It means that as the group experiences various leadership needs, group members are willing to take on those functions naturally and willingly. Many groups find that as they begin to get under way, certain members seem to do most of the talking. Others say very little or nothing at all. Our goal is to have all members participating actively. This means that the big talkers may have to talk less (and perhaps put their verbal skills to use in helping the group) and that small talkers may need to talk more.

Sub-Grouping and Quiet Members

There is a popular myth that says it is all right for a person to be silent if he or she wants to because one can still learn a lot. Part of this myth is true. It is true that you can sit silently in a group for ten weeks and learn something. But you are not likely to grow interpersonally during that time because it is impossible to experience interpersonal growth without interpersonal exchange. And there is a further problem with being silent. It is very difficult for other group members to know how to react to someone who doesn't say anything. Group members may wonder whether the person's silence means he or she is not interested in getting involved, or disapproves of what is going on in the group, or is simply shy and needs to be encouraged to participate more actively.

We certainly acknowledge that some people are quieter than others and don't feel totally comfortable interacting in a group. Many people need some warm-up time before they can talk comfortably in their group. As group members come to trust one another, it makes it easier for all of them to contribute actively. Especially during the first half of the semester, we structure groups to spend a portion of each session working in smaller clusters of two or three persons, which we call sub-grouping. Some students wonder how ten people can become a group if they don't spend all their time sitting around in a circle as a whole group. But we have learned that breaking groups down into these smaller units accomplishes a number of important tasks needed for an effective group. Here are some of the reasons our groups often spend time in sub-groups.

- Working in pairs gives students a chance to learn quickly a great deal about another member and to begin forming a relationship of substance.

- The amount of talking that goes on in sub-groups is many times greater than when the group works together as a whole. Many students find it easier to talk with one or two others. As participants develop more trusting feelings about one another through working in sub-groups, it allows them to carry over these trusting feelings to the whole group.

- Individuals who know that they are on the quiet side feel more comfortable when sharing ideas and feelings. Getting to know individuals in this way helps the more verbal participants encourage and facilitate open discussion in the large group.

A DISTRIBUTED FUNCTIONS MODEL OF GROUP LEADERSHIP

There are a few aspects of leadership that are useful to understand as you begin working with your group. Of the several well-known approaches to leadership, we subscribe to the one that is called distributed functions. This concept of leadership says that all effective groups require a number of functions to be performed, and that to work best, the functions must be distributed among all the members. These functions can be divided into two categories: Task Functions and Maintenance Functions.

Task Functions

Task functions include behaviors that help the group accomplish its tasks (surprise!) and include things like the following:

- Giving information and opinions, providing facts and ideas.

- Seeking information, opinions, facts, ideas, or feelings from other groups.

- Proposing goals or tasks that get the group started. "Well, suppose we make a list of all the lines we've heard, and see what they have in common."

- Summarizing related information or helping to restate major points.

- Diagnosing the difficulties the group may be having, perhaps by pointing out apparent blocks preventing it from accomplishing its goal.

Maintenance Functions

Maintenance functions are those which help the group maintain its interpersonal cohesiveness. Maintenance functions involve the processes within the group and include things like these:

- Encouraging participation, recognizing contributions, demonstrating acceptance and openness to the ideas of others.

- Helping members analyze and reconcile their differences.

- Relieving tension by getting the group to laugh, suggesting breaks, and making the group fun.

- Watching the process in which the group is working and suggesting ways to improve its effectiveness.

- Building trust by being accepting and open and by reinforcing risk taking by other participants.

Decision Making

If they are to function smoothly, groups need to be able to make decisions efficiently and to the satisfaction of all members. One of the best ways to do this is by consensus, which means that everyone agrees. Coming to consensus does not mean that everyone gets exactly what they want, but rather that everyone fully accepts what the group decides. Decision making by consensus promotes commitment to the group because it is a process whose only goal is agreement by all.

Conflicts of Ideas

Another myth about groups is that they should have no conflict. Quite the contrary is true. Conflicts among those with opposing ideas and opinions should not be discouraged, because they intensify the involvement of the group. This does not mean that people should be fighting with each other, but rather that it is important for people with opposing views to debate these views openly and forcefully with one another. Honest, open debate does not discourage or harm relationships; it enhances them. Groups are a way for participants to practice such skills in a supportive and trusting environment.

Interpersonal Effectiveness

Many skills are involved in becoming interpersonally competent—skills like empathetic listening, expressing feelings, the ability to deal with anger, showing concern and respect for others, conveying ideas concretely, expressing warmth, being genuine, being able to confront others, and self-disclosure. Since individual group members possess varying degrees of these skills, it becomes a task of the group to help every member identify and improve on weaker areas.

THE GROUP FACILITATOR

Each discussion group is facilitated by a student who has taken the Human Relationships and Sexuality course. Most of them are currently enrolled in another course, Facilitating Human Sexuality Discussion Groups, or have taken this course in a previous semester. Facilitators' jobs are difficult because at the same time they are learning about groups they are also responsible for facilitating one.

Facilitators have a number of roles to fulfill. They are responsible for planning, facilitating, and evaluating each group session. They attend a weekend retreat, evaluate projects written by students in the sexuality course, and write numerous reports. They provide an important communication link between me and you, since they are working with me on a more individualized basis.

It is not unusual for some group participants to assume that it is the facilitator's responsibility to make sure the group experience is a satisfying one. These are the same individuals who come away from the experience feeling that they got nothing out of it, or that it was a waste of their time. It is important at the outset to understand that the facilitator is not responsible for making your group experience a satisfying one for you. You are. The extent to which you benefit from the group depends on the extent of your own personal involvement as well as the involvement of each other group member. This does not mean that your facilitator will not work very hard to contribute to the group's effectiveness. He or she will spend a good bit of time outside of each session to see that this happens. But it does mean that if you sit back with the expectation that the facilitator is going to make things happen, you will be very disappointed with the outcome.

The key point here is that each group participant brings some special abilities, ideas, insights, and skills to a group, and it is the entire group's responsibility to see that each of these contributions is utilized to its fullest. The facilitator is learning about and expanding on a set of specific skills related to facilitating. Facilitators use their specialized skills to help a group move effectively toward its goals. The emphasis in the last sentence is on the word *help*. That's the facilitator's special contribution. Each participant is equally responsible to make his or her own contributions.

GROUP MEETING GUIDELINES

Your group leader is responsible for conducting meetings according to the following guidelines. Failure to follow these guidelines is a violation of the contract signed by the leader, and as a group participant you can help avoid this possibility by being supportive of the guidelines.

1. Meetings are to be held on the scheduled day and at the scheduled time only. If for some reason a meeting needs to be changed, the leader must consult with me for approval. Meetings are to be held regardless of the number of participants who show up, and may not be canceled or rescheduled because of exams, paper deadlines, or other reasons except the leader's illness. If the leader is unable to conduct a meeting because of illness, he or she must notify me and the group participants.

2. Meeting plans are to be followed as written, with no changes, deletions, or additions. Double meetings (in which two sessions are conducted back-to-back) are not permitted.

3. The use of drugs and alcohol is strictly forbidden at all group meetings. Under no circumstances are meetings to be conducted in bars or restaurants.

4. Falsifying reports for attendance, post-meeting summaries, and journals will result in the filing of academic dishonesty charges against the leader.

(Reprinted by permission of the author.)

A BIBLIOGRAPHY FOR TEACHING
HUMAN SEXUALITY

Many of the "how to" manuals that help to teach human sexuality appear to be the cumulation of the author's experience, personality, and materials and ideas collected over the years. Though *The Resource Book* incorporates these elements, it also adds the component of research. When combined, these elements provide a framework which we hope you find helpful in planning your course.

D'Augelli, Anthony. "Teaching Lesbian/Gay Development: From Oppression to Exceptionality." *Journal of Homosexuality,* 1992, 22, 213–227.

Barbour, J. R. "A Course in Facilitating Human Sexuality Discussion Groups." *Journal of Sex Education and Therapy,* 1989a, 15, 114–120.

_____. "Teaching a Course in Human Relationships and Sexuality: A Model for Personalizing Large Group Instruction." *Family Relations,* 1989b, 38, 142–148.

Fitzpatrick, Jean Grasso. "Teaching Values." *Parents,* 1995, 70(6) 34–38.

Levine, M. P., and P. Rust. *The Sociology of Sexuality and Homosexuality—Syllabi and Teaching Materials.* Washington, D. C.: American Sociological Association, 1990.

Rosen, Ellen, and Linda Petty. "Teaching Human Sexuality Using Guided Design." *Journal of Sex Education and Therapy,* 1989, 15, 121–126.

Ross, Susan. "Why It's So Hard to Talk About Sex." *US Catholic,* 1995, 60(2), 16–23.

Sollie, Donna, and Julie Kaetz. "Teaching University Level Family Studies Courses." *Family Relations,* 1992, 41, 18–24.

Sprecher, Susan, and O. Pocs. "Teaching Sexuality: Two Techniques for Personalizing the Large Class." *Teaching Sociology,* 1987, 15, 268–272.

Strouse, Jeremiah S., Laurice A. Krajewski, and Shannon M. Gilin. "Utilizing Undergraduate Students as Peer Discussion Facilitators in Human Sexuality Classes." *Journal of Sex Education & Therapy,* 1990, 16(4), 227–235.

Walker-Hirsch, Leslie, and Marilyn P. Champagne. "Circles Revisited: Ten Years Later." Special Issue: Sexuality and Developmental Disability." *Sexuality & Disability,* 1991, 9(2),143–148.

Weis, David, et al. "Individual Changes in Sexual Attitudes and Behavior within College-Level Human Sexuality Courses." *Journal of Sex Research,* 1992, 39, 43–59.

Wells, Joel W. "What Makes a Difference? Various Teaching Strategies to Reduce Homophobia in University Students." *Annals of Sex Research,* 1991, 4(3–4), 229–238.

Whately, Marianne. "Images of Gays and Lesbians in Sexuality and Health Textbooks." *Journal of Homosexuality,* 1992, 22, 197–211.

A BASIC BIBLIOGRAPHY
FOR LECTURE PREPARATION

The books listed below were selected for their usefulness in preparing lectures on human sexuality. Don't be overwhelmed by this list. It is not a reading list of books every human sexuality instructor is supposed to know; it is not even representative. Rather, it is a list of books we think might be helpful in preparing lectures on various topics, especially if you are unfamiliar with a topic. At the end of the book list, you will find a list of journals that may contain articles of interest to you.

At the end of each chapter in the textbook you will also find an annotated list of relevant books. In addition, the individual chapter material in Part II contains a more detailed list of references for each chapter.

BOOKS

Abramson, Paul R., and Steven Pinkerton (eds.). *Sexual Nature, Sexual Culture.* Chicago: University of Chicago Press, 1995. A collection of scholarly essays examining the contributions of nature and nurture to the development of human sexuality.

Arndt, William B., Jr. *Gender Disorders and the Paraphilias.* Madison, CT: International Universities Press, Inc., 1991. A comprehensive look at transvestism, transsexuality, and the paraphilias.

Barbach, Lonnie. *For Each Other: Sharing Sexual Intimacy.* New York: New American Library, 1984. One of the most widely read books on female sexuality by a popular sex therapist.

Blumstein, Philip, and Pepper Schwartz. *American Couples: Money, Work, Sex.* New York: Pocket Books, 1985. An important study that integrates heterosexual, gay, and lesbian sexuality into a seamless work.

Boston Lesbian Psychologies Collective. *Lesbian Psychologies.* Urbana, IL: University of Illinois Press, 1988. Outstanding collection of essays on lesbian sexuality and relationships.

Boston Women's Health Book Collective. *The New Our Bodies Our Selves for the New Century.* New York: Touchstone, 1998. New edition of the landmark work on female sexuality and health.

Brandt, Allan M. *No Magic Bullet: A Social History of Venereal Disease in the United States Since 1880.* New York: Oxford University Press, 1985. The best history available of the social and political aspects of sexually transmitted diseases.

Bullough, Vern L. *Sexual Variance.* Chicago: University of Chicago Press, 1976. A comprehensive history of the changing Western and Mideastern attitudes toward sexuality, especially in terms of what is defined as "sinful" or "abnormal."

Bullough, Vern L., and Bonnie Bullough. *Human Sexuality: An Encyclopedia.* New York: Garland Publishing Co., 1994. A broad-based text exploring a wide variety of sexual topics.

Buss, David. *The Evolution of Desire: Strategies of Human Mating.* New York: Basic Books, 1994. This sociobiological approach uses animal reproductive behavior to understand human sexual behavior.

Chapple, Steve, and David Talbot. *Burning Desires: Sex in America.* New York: Doubleday, 1989. An informative, entertaining tour of contemporary American sexuality by two journalists.

Davis, Clive M., William L. Yarber, and Sandra Davis (eds.). *Sexuality-Related Measures: A Compendium.* Lake Mills, Iowa, 1988. Published by the authors. (To order, contact Clive Davis, Department of Psychology, Syracuse University, Syracuse, NY 13244.) More than 270 pages of testing instruments reproduced with commentary.

Davis, Murray. *Smut: Erotic Reality/Obscene Ideology.* Chicago: University of Chicago Press, 1985. A powerful sociological examination of "pornography."

DeCecco, John (ed.). *Sex, Cells, and Same-Sex Desire: The Biology of Sexual Preference.* Binghamton, WA: Harrington Park Press, 1995.

Delacoste, Frederique, and Priscilla Alexander. (eds.). *Sex Work: Writings by Women in the Sex Industry.* Pittsburgh, PA: Cleis Press, 1991. A unique perspective on sexually oriented material, prostitution, and erotic dancing.

D'Emilio, John, and Estelle Freedman. *Intimate Matters* (2nd ed.). Chicago: University of Chicago Press, 1996. The most complete scholarly history of American sexuality to date.

Dines, Gail, and Jean Humes (eds.). *Gender, Race and Class in the Media*. Thousand Oaks, CA: Sage Publications, 1994. An excellent introduction to popular culture and the media.

Division for Church in Society of the Evangelical Lutheran Church in America. *Human Sexuality and the Christian Faith: A Study for the Church's Reflection and Deliberation*. Minneapolis, MN: ELCA, 1991. A valuable 55-page document that evenhandedly discusses current biblical controversies centering around the Bible and human sexuality. Permission is granted by ELCA to reproduce it in whole or in part if each copy displays the copyright. (Available for $1 from ELCA Distribution Service, 426 South Fifth Street, Minneapolis, MN 55440; telephone: 1-800-328-4648).

Donnerstein, Edward, et al (eds.). *The Question of Pornography*. New York: Free Press, 1987. A review of the scientific research on sexually oriented material, its effects, and the legal issues involved.

Faderman, Lilian. *Odd Girls and Twilight Lovers: A History of Lesbian Life in Twentieth-Century America*. New York: Penguin, 1991. A well-written social history of being lesbian in America.

Foucault, Michel. *The History of Sexuality: An Introduction*. New York: Vintage Books, 1980 (paperback). One of the most intellectually influential books on sexuality in the last twenty-five years, whether or not one agrees with the author.

Francoeur, Robert T. (ed.). *Taking Sides: Clashing Views on Controversial Issues in Human Sexuality* (5th ed.). Madison, WI: Dushkin Publishing Company, 1996. Point-counterpoint discussions that help readers clarify their values.

Gagnon, John, and William Simon. *Sexual Conduct: The Social Sources of Human Sexuality*. Chicago: Aldine Publishing Co., 1973. The most important statement of the social interactionist approach to human sexuality.

Garber, Marjorie. *Vested Interests: Cross-Dressing and Cultural Anxiety*. New York: Routledge, 1991. A provocative study of the role of cross-dressing in contemporary culture. Cross-dressers, the author argues, call attention to cultural inconsistencies about being male and female in our society.

Geer, James, and William O'Donohue (eds.). *Theories of Human Sexuality*. New York: Plenum Press, 1987. A collection of essays briefly describing various theories of human sexuality.

Gordon, Linda. *Woman's Body, Woman's Right: A Social History of Birth Control in America*. New York: Penguin, 1977 (paperback). A well-written, sometimes surprising history of birth control.

Gregor, Thomas. *Anxious Pleasures: The Sexual Lives of an Amazonian People*. Chicago: University of Chicago Press, 1985. An exceptional look at the sexual behavior, beliefs, and mores of the Mehinaku. A one-hour documentary, "We Are the Mehinaku," is also available.

Groth, Nicholas. *Men Who Rape: The Psychology of the Offender*. New York: Plenum Books, 1979. A leading rape researcher explores background and psychological dynamics of stranger rapists.

Gullotta, Thomas, Gerald Adams, and Raymond Montemayor. *Adolescent Sexuality*. Newbury Park, CA: Sage Publications, 1992. A concise overview of adolescent sexuality studies.

Hasbany, Richard (ed.). *Homosexuality and Religion*. New York: Haworth Press, 1990. An examination of recent Christian and Jewish positions on homosexuality as well as current biblical and theological scholarship.

Hatcher, Robert, et al. *Contraceptive Technology*. New York: Irvington Publishers, 1993 (paperback; revised regularly). The most comprehensive and technically reliable book on developments in contraceptive technology.

Heiman, Julia, and Joseph LoPiccolo. *Becoming Orgasmic: A Sexual Growth Program for Women*. Englewood Cliffs, NJ: Prentice-Hall, NJ: 1989. A widely used program for developing sexual responsiveness.

Heins, Marjorie. *Sex, Sin, and Blasphemy: A Guide to America's Censorship Wars*. New York: New Press, 1993. An overview of current censorship battles in film, popular music, and the arts by the director of the ACLU Art Censorship Project.

Holmes, King, et al. *Sexually Transmitted Diseases* (3rd ed.). New York: McGraw-Hill, 1998. The definitive reference work on sexually transmitted diseases (including HIV/AIDS) by leading researchers in the United States and Europe.

Hunter, James Davison. *Culture Wars: The Struggle to Define America*. New York: Basic Books, 1991. Background on the conflict over moral values between liberals and the religious right that influence, among other things, the debate about abortion, homosexuality, and sex education.

Irvine, Janice. *Disorders of Desire: Sex and Gender in Modern American Sexology*. Philadelphia: Temple University Press, 1991. A critical examination of sexology, including the Kinsey studies, the work of William Masters and Virginia Johnson, sex therapy, and gender research, especially gay/lesbian sexuality and transsexuality; uses a feminist gender perspective.

Isensee, Rik. *Love Between Men: Enhancing Intimacy and Keeping Your Relationship Alive*. New York: Prentice-Hall Press, 1990. A best-selling self-help book for gay men.

Janus, Samuel, and Cynthia Janus. *The Janus Report*. New York: John Wiley & Sons, 1993. A nationwide representative study of the sexual behavior of 2700 Americans that contains much valuable information about contemporary sexuality.

Jones, James. *Bad Blood: The Tuskegee Syphilis Experiment—A Tragedy of Race and Medicine*. Rev. ed. New York: Free Press, 1993. A chilling account of the infamous 40-year Public Health Service experiment that used African Americans as guinea pigs. The distrust it engendered of health agencies continues to be a major factor in the response of African Americans to AIDS.

Journal of Social Issues 48:1 (1992). Special issue devoted to sexual aggression and rape.

Kitzinger, Sheila. *The Complete Book of Pregnancy and Childbirth*. New York: Knopf, 1996. A comprehensive, sensitive, and down-to-earth manual for those who are contemplating pregnancy or those who want to understand more about its physiological and psychological aspects.

Kroll, Ken, and Erica Levy Klein. *Enabling Romance: A Guide to Love, Sex, and Relationships for the Disabled*. Bethesda, MD: Woodbine House, 1995. Interviews with hundreds of men and women with disabilities discuss stereotypes, different ways of being sexual, use of sex toys, and strengthening relationships.

Laumann, Edward, John Gagnon, Robert Michael, and Steven Michaels. *The Social Organization of Sexuality*. Chicago: University of Chicago Press, 1994. A large-scale study of the sexual habits and practices of Americans.

Leiblum, Sandra, and Raymond Rosen (eds.). *Principles and Practice of Sex Therapy*. New York: Guilford Press, 1989. A collection of essays on various aspects of sex therapy designed for professionals.

Lehrman, Karen. *The Lipstick Proviso: Women, Sex and Power in the Real World*. New York: Anchor/Doubleday, 1997. An inspiring celebration of autonomy, beauty, and the true diversity that exists among women.

Lips, Hilary. *Sex and Gender* (3rd ed.). Mountain View, CA: Mayfield Publishing Co., 1997. An excellent introduction to gender and gender roles.

Lister, Larry (ed.). *Human Sexuality, Ethnoculture, and Social Culture*. New York: Haworth Press, 1987. Essay on sexuality and ethnicity, including African Americans, Mexican Americans, Puerto Ricans, and Japanese Americans.

Loulan, JoAnn. *Lesbian Sex*. San Francisco: Spinsters Press, 1983. A thoughtful self-help book by the Dr. Ruth of lesbian sexuality.

Margulis, Lynn, and Dorion Sagan. *Mystery Dance: On the Evolution of Human Sexuality*. New York: Simon and Schuster, 1991. Literate, often charming essays from a sociobiological perspective.

McGoldrick, M., J. K. Pearce, and J. Giordano (eds.). *Ethnicity and Family Therapy*. New York: Guilford Press, 1982. A collection of essays that provide excellent historical and family background material for America's diverse ethnic groups.

McKinney, Kathleen, and Susan Sprecher (eds.). *Human Sexuality: The Societal and Interpersonal Context*. New York: Ablex Publishing Company, 1989. Sociologically oriented essays on human sexuality.

———. *Sexuality in Close Relationships*. Hillsdale, NJ: Lawrence Earlbaum Associates, 1991. A collection of essays from the close relationships perspective.

Michael, Robert, John Gagnon, Edward Laumann, and Gina Kolata. *Sex in America: A Definitive Survey*. Boston: Little, Brown & Co., 1994. A summary of Laumann et al.'s large-scale survey of sexual practices for the general public.

Parker, Richard, and John Gagnon (eds). *Conceiving Sexuality: Approaches to Sex Research in a Postmodern World*. New York: Routledge, 1995.

Parrinder, Geoffrey. *Sex in the World's Religions*. New York: Oxford University Press, 1980. An overview of attitudes and beliefs of the major religions.

Parrot, Andrea. *Coping with Date Rape and Acquaintance Rape*. New York: Rosen Publishing Group, 1996. A collection of scholarly articles on date rape.

Pittman, Frank. *Private Lives: Infidelity and the Betrayal of Intimacy*. New York: W. W. Norton, 1989. An intelligent, thoughtful look at extramarital relationships.

Reiss, Ira. *Journey into Sexuality*. Englewood Cliffs, NJ: 1986. A sociological investigation of sexuality by a leading researcher.

_____. *An End to Shame: Shaping Our Next Sexual Revolution*. Buffalo, NY: Prometheus Books, 1990. Reflections and arguments on what is needed for a sex-positive culture.

Rieff, Philip. *Freud: The Mind of a Moralist*. Chicago: University of Chicago Press, 1979. An outstanding study of Freud and his dark view of the world, women, and sexuality.

Robinson, Paul. *The Modernization of Sex*. New York: Harper & Row, 1976. An important study of Havelock Ellis, Alfred Kinsey, and Masters and Johnson by an intellectual historian.

Rubin, Lillian. *Erotic Wars: What Happened to the Sexual Revolution?* New York: Farrar, Straus, 1990. An interpretation of the sexual relationships between men and women.

Russell, Diana E. H. *Sexual Exploitation: Rape, Child Sexual Abuse and Workplace Harassment*. Newbury Park, CA: Sage Publications, 1984. A synthesis of research on the various forms of sexual exploitation.

Satir, Virginia. *The New Peoplemaking*. Rev. ed. Palo Alto, CA: Science and Behavior Books, 1988 (paperback). One of the most influential books of the last twenty-five years on communication.

Shilts, Randy. *And the Band Played On: People, Politics, and the AIDS Epidemic*. New York: St. Martin's Press, 1987. The compelling story behind the "discovery" of AIDS and the politics and prejudice that undermined an effective public health response.

Sprecher, Susan, and Kathleen McKinney. *Sexuality*. Newbury Park, CA: Sage Publications, 1993. A concise overview of human sexuality from the close relationships perspective.

Steinberg, David (ed.). *The Erotic Impulse: Honoring the Sensual Self*. Los Angeles: Jeremy Tarcher, 1992. An impressive and highly intelligent collection of essays, stories, and reflections on eroticism.

Sternberg, Robert, and Michael Barnes (eds.) *The Psychology of Love*. New Haven, CT: Yale University Press, 1988. An excellent collection of essays by some of the leading researchers into love.

Suggs, David N., and Andrew W. Miracle. *Culture and Human Sexuality*. Pacific Grove: Brooks/Cole Publishing Co., 1993. A fine collection of cross-cultural essays on human sexuality.

Symons, Donald. *The Evolution of Human Sexuality*. New York: Oxford University Press, 1979. The most thorough book on the sociobiology of human sexuality.

Tavris, Carol. *The Mismeasure of Woman*. New York, Norton, 1992. An examination of various misconceptions and biases that affect our understanding of women. Includes critiques of sociobiology, the G-spot, premenstrual and postmenstrual syndromes, and the codependency and addiction movements.

Ting-Toomey, S. and Felipe Korzenny (eds.). *Cross-Cultural Interpersonal Communication*. Newbury Park, CA: Sage Publications, 1991. Useful background material for differing multicultural and cross-cultural communication patterns.

Tribe, Laurence. *Abortion: The Clash of Absolutes*. New York: W. W. Norton, 1990. A balanced, comprehensive examination of the legal, social, medical, and moral questions surrounding abortion by a leading constitutional scholar.

Vance, Carole. *Pleasure and Danger: Exploring Female Sexuality*. Boston: Routledge & Kegan Paul, 1984. A provocative collection of essays dealing with female sexuality from a feminist perspective.

Weber, Ann L., and John Harvey (eds.). *Perspectives on Close Relationships*. Boston: Allyn & Bacon, 1994. A collection of essays by leading scholars on various aspects of intimate relationships.

Weeks, Jeffrey. *Sexuality and Its Discontents: Meanings, Myths, and Modern Sexualities*. London: Routledge & Kegan Paul, 1985 (paperback). An excellent study on the changing meanings of sexuality from a social construction perspective

Weg, Ruth (ed.). *Sexuality in the Later Years: Roles and Behavior.* New York: Academic Press, 1983. Anthropological, psychological, and sociological perspectives.

Weideger, Paula. *Menstruation and Menopause: The Physiology and Psychology, the Myth and the Reality.* New York: Delta Books, 1977 (paperback). A thorough discussion of menstruation and menopause; especially strong on taboos and myths.

Weinberg, Martin, Collin Williams, and Douglas Pryor. *Dual Attraction: Understanding Bisexuality.* New York: Oxford University Press, 1994. The first major scientific study on the nature of bisexuality.

Weinberg, Thomas, and G. W. L. Kamel (eds.). *S and M: Studies in Sadomasochism.* New York: Prometheus Books, 1983. A collection of essays on S&M that views it as atypical rather than pathological.

Zilbergeld, Bernie. *The New Male Sexuality Book.* New York: Bantam Books, 1992. An updated version of the classic work on male sexuality, describing sexual myths, communication, and sexual expression.

JOURNALS

If we were to choose five journals with which to be stranded on a desert island (and still keep up with the field), they would be the ones listed below (alphabetical order). They should be part of your library's basic journal collection.

> *Archives of Sexual Behavior*
>
> *Family Planning Perspectives*
>
> *Journal of Homosexuality*
>
> *Journal of Sex & Marital Therapy*
>
> *Journal of Sex Research*

Most of the useful journals listed below are not directly related to human sexuality but often have relevant articles.

> *Adolescence*
>
> *American Journal of Public Health*
>
> *Family Life Educator*
>
> *Family Relations*
>
> *Health Education*
>
> *Hispanic Journal of Behavioral Sciences*
>
> *JAMA: Journal of The American Medical Association*
>
> *Journal of American Public Health*
>
> *Journal of Black Psychology*
>
> *Journal of Black Studies*
>
> *Journal of Marital and Family Therapy*
>
> *Journal of Marriage and the Family*
>
> *Journal of Psychology & Human Sexuality*
>
> *Journal of Sex Education and Therapy*
>
> *Journal of Social Issues*
>
> *Journal of Social and Personal Relationships*
>
> *Journal of Social Work & Human Sexuality*
>
> *Journal of the History of Sexuality*
>
> *New England Journal of Medicine*
>
> *Sage: A Scholarly Journal of Black Women*
>
> *Sex Roles*
>
> *Sexually Transmitted Diseases*
>
> *SIECUS Reports*
>
> *Women and Health*

HUMAN SEXUALITY FILMS AND VIDEOS

The list of films and videos represents a large selection of the most relevant media material currently available. New material constantly comes on the market. Each year the January issue of *Family Relations* publishes the results of the National Council on Family Relations Media Competition, which lists around a hundred award-winning films/videos, many of which are relevant to human sexuality. The journal provides a brief synopsis and set of learning objectives for each work.

Mayfield Relationships and Intimacy Videotape is available to adopters. You may choose to use the video segments with the text chapters as follows:

	Text Chapter	Suggested Video Segment(s)
1	Perspectives on Human Sexuality	Beyond Macho
2	Studying Human Sexuality	
3	Female Sexual Anatomy, Physiology, and Response	A Practical Guide to STDs
4	Male Sexual Anatomy, Physiology, and Response	A Practical Guide to STDs
5	Gender and Gender Roles	Beyond Macho
		Florence and Robin
6	Sexuality Over the Life Span	
7	Love, Intimacy, and Sexuality	Interracial Marriages
		Beyond Macho
8	Communicating About Sex	
9	Sexual Expression	
10	Atypical and Paraphiliac Sexual Behavior	
11	Contraception and Birth Control	
12	Conception, Pregnancy, and Childbirth	
13	The Sexual Body in Health and Illness	A Practical Guide to STDs
14	Sexual Enhancement and Therapy	
15	Sexually Transmitted Diseases	A Practical Guide to STDs
16	HIV and AIDS	AIDS: No-Nonsense Answers
		AIDS: The Women Speak
17	Sexual Coercion: Harassment, Aggression, and Abuse	Date Rape
18	Commercial Sex: Sexually Oriented Material and Prostitution	

Check with your college's media library or resource center for a listing of its holdings, often organized by category. If they do not have the material you want, they will often be able to help you locate and order it. They are a valuable resource that you should feel free to use, especially if you are having problems locating relevant materials.

Give yourself plenty of time in ordering your films/videos. If you can place your orders well before classes begin, the better off you will be.

FILM DISTRIBUTORS

The major film/video distributors for relevant human sexuality materials are listed below. Give them as much leeway as possible in filling your requests, preferably six to eight weeks.

AIMS Multimedia, 9710 DeSoto Ave., Chatsworth, CA 91311-4409 (800) 367-2467

Altschul Group, 1560 Sherman Ave., Ste. 100, Evanston, IL 60201 (800) 421-2363

Better World Society, 1140 Connecticut Ave., N.W., Washington, D.C. 20036

Carle Medical Communications, 110 West Main St., Urbana, IL 61810

Churchill Media, 12210 Nebraska Ave., Los Angeles, CA 90025 (818) 778-1978

The Cinema Guild, 1697 Broadway, Suite 802, New York, NY 10019 (800) 723-5522

Columbia Tristar Video, 3400 Riverside Dr., Burbank, CA 91505 (818) 972-8193

Coronet/MTI, 2349 Chassee Dr., St. Louis, MO 63146 (800) 221-1274

Encyclopedia Britannica, 310 S. Michigan Ave., Chicago, IL 60604 (312) 347-7900

ETR Associates, P.O. Box 1830, Santa Cruz, CA 95061-4284 (800) 321-4407

Facets Multi Media, 1517 West Fullerton Ave., Chicago, IL 60614 (800) 331-6197

Fanlight Productions, 47 Halifax St., Boston, MA 02130 (617) 524-0980

Filmakers Library, 124 E. 40th St., New York, NY 10016 (212) 808-4980

Films for the Humanities and Sciences, Inc., P.O. Box 2053, Princeton, NJ, 08543 (800) 257-5126

The Glendon Association, Suite 3000, 2049 Century Park East, Los Angeles, CA 90067

HBO Home Video, 1114 6th Ave., New York, NY 10036 (212) 512-7400

Human Relations Media, 175 Tomkins Ave., Pleasantville, NY 10570 (914) 769-6900

Indiana University Audio Visual Center, Bloomington, IN 47405-5901 (800) 552-8620

Kent State University Audio Visual Services, P.O. Box 51901, Kent, OH 44242-0001 (800) 338-5718

Lorimar, 17942 Cowan, Irvine, CA 92714

Multi-Focus, Inc., 1525 Franklin Street, San Francisco, CA 94109 (415) 673-5100

New Day, 22 D Hollywood Ave., Hohokus, NJ 07423 (212) 645-8210

NEWIST/CESA 7, University of Green Bay, IS 1110, 2420 Nicolet Dr., Green Bay, WI 54311

PBS Video, 1320 Braddock Place, Alexandria, VA 22314-1698 (800) 344-3337

PCR: Films and Video in the Behavioral Sciences, Penn State Audio-Visual Services, Special Services Building, Pennsylvania State University, University Park, PA 16802 (800) 826-0132

Polymorph, 95 Chapel St., Newton, MA 02158 (800) 370-3476

Rape Treatment Center, Santa Monica Hospital, 1250 16th St., Santa Monica, CA 90404 (310) 319-4000

RCA Columbia, 2901 W. Alameda Ave., Burbank, CA 91505

The Sexuality Library, 938 Howard St., San Francisco, CA 94103 (415) 974-8990

SVE/Churchill Media, 6677 NW Highway, Chicago, IL 60031 (800) 334-7830

Swank Motion Pictures, 201 S. Jefferson, P.O. Box 231, St. Louis, MO 63166 (800) 876-5577

University of California, Los Angeles, Office of Instructional Development, Media Services, 10962 Leconte Avenue, Los Angeles, CA 90024 (310) 206-1211

University of Minnesota Film and Video, 1313 Fifth Street, S.E., Suite 108, Minneapolis, MN 55414 (800) 847-8251. The film and video library publishes a comprehensive catalog that is a useful resource. Call for a free copy.

Varied Directions International, 69 Elm St., Camden, ME 04843 (207) 236-8506

Vida Health Communications, 6 Bigelow Street, Cambridge, MA 02139 (617) 864-4334

Vidmark Entertainment, 2644 30th St., Santa Monica, CA 90405 (310) 314-2000

EROTIC/EXPLICIT FILMS

"Achieving Sexual Maturity" (1973, 22 min., 16mm, Kent State University). This film deals with sexual anatomy using explicit live photographs of nude adults. It uses graphics and diagrams to explain physiology and internal anatomy. Chronologically presents conception, embryonic development, childhood, puberty, adolescence, and adulthood in both males and females. Using live photography, the film describes ovulation, menstruation, ejaculation, and masturbation. Explicit.

"The Better Sex Video Series" (VHS, The Townsend Institute, Dept. ZMJ8, P.O. Box 5310, Lighthouse Point, FL 33074). Three videos that explicitly show methods of improving intimacy, gentleness, and communication. The videos show demonstrations of the techniques discussed. Explicit.

"Her Fantasy Love Scenes" (1991, 106 min., VHS, The Sexuality Library). This feminist erotic video portrays vignettes of women who "call all the erotic shots." This role reversal is designed to let women do the objectifying. There are no "gynecological" or penetration shots. Explicit.

"Love in Later Life" (1983, 30 min., VHS and 16mm, Multi-Focus, Inc.). This film was created to counter taboos and prejudices which rule out sexuality for older people and define physical beauty in terms of youth. A couple, now in their seventies, discusses physical intimacy and joy in each other's bodies. Contains nudity.

"Selfloving" (1992, 60 min., VHS, Multi-Focus, Inc.). A video portrait of a women's sexuality seminar where 10 women, from age 28 to 60, interact in the nude to confront false modesty. They discuss their search for sexual expression and engage in pleasure rituals designed to enhance sexual self-knowledge. Explicit.

"The Squeeze Technique" (1972, 10 min., VHS and 16mm, Multi-Focus, Inc.). Demonstrates the squeeze technique and gives background information on premature ejaculation. Explicit.

LIST OF STUDENT WORKSHEETS
AND HANDOUTS

LIST OF TRANSPARENCY MASTERS

The 57 transparency masters, which appear in the support material for each chapter, serve to reinforce key graphic material and concept summaries presented in the textbook. Some are reproduced directly from the chapters of the textbook, while others have been selected from recently published research and books. We are especially grateful to Mayfield Publishing Company for providing illustrations from Paul M. Insel and Walton T. Roth's *Core Concepts in Health,* eighth edition, 1998.

TEACHING ABOUT SEXUALITY
AND POPULAR CULTURE

In class, you often hear students talk about what they just learned about sexuality on a talk show, in an advice column, or in a news or magazine article. Although the media is one of the most important sources of information about human sexuality, students often show little ability to critically evaluate what they read, hear, and see. As such, their knowledge, attitudes, and values are often uncritically shaped by Dr. Ruth, Ann Landers, *Playboy* and *Cosmopolitan*, the 10 o'clock news, Sharon Stone movies, cop shows, rock and rap, MTV, Geraldo and Oprah, and a host of other personalities and programs.

As anthropologist Michael Moffatt (1989), who studied student life at Rutgers University, wrote:

> The direct sources of students' sexual ideas were located almost entirely in mass consumer culture: the late-adolescent/young adult exemplars displayed in movies, popular music, advertising, and on TV; Dr. Ruth, sex manuals, *Playboy, Penthouse, Cosmopolitan, Playgirl,* etc.; Harlequins and other pulp romances (females only); the occasional piece of real literature; sex education and popular psychology as it had filtered through these sources, as well as through public schools as it continued to filter through the student-life infrastructure of the college; classic soft-core and hard-core pornographic movies; books; and videocassettes.

Because the mass media has such an important role in shaping students' understanding of human sexuality, it is important that we introduce the tools for students to evaluate the information and messages disseminated by popular culture.

In many ways, teaching about sex and popular culture is one of the easiest—and most important—things you can do. Students are immersed in popular culture: They watch TV, listen to rock and rap, go to movies, read *Playboy* and *Cosmopolitan*. You can integrate their world of entertainment into the very serious task of learning about human sexuality. What follows are ideas and strategies for teaching about sex and popular culture.

The Framework

We set the framework for studying sexuality and popular culture in Chapters 1 and 2. In Chapter 1, "Perspectives on Human Sexuality," we discuss media portrayals of sexuality, especially television, films, music videos, and romance novels, to introduce students to the different ways the media treats sexuality. Media messages about sexuality, which may have been invisible to the student as media consumer, are made visible. Once these messages become visible, they are subject to critical examination.

In Chapter 2, we begin the study of sex research by discussing the role of "sex experts" and advice columnists in the media. We offer general guidelines for evaluating what we call "pop sex." We next introduce critical thinking skills that are especially relevant to the discussion of human sexuality. These guidelines and critical thinking skills provide the basis for students to evaluate sexuality and popular culture throughout the remainder of the course.

Teaching Ideas

The suggestions that follow are general ideas that you may want to incorporate into your course.

Current Events. Every day, TV news, newspapers, and magazines contain stories about sexuality: child sexual abuse, prostitution, rape, medical advances, transsexuality, and so on. In class, ask students to comment on these stories: What type of sex is usually discussed? What information is presented? At the time of this writing, stories about Dennis Rodman, the cross-dressing Chicago Bulls basketball player, and Madonna, a single mother, are dominating the media. These stories can be take-off points for what we know about transvestism or children born outside of marriage.

Film/TV Excerpts. You can take short excerpts from films on videocassette or TV programs to illustrate points. In discussing sexual harassment, for example, a 5-minute excerpt of the trucker scene from "Thelma and Louise" can be used as a starting point. In discussing sexual physiology, "What Happens During Ejaculation," a vignette from Woody Allen's "Everything You Ever Wanted to Know About Sex," can lighten up a sometimes tedious discussion. It further introduces the point that physiological processes may sometimes be anthropomorphized (hero sperm "wins" princess egg). A clip from "The Crying Game" or "The Birdcage" can be used to discuss popular images of cross-dressing and transvestism. A scene from "Seinfeld" on masturbation can illustrate how masturbation is presented—and avoided—on television. A discussion of transsexuality can be introduced with an excerpt from a talk show such as Geraldo or Howard Stern, which can raise questions on the kinds of information transmitted in such shows. An excerpt from a show featuring Dr. Ruth can point to the differences between "sex experts" and sex researchers.

Such film/TV excerpts serve several functions. First of all, they demonstrate various sexual themes or stereotypes found in popular culture. Second, they are immensely powerful in stimulating class discussion. Third, they act as a change of pace in lectures, getting student attention and motivating them for further learning.

Rock, Rap, and Music Videos. Music is a major aspect of student life that conveys powerful images of sexuality and male/female relationships. Recording a few minutes of MTV music videos to show in class is a powerful window into the student world. Madonna's music video of "Justify Your Love" is controversial because of its gender bending and can be used to discuss gender roles and cross-dressing. 2 Live Crew's "Nasty as They Wanna Be" is an excellent vehicle for discussing sexism in music. Prince's "Darling Nikki," about masturbation, provoked Tipper Gore into founding a group to censor popular music.

Excerpts from music videos or recordings serve many of the same functions as film/TV excerpts. In addition, they are rarely longer than a couple of minutes and generally require no editing.

Advertising. Print advertising and radio and TV commercials utilize sex to sell. Slides or recordings of such advertising can be used in lectures in many ways. Ads using models who are thin, young, and usually white can be used to discuss cultural standards of female attractiveness. Naked models selling blue jeans raises the question: What is the relation between nudity and blue jeans? Periodically, advertising campaigns feature bondagelike situations: What does this tell us about domination and submission activities in our culture?

Student-Generated Material on Popular Culture. Students can be encouraged to bring in videocassettes, music tapes or CDs, magazine covers, and advertising that relates to lecture topics. Before discussing sexual scripts, for example, ask students to bring to class different pop culture examples that illustrate typical male/female scripts. These can be discussed in class, in small groups, or in sections. Such student-generated material encourages students to actively examine popular culture and enrich class discussion at the same time.

Students as Active Consumers of Popular Culture. Students can be asked to report on various media to see how each medium presents sexuality. Over the course of instruction, they can be asked to report on a television program, a movie, a music video, a commercial or print ad, a newspaper or magazine article, and so on. The report could be as simple as filling out a one-page pop culture response paper (copies of which you will find in a number of chapter materials) or writing a short paper. The more media that students report on over the course period, the more likely they are to become discerning consumers.

TEACHING ABOUT GAY MEN, LESBIANS, AND BISEXUALS

A unique feature of our textbook is the integration of lesbian/gay/bisexual research and issues through the text. This integration makes it significantly easier to teach about gay, lesbian, and bisexual relationships. As relevant topics appear in the textbook, gay/lesbian/bisexual research is included. This permits a seamless discussion of human sexuality.

Although textbooks have traditionally segregated gay/lesbian/bisexual material to a separate chapter, such segregation is artificial. Within actual classroom situations, instructors find themselves frequently referring to or being asked about gay/lesbian/bisexual relationships long before the chapter on homosexuality (or, as it is sometimes euphemistically called, "sexual orientation") arrives in the middle of the book. Lesbian/gay/bisexual relationships naturally fall within discussions of love, sexual expression, the media, and a host of other topics. By the time the instructor reaches the chapter on homosexuality, much of its material has already been covered and the chapter is redundant.

It's important to realize that some of your students are gay, lesbian, or bisexual. They may or may not be "out" in class. Many of these students may have been struggling for some time to accept their orientation. They may have spent considerable energy dealing with fears of deviance; they may have hidden their orientation from families, friends, and peers. Others may be questioning their orientation, and the class may be helpful for them in establishing their identity as heterosexual, gay, lesbian, or bisexual. In college, especially in a human sexuality course, they often seek to learn more about homosexuality. For them, a human sexuality course may be critical in affirming themselves and their self-worth (D'Augelli, 1992).

It is also important to recognize that anti-gay prejudice continues to be sanctioned in our society. Consequently, many students enter a human sexuality course with numerous stereotypes and prejudices that may interfere with their learning. Students need to approach the subject with as much openness as they can muster.

To enable you to deal with problems of anti-gay/lesbian/bisexual prejudice, we structure several important themes in Chapters 1 and 2. In Chapter 1, we introduce images of gay men, lesbians, and bisexuals in films to allow a discussion of stereotypes. Next, we discuss historical and cultural examples (Greece and the Sambians) of societies which accepted same-sex relationships. Finally, we explore concepts of sexual variation as culturally relative.

In Chapter 2, we introduce critical thinking skills that allow students to evaluate the information regarding sexuality, including homosexuality. We also discuss the work of Havelock Ellis, Alfred Kinsey, and Evelyn Hooker as milestones in the "depathologization" of homosexuality. (It is important to stress that mainstream psychology, psychiatry, and sociology believe that there is nothing pathological about homosexuality.) These two chapters help set the groundwork for dealing with anti-gay prejudice. The best discussion on the topic of bisexuality is found in the Chapter 6 box titled "Bisexuality: The Nature of Dual Attraction." Here, the process of bisexual identity formation is discussed along with types of bisexuals and the nature of bisexual relationships.

Much anti-gay prejudice finds its justification in religious teachings. But traditional religious teachings are undergoing considerable rethinking in many denominations and faiths, especially in light of evidence that homosexuality is not "chosen." The student handout "Sexuality, Science, and the Bible: When Religious Beliefs Are Challenged" by the Rev. Sandra Dager (Chapter 2) helps students explore their religious beliefs in reference to sexuality, including homosexuality.

We have included in Chapter 17 a student handout with excerpts from the Evangelical Lutheran Church's re-evaluation of human sexuality and the Bible. The handout, entitled "Homosexuality and the Christian Faith," is representative of much of the questioning that religious doctrines are undergoing in reference to homosexuality. It also raises questions that may be of value to those instructors or students who wish to discuss religion and homosexuality. You may photocopy this excerpt without permission as long as you include the following: "Copyright © November

1991. Evangelical Lutheran Church of America." (The complete document may be ordered for $1.00 from ELCA Distribution Service, 426 South Fifth Street, Minneapolis, MN 55440. Telephone: 800-328-4648.)

An effective teaching tool for destroying stereotypes is to bring gay/lesbian/bisexual students into the classroom for a panel discussion. Their coming-out stories and other experiences are powerful teaching tools that allow heterosexual students to see fundamental "sameness" as well as bringing out some of the consequences of prejudice.

ETHNICITY AND HUMAN SEXUALITY

Human sexuality cannot be fully understood without considering ethnic variation. Unfortunately, research on sex and ethnicity has been slow to emerge. The overwhelming majority of existing ethnic research focuses on African Americans and Latinos. (At the end of this essay we have appended a bibliography on ethnicity and sexuality as well as a list of journals and periodicals relating to ethnicity.)

Until the last few years, sex research on African Americans and Latinos has generally approached these groups from a "problems" perspective. Most research on sexuality and ethnicity, which was government funded, has focused on adolescent sexuality, especially fertility issues (such as birth control and pregnancy) and STDs. As a result, we know very little about sexual attitudes, values, and behaviors of the majority of adult African Americans and Latinos. (See, for example, Graham, S., 1992. "Most of the Subjects Were White and Middle Class—Trends in Published Research on African Americans in Selected APA Journals, 1970–1989." *American Psychologist* 47(5), 629–639.)

Teaching Considerations

It is important to begin class by acknowledging the lack of ethnic research, pointing out that most existing research is from a "problems" perspective. As ethnicity is a sensitive subject area for many, acknowledge that uncertainties may exist for both students and instructors. Unresolved tensions may exist regarding ethnic issues, which are important to bring out into the open. Discuss why it is difficult to discuss ethnic issues, especially those revolving around sexuality.

Because little research exists, and many students may have had little contact with those of different ethnicity, a starting point is stereotypes. Try to elicit what types of stereotypes students have of different ethnic groups. (This might be facilitated by having students anonymously list different stereotypes on 3 x 5 cards and turning them in. The instructor can then list the stereotypes on the blackboard and begin a discussion of them.) What are the sources of these stereotypes? What are media stereotypes of different ethnic groups? (Chapter 2 discusses stereotypes in the section on critical thinking.)

It is useful to point out to students that ethnic groups are not monolithic. There are (1) socioeconomic differences that affect values and behaviors, (2) subcultures within an ethnic group, such as Mexican American, Puerto Rican, and Cuban American among Latinos, that are important, and (3) degrees of assimilation.

If you have members of underrepresented groups in your class, students may turn to them as having special "expertise," making them representatives of their group. No individual can speak as a representative for her or his ethnic group. Few students feel comfortable as cultural representatives of their group. Instead, invite individuals with expertise about different or specific ethnic groups.

It is also important to note that some culture groups, such as Native American and Asian American, discourage speaking in front of others, especially for women. Small group discussions and activities provide such students with a less threatening setting to test their thinking and ideas.

Research increasingly focuses on ethnic groups over race. Students may be confused about the differences between the two concepts. "Race" refers to a large number of people defined as distinct because of genetically transmitted physical characteristics, especially facial structure and skin color. An "ethnic group" is a large group of people distinct from others because of cultural characteristics such as language, religion, and customs transmitted from one generation to another. The term "African American," used increasingly in place of "Black," reflects the growing significance of ethnicity over race (skin color). (See T. W. Smith, 1992. "Changing Racial Labels—From Negro to Black to African American," *Public Opinion Quarterly,* 56(4), 496–514.) Also, students may be confused about the use of "Latino" and "Hispanic." The two can generally be used interchangeably, but we prefer "Latino" because it emphasizes broader Latin roots rather than Spanish. (Brazilians, for example, are included in the term "Latino" but not "Hispanic," as their heritage is Portuguese, not Spanish.)

Although empirical research is critical to understanding ethnicity, the texture of ethnic life cannot be adequately captured through objective studies. For that reason, we believe that novels and short stories add a valuable dimension and sensitivity to one's understanding. Some novels and collections of short stories you might want to consider reading include Terry McMillan's *Waiting to Exhale,* Miram DeCosta-Willis's (ed.) *Erotique Noire/Black Erotica,* Edward Simmen's (ed.) *North of the Rio Grande,* and Amy Tan's *Joy Luck Club.* Al Santoli's *New Americans: An Oral History* provides insight into the lives of recent immigrants.

African Americans

In studying African American sexuality, several factors need to be considered: (1) sexual stereotypes, (2) Black subculture, and (3) socioeconomic status.

Stereotypes about African American sexuality are common among Whites. One of the most common stereotypes is the depiction of African Americans as sexually driven. Black stereotypes about Whites include their being "uptight." These can be explored in lecture and class discussion.

Socioeconomic status is an important element in African American sexual values and behaviors (Staples and Johnson, 1993). Middle-class Blacks, representing 37% of African Americans, share many sexual attitudes and values with middle-class Whites. The subculture of urban Blacks of lower socioeconomic status is deeply influenced by poverty, racial discrimination, and structural subordination. In contrast to middle-class Whites and Blacks, low-income Blacks are more likely to engage in sexual intercourse at an earlier age and to have children outside of marriage.

The African American subculture is important to understanding the context of Black sexuality. Differences between African Americans and Whites may be the result of the Black adaptation to historical and social forces, including their African heritage, slave legacy, discrimination, and the resulting poverty. Generally speaking, Black sexuality is more permissive than White or Latino sexuality. Premarital sexual activity is not considered immoral or stigmatized as it is in middle-class White communities. Because sexual activity is regarded as natural, premarital sex is viewed as appropriate as relationships become more involved.

Several considerations may be useful when teaching about Black sexuality: (1) Acknowledge that there is little research outside of a "problem" framework. (2) Examine Black sexuality from an African American cultural context. (3) Utilize a cultural equivalence perspective that views the attitudes, values, and behaviors of one ethnic group as similar to those of another ethnic group and that rejects differences between Blacks and Whites as signs of inherent deviance.

Latinos

Latinos are the fastest growing and second largest ethnic group in the United States. Between 1980 and 1990, the Latino population increased by 35%, mostly as a result of immigration from Mexico. At this time there is a growing backlash against immigrants, which may account for, among other things, the very little research done on Latino sexuality.

Two common sexual stereotypes depict Latinos as sexually permissive and Latino males as pathologically "macho" or hyper-masculine (Becerra, 1988) (Espín, 1984). Like African Americans, Latino males are stereotyped as being promiscuous, engaging in excessive and indiscriminate sexual activities. No research, however, validates this stereotype.

There are three important factors to consider when studying Latinos: (1) diversity of ethnic groups, (2) socioeconomic status, and (3) degree of acculturation.

Latinos are comprised of numerous ethnic subgroups, the largest of which are Mexican Americans, Puerto Ricans, and Cubans (Vega, 1991). Each group has its own unique background and cultural traditions that affect members' sexual attitudes and behaviors.

Socioeconomic status is important, as middle-class Latino values appear to differ from those of low-income Latinos. The birth rate to single women, for example, is significantly higher among low-income Latinos than among those of the middle class. Furthermore, Latino ethnic groups rank differently on the socioeconomic scale. The middle class is strongest among Cuban Americas, followed by Puerto Ricans, and then Mexican Americans.

The degree of acculturation to this culture may be the most important factor affecting sexual attitudes and behavior among Latinos. Acculturation can be viewed on a continuum: traditional on one pole, bicultural in the middle, and acculturated on the other pole. Traditional Latinos were born and raised in Latin America; adhere to the norms, customs, and values of their original homeland; speak mostly their native language; and have strong religious ties.

Bicultural Latinos may have been born in either Latin America or the United States, speak both Spanish and English, function well in both Latino and Anglo cultures, and have moderate religious ties. Acculturated Latinos do not identify with their Latino heritage, speak only English, and have moderate (or less) religious ties.

Asian and Pacific Islander Americans

Asian and Pacific Islander Americans represent about 3.5 percent of the total population in the United States today. The two oldest and largest groups are Japanese Americans and Chinese Americans. Other groups include Vietnamese, Laotians, Cambodians, Koreans, Filipinos, Asian Indians, Native Hawaiians, and other Pacific Islanders. Numbering over nine million people, they speak more than thirty different languages and represent a similar number of distinct cultures.

Significant differences in attitudes, values, and practices exist among these groups, making it difficult to speak in general terms without stereotyping and oversimplifying. In general, Asian Americans are less individualistic and more relationship-oriented than other cultures. Individuals are seen as the products of their relationships to nature and other people (Shon & Ja, 1982). Asian Americans are less verbal and expressive in their interactions and often rely on indirection and nonverbal communication such as silence and avoidance of eye contact as signs of respect (Del Carmen, 1990).

Because harmonious relationships are highly valued, Asian Americans have a greater tendency to avoid direct confrontation and conflict; verbal communication is often indirect or ambiguous. Consequently, Asian Americans rely on each other to interpret the meaning of a conversation or nonverbal cue.

Self-disclosure is often viewed less favorably in Eastern cultures than in Western. Not surprisingly then, it has been found that people in the United States tend to disclose much more about themselves in social actions than do the Japanese. Furthermore, quick self-disclosure of personal information may give the impression of emotional imbalance.

Along with the vast religious differences among Asian Americans come major distinctions about sexual attitudes and practices. Like Latinos, however, the degree of acculturation to the culture may be the most important factor affecting sexual attitudes and behaviors. Those who were born and raised in their original homeland tend to adhere to their norms, customs, and values more closely than those who were raised in the United States.

BIBLIOGRAPHY: ETHNICITY AND SEXUALITY

Ahn, H. N., and N. Gilbert. "Cultural Diversity and Sexual Abuse Prevention." *Social Service Review,* Sept. 1992, 66(3), 410–428.

Aneshensel, Carol, E. Fielder, and R. Becerra. "Fertility and Fertility-Related Behavior among Mexican-American and Non-Hispanic White Females." *Journal of Health and Social Behavior,* March 1989, 30(1), 56–78.

Baldwin, J. D., S. Whitely, and J. I. Baldwin. "The Effect of Ethnic Group on Sexual Activities Related to Contraception and STDs." *Journal of Sex Research,* May 1992, 29(2), 189–206.

Bean, F., and M. Tienda, M. *The Hispanic Population of the United States.* New York: Russell Sage Foundation, 1987.

Becerra, R. "The Mexican American Family." In C. Mindel et al. (eds.) *Ethnic Families in America: Patterns and Variations* (3d ed.). New York: Elsevier North Holland, Inc., 1988.

Belcastro, P. "Sexual Behavior Differences between Black and White Students." *Journal of Sex Research,* Feb. 1985, 21(1), 56–67.

Billy, J., K. Tanfer, W. R. Grady, and D. H. Klepinger. "The Sexual Behavior of Men in the United States." *Family Planning Perspectives,* March 1993, 25(2), 52–60.

Binion, V. "Psychological Androgyny: A Black Female Perspective." *Sex Roles,* April 1990, 22(7–8).

Blackwood, E. "Sexuality and Gender in Certain Native American Tribes: The Case of Cross-Gender Females." *Signs,* 1984, 10, 27–42.

Boles, A. J.. and H. Curtis-Boles. "Black Couples and the Transition to Parenthood." *The American Journal of Social Psychiatry,* Dec. 1986, 6(1), 27–31.

Bond, S., and T. F. Cash. "Black Beauty—Skin Color and Body Images Among African-American College Women." *Journal of Applied Social Psychology*, 1992, 22(11), 874–888.

Bonilla, L., and J. Porter. "A Comparison of Latino, Black, and Non-Hispanic White Attitudes Toward Homosexuality." *Hispanic Journal of Behavioral Sciences,* 1990, 12, 437–452.

Bowser, B. P., M. T. Fullilove, and R. E. Fullilove. "African-American Youth and AIDS High-Risk Behavior: The Social Context and Barriers to Prevention." *Youth and Society,* Sept. 1990, 22(1), 54–66.

Brown, J. D., and K. Campbell. "Race and Gender in Music Videos: The Same Beat but a Different Drummer." *Journal of Communications,* 1986, 36(1), 94–106.

Brown, J. D., and L. Schulze. "The Effects of Race, Gender, and Fandom on Audience Interpretations of Madonna's Music Videos." *Journal of Communications,* 1990, 40, 88–102.

Bryant, Z. L., and M. Coleman. "The Black Family as Portrayed in Introductory Marriage and Family Textbooks." *Family Relations,* July 1988, 37(3), 255–259.

Butts, J. D. "Adolescent Sexuality and Teenage Pregnancy from a Black Perspective." T. Ooms (ed.). *Teenage Pregnancy in a Family Context*. Philadelphia, PA: Temple University Press, 1981.

Callender, C., et al. "The North American Berdache." *Current Anthropology,* Aug. 1983, 24(4), 443–456.

Caplan, A. L. "Twenty Years After. The Legacy of the Tuskegee Syphilis Study. When Evil Intrudes." *Hastings Center Report,* Nov. 1992, 22(6), 29–32.

Carrier, J. "Miguel: Sexual Life History of a Gay Mexican American." G. Herdt (ed.). *Gay Culture in America: Essays from the Field*. Boston: Beacon Press, 1992.

Carrier, J., C. Joseph, B. Nguyen, and S. Su. "Vietnamese American Sexual Behaviors and the HIV Infection." *Journal of Sex Research,* Nov. 1992, 29(4), 547–560.

Chapman, A. "Male-Female Relations: How the Past Affects the Present." H. McAdoo (ed.). *Black Families* (2d ed.). Beverly Hills, CA: Sage Publications, 1988.

Chrisman, R., and R. Allen (eds.). *Court of Appeal: The Black Community Speaks Out on the Racial and Sexual Politics of Clarence Thomas vs. Anita Hill*. New York: Ballantine, 1992.

Cochran, S. D., V. M. Mays, and L. Leung. "Sexual Practices of Heterosexual Asian-American Young Adults: Implications for Risk of HIV Infection." *Archives of Sexual Behavior,* Aug. 1991, 20(4), 381–394.

Collier, M. J. "Conflict Competence within African, Mexican, and Anglo American Friendships." S. Ting-Toomey and Felipe Korzenny (eds.). *Cross-Cultural Interpersonal Communication*. Newbury Park, CA: Sage Publications, 1991.

Collins, P. H. "The Meaning of Motherhood in Black Culture." R. Staples (ed.). *The Black Family* (5th ed.). Belmont, CA: Wadsworth Publishing Co., 1994.

Cortese, A. "Subcultural Differences in Human Sexuality: Race, Ethnicity, and Social Class." K. McKinney and S. Sprecher (eds.). *Human Sexuality: The Societal and Interpersonal Context*. Norwood, NJ: Ablex Publishing Corporation, 1989.

Crawford, I., et al. "Attitudes of African-American Baptist Ministers toward AIDS." *Journal of Community Psychology,* 1992, 20(4), 304–308.

DeCosta-Willis, Miram, et al. (eds.). *Erotique Noire/Black Erotica*. New York: Doubleday, 1992.

Del Carmen, R. "Assessment of Asian-Americans for Family Therapy." F. Serafica, et al. (eds.). *Mental Health of Ethnic Minorities*. New York: Praeger, 1990.

Demb, J. M. "Abortion in Inner-City Adolescents: What the Girls Say." *Family Systems Medicine,* 1991, 9, 93–102.

Drugger, K. "Social Location and Gender-Role Attitudes: A Comparison of Black and White Women." *Gender & Society,* Dec. 1988, 2(4), 425–448.

Durant, R., R. Pendergast, and C. Seymore. "Contraceptive Behavior Among Sexually Active Hispanic Adolescents." *Journal of Adolescent Health,* 11(6), Nov. 1990, 490–496.

Espín, O. M. "Cultural and Historical Influences on Sexuality in Hispanic/Latin Women: Implications for Psychotherapy." C. Vance (ed.). *Pleasure and Danger: Exploring Female Sexuality.* Boston: Routledge and Kegan Paul, 1984.

Falicov, C. "Mexican Families." M. McGoldrick, et al. (eds.). *Ethnicity and Family Therapy.* New York: Guilford Press, 1982.

Fossett, M. A., and K. J. Kiecolt. "Mate Availability and Family Structure among African Americans in Metropolitan Areas." *Journal of Marriage and the Family,* 1992, 55(2), 288–302.

Franklin, D. L. "The Impact of Early Childbearing on Development Outcomes: The Case of Black Adolescent Parenting." *Family Relations,* 1988, 37, 268–274.

Gibson, J. and J. Kempf. "Attitudinal Predictors of Sexual Activity in Hispanic Adolescent Females." *Journal of Adolescent Research,* 1990, 5(4), 414–430.

Griswold Del Castillo, R. *La Familia: Chicano Families in the Urban Southwest, 1848 to the Present.* South Bend, IN: University of Notre Dame, 1984.

Guerrero Pavich, E. "A Chicana Perspective on Mexican Culture and Sexuality." L. Lister (ed.). *Human Sexuality, Ethnoculture, and Social Work.* New York: Haworth Press, 1986.

Gump, J. "Reality and Myth: Employment and Sex Role Ideology in Black Women." F. Denmark and J. Sherman (eds.). *The Psychology of Women.* New York: Psychological Dimensions, 1980.

Gutman, H. *The Black Family: From Slavery to Freedom.* New York: Pantheon, 1976.

Hatchett, S. J. "Women and Men." J. S. Jackson (ed.). *Life in Black America.* Newbury Park, CA: 1991.

Hines, P. M., and N. Boyd-Franklin. "Black Families." M. McGoldrick, et al. (eds.). *Ethnicity and Family Therapy.* New York: Guilford Press, 1982.

Holloway, Marguerite. "A Global View." *Scientific American,* 1994, 271(2), 76–85.

Howard, J. "A Structural Approach to Interracial Patterns in Adolescent Judgments about Sexual Intimacy." *Sociological Perspectives,* Jan. 1988, 31(1), 88–121.

Jackson, J. S. (ed.). *Life in Black America.* Newbury Park, CA: Sage Publications Co., 1991.

Jemmott, J. B., I.. L. S. Jemmott, and G. T. Fong. "Reductions in HIV Risk-Associated Sexual Behaviors among Black Male Adolescents: Effects of an AIDS Prevention Intervention." *American Journal of Public Health,* March 1992, 82(3), 372–377.

Jones, J. H. "Twenty Years After. The Legacy of the Tuskegee Syphilis Study. AIDS and the Black Community." *Hastings Center Report,* Nov. 1992, 22(6), 38–40.

Jones, J. H. *Bad Blood: The Tuskegee Syphilis Experiment* (rev. ed.). New York: Free Press, 1993.

Jorgensen, S., and R. Adams. "Predicting Mexican-American Family Planning Intentions: An Application and Test of a Social Psychological Model." *Journal of Marriage and the Family,* Feb. 1988, 50, 107–119.

Kalichman, S. C., et al. "Culturally Tailored HIV-AIDS Risk-Reduction Messages Targeted to African American Urban Women." *Journal of Consulting and Clinical Psychology,* 1993, 61(2), 291–295.

Keller, C., and D. Bergstom. "Value Orientations in African American Women." *Perceptual and Motor Skills,* 1993, 76(1), 319–322.

Kim, Young Yun (ed.). *Interethnic Communication: Current Research.* Newbury Park, CA: Sage Publications, 1991.

Kline, A., E. Kline, and E. Oken. "Minority Women and Sexual Choice in the Age of AIDS." *Social Science and Medicine,* Feb. 1992, 34(4), 447–457.

Lantz, H. "Family and Kin as Revealed in the Narratives of Ex-Slaves." *Social Science Quarterly,* March 1980, 60(4), 667–674.

Lawrence III, C. "Cringing at the Myths of Black Sexuality." R. Chrisman and R. Allen (eds.). *Court of Appeal: The Black Community Speaks Out on the Racial and Sexual Politics of Clarence Thomas vs. Anita Hill.* New York: Ballantine, 1992.

Lester, J. "Men: Being a Boy." *Ms.,* July 1973, 112–113.

Lieberson, S. and M. Waters. *From Many Strands: Ethnic and Racial Groups in Contemporary America.* New York: Russell Sage Foundation, 1988.

Lim, S. "Asian-American Literature: Race, Class, Gender, and Sexuality." *Multicultural Review,* 1994, 3(2), 46–52.

Lister, L. (ed.). *Human Sexuality, Ethnoculture, and Social Work*. New York: Haworth Press, 1986.

Marin, G., and B. V. Marin. "A Comparison of Three Interviewing Approaches for Studying Sensitive Topics with Hispanics." *Hispanic Journal of the Behavioral Sciences,* Nov. 1989, 11(4), 330–340.

Marin, G. and B. V. Marin. *Research with Hispanic Populations*. Newbury Park, CA: Sage Publications, 1991.

Mays, V. M., S. D. Cochran, G. Bellinger, and R. G. Smith. "The Language of Black Gay Men's Sexual Behavior: Implications for AIDS Risk Reduction." *Journal of Sex Research,* Aug. 1992, 29(3), 425–434.

Mays, V. M., J. A. Flora, C. Schooler, and S. D. Cochran. "Magic Johnson's Credibility among African-American Men". *American Journal of Public Health,* Dec. 1992, 82(12), 1692–2693.

McGoldrick, M. "Normal Families: An Ethnic Perspective." F. Walsh (ed.). *Normal Family Processes*. New York: Guilford Press, 1982.

McGoldrick, M., J. K. Pearce, and J. Giordano (eds.). *Ethnicity and Family Therapy*. New York: Guilford Press, 1982.

McIntosh, E. "An Investigation of Romantic Jealousy among Black Undergraduates." *Social Behavior and Personality*, 1989, 17(2), 135–141.

McLaurin, M. *Celia: A Slave*. Athens, GA: University of Georgia Press, 1991.

Mindel, C. H., R. W. Haberstein, and Roosevelt Wright, Jr. (eds.). *Ethnic Families in America: Patterns and Variations* (3d ed.). New York: Elsevier North Holland, 1988.

Murry, V. M. "Socio-Historical Study of Black Female Sexuality: Transition to First Coitus." R. Staples (ed.). *The Black Family* (5th ed.). Belmont, CA: Wadsworth Publishing Co., 1994.

Norris, A. E., and K. Ford. "Beliefs about Condoms and Accessibility of Condoms in Hispanic and African American Youth." *Hispanic Journal of Behavioral Sciences,* 1992, 14(3), 373–382.

Oggins, J., D. Leber, and J. Veroff. "Race and Gender Differences in Black and White Newlyweds' Perceptions of Sexual and Marital Relations." *Journal of Sex Research,* 1993, 30(2), 152–160.

Ortiz, S., and J. M. Casas. "Birth Control and Low-Income Mexican-American Women: The Impact of Three Values." *Hispanic Journal of the Behavioral Sciences,* Feb. 1990, 12(1), 83–92.

Ostrow, D. G., et al. "Racial Differences in Social Support and Mental Health in Men with HIV Infection: A Pilot Study." *AIDS Care,* 1991, 3(1), 55–62.

Padilla, E. R., and K. E. O'Grady. "Sexuality among Mexican Americans: A Case of Sexual Stereotyping." *Journal of Personality and Social Psychology,* 1987, 52, 5–10.

Peterson, J. L. "Black Men and Their Same-Sex Desires and Behaviors." G. Herdt (ed.). *Gay Culture in America: Essays from the Field*. Boston: Beacon Press, 1992.

Price, J. H., and P. A. Miller. "Sexual Fantasies of Black and White College Students." *Psychological Reports,* 1984, 54, 1007–1014.

Priest, R. "Child Sexual Abuse Histories Among African-American College Students: A Preliminary Study." American Journal of Orthopsychiatry, July 1992, 62(3), 475–477.

Quinn, S. C. "AIDS and the African American Woman: The Triple Burden of Race, Class, and Gender." *Health Education Quarterly,* 1993, 20(3), 305–320.

Raisbaum, H. "El Rol Sexual Femenino en los Medios de Comunicación Masiva: Un Estudio Comparativo de Telenovelas Mexicanas y Estadounidenses." *Revista Mexicana de Psicología,* July 1986, 3(2), 188–196.

Rao, K., et al. "Child Sexual Abuse of Asians Compared with Other Populations." *Journal of the American Academy of Child and Adolescent Psychiatry*, Sept. 1992, 31(5), 880 ff.

Rice, R. J., P. L. Roberts, H. H. Handsfield, and K. K. Holmes. "Sociodemographic Distribution of Gonorrhea Incidence: Implications for Prevention and Behavioral Research." *American Journal of Public Health,* Oct. 1991, 81(10), 1252–1258.

Salgado de Snyder, V. N., R. Cervantes, and A. Padilla. "Gender and Ethnic Differences in Psychosocial Stress and Generalized Distress among Hispanics." *Sex Roles,* April 1990, 22(7), 441–453.

Schinke, S. P., G. J. Botvin, M. A. Orlandi, R. F. Schilling, and A. N. Gordon. "African-American and Hispanic-American Adolescents, HIV Infection, and Preventative Intervention." *AIDS Education and Prevention,* Dec. 1990, 2(4), 305–312.

Shon, S., and D. Ja. "Asian Families." M. McGoldrick, et al. (eds.). *Ethnicity and Family Therapy*. New York: Guilford Press, 1982.

Simpson, Rennie. "The Afro-American Female: The Historical Context of the Construction of Sexual Identity." Ann Snitow, [et al.] (eds.). *Powers of Desire: The Politics of Sexuality.* New York: Monthly Review Press, 1983.

Sluzki, C. "The Latin Lover Revisited." M. McGoldrick, et al. (eds.). *Ethnicity and Family Therapy.* New York: Guilford Press, 1982.

Smith, E. A. and J. R. Udry. "Coital and Non-coital Sexual Behaviors of White and Black Adolescents." *American Journal of Public Health,* 1985, 75, 1200–1203.

Smith, E. J. "The Black Female Adolescent: A Review of the Educational, Career, and Psychological Literature." *Psychology of Women Quarterly,* 1982, 6, 261–288.

Smith, J. E., and J. Krejci. "Minorities Join the Majority: Eating Disturbances among Hispanic and Native American Youth." *International Journal of Eating Disorders,* 1991, 10, 179–186.

Sorenson, S. B., and J. M. Siegel. "Gender, Ethnicity, and Sexual Assault: Findings from a Los Angeles Study." *Journal of Social Issues,* March 1992, 48(1), 93–104.

South, S., and R. Felson. "The Racial Patterning of Rape." *Social Forces,* Sept. 1990, 69(1), 71–93.

St. Lawrence, J. S. "African-American Adolescents' Knowledge, Health-Related Attitudes, Sexual Behavior and Contraceptive Decisions—Implications for the Prevention of Adolescent HIV Infection." *Journal of Consulting and Clinical Psychology,* 1993, 61(1), 104–112.

Stack, C. B. *All Our Kin: Strategies for Survival in a Black Community.* New York: Harper and Row, 1974.

Staples, R. "The Black American Family." C. Mindel, et al. (eds.). *Ethnic Families in America: Patterns and Variations* (3d ed.). New York: Elsevier North Holland, Inc., 1988.

Staples, R., and L. B. Johnson. *Black Families at the Crossroads: Challenges and Prospects.* San Francisco, CA: Jossey-Bass Publishers, 1993.

Stein, J. A., S. A. Fox, and P. J. Murata. "The Influence of Ethnicity, Socioeconomic Status, and Psychological Barriers on Use of Mammography." *Journal of Health and Social Behavior,* June 1991, 32(2), 101–113.

Sue, D. W., and D. Sue. *Counseling the Culturally Different: Theory and Practice.* New York: John Wiley & Sons, 1992.

Suggs, D. N., and A. W. Miracle (eds.) *Culture and Human Sexuality: A Reader.* Pacific Grove, CA: Brooks/Cole Publishing Co., 1993.

Taylor, R. J., L. M. Chatters, B. Tucker, and E. Lewis. "Developments in Research on Black Families." A. Booth (ed.). *Contemporary Families: Looking Forward, Looking Back.* Minneapolis: National Council on Family Relations, 1991.

Thomas, S. B., and S. C. Quinn. "The Tuskegee Syphilis Study, 1932 to 1972: Implications for HIV Education and AIDS Risk Education Programs in the Black Community." *American Journal of Public Health,* Nov. 1991, 81(11), 1498–1504.

Thompson, B. W. "'A Way Outa No Way': Eating Problems Among African-American, Latina, and White Women." *Gender & Society,* Dec. 1992, 6(4), 546–561.

Thompson, V. L. S., and S. D. West. "Attitudes of African American Adults Toward Treatment in Cases of Rape." *Community Mental Health Journal,* 1992, 28(6), 531–536.

Ting-Toomey, Stella. "Conflict Communication Styles in Black and White Subjective Cultures." Kim, Young Yun (ed.). *Interethnic Communication: Current Research.* Newbury Park, CA: Sage Publications, 1991.

_____, and Felipe Korzeny (eds.). *Cross-Cultural Interpersonal Communication.* Newbury Park, CA: Sage Publications, 1991.

Torres, A., and S. Singh. "Contraceptive Practice among Hispanic Adolescents." *Family Planning Perspectives,* July 1986, 18(4), 193–194.

True, R. H. "Psychotherapeutic Issues with Asian American Women." *Sex Roles,* April 1990, 22(7), 477–485.

Tucker, M. B., and R. J. Taylor. "Demographic Correlates of Relationship Status among Black Americans." *Journal of Marriage and the Family,* 1989, 51, 655–665.

Twinam, A. "Honor, Sexuality, and Illegitimacy in Colonial Spanish America." A. Lavrin (ed.). *Sexuality and Marriage in Colonial Latin America.* Lincoln, NE: University of Nebraska Press, 1989.

U. S. Bureau of the Census, "The Hispanic Population in the United States." *Current Population Reports,* Series P–20. Washington, D. C.: U. S. Government Printing Office, 1991.

Vasquez-Nuthall, E., et al. "Sex Roles and Perceptions of Femininity and Masculinity of Hispanic Women: A Review of the Literature." *Psychology of Women Quarterly,* 1987, 11, 409–426.

Vega, W. "Hispanic Families." A. Booth (ed.). *Contemporary Families: Looking Forward, Looking Back.* Minneapolis: National Council on Family Relations, 1991.

Weinberg, M. S., and C. J. Williams. "Black Sexuality: A Test of Two Theories." *Journal of Sex Research,* May 1988, 25(2), 197–218.

White, J., and T. Parham. *The Psychology of Blacks: An African-American Perspective* (2d ed.). Englewood Cliffs, NJ: Prentice-Hall, 1990.

Williams, W. L. "Persistence and Change in the Berdache Tradition Among Contemporary Lakota Indians." *Journal of Homosexuality*, June 1985, 11(3–4), 191–200.

Wilson, P. "Black Culture and Sexuality." *Journal of Social Work and Human Sexuality,* March 1986, 4(3), 29–46.

Wyatt, G. E. "Examining Ethnicity versus Race in AIDS Related Sex Research." *Social Science and Medicine,* 1991, 33(1), 37–45.

———. "The Sociocultural Context of African American and White American Women's Rape." *Journal of Social Issues,* March 1992, 48(1), 77–91.

Wyatt, G. E., et al. "Kinsey Revisited II: Comparisons of the Sexual Socialization and Sexual Behavior of Black Women over 33 Years." *Archives of Sexual Behavior,* Aug. 1988, 17(4), 289–332.

Wyatt, G. E., and S. Lyons-Rowe. "African American Women's Sexual Satisfaction as a Dimension of Their Sex Roles." *Sex Roles,* April 1990, 22(7–8), 509–524.

ETHNIC STUDIES INDEXES, JOURNALS, AND PERIODICALS

This list contains the titles of periodicals primarily concerned with African Americans, Latinos, Asian Americans, and Native Americans.

The following periodical indexes are also useful:

Chicano Periodical Index

HAPI: Hispanic American Periodicals Index

Index to Periodical Articles by and about Blacks

Sage Race Relations Abstracts

African American Journal and Periodicals

Also see Geary, J. W. "A Selected Undergraduate Guide to African-American Periodicals." *Serials Librarian,* 1993, 23(1), 65–70.

Black American Literature Forum

Black Law Journal

The Black Nation

Black Scholar

Callaloo: Journal of Afro-American and African Arts and Letters

College Language Association (CLA) Journal: Afro-American, African and Caribbean Literature

Ebony

Essence

Freedomways

Journal of Black Psychology

Journal of Black Studies
Journal of Negro Education
Journal of Negro History
Kokay I
Negro History Bulletin
Obsidian II: Black Literature in Review
Phylon, a Review of Race & Culture
Review of Black Political Economy
SAGE: A Scholarly Journal of Black Women
*Western Journal of Black Studie*s

Latino Journals and Periodicals

Aztlan
Bilingual Review, La Revista
El Chicano
Chicano Law Review
Hispanic Journal of Behavioral Sciences
Hispanic Link Weekly Report
Revista Mujeres
El Tecolote

Asian American Journals and Periodicals

Amerasia Journal
Asiaweek: Journal for the Asian American Community
Focus on Asian Studies
P/AAMHRC (Pacific/Asian American Mental Health Research Center) Research Review
Pacific Citizen
Pacific Ties
Vietnam Forum

Native American Journals and Periodicals

Akwesasne Notes
American Indian Art Magazine
American Indian Culture and Research Journal
American Indian Law Review
American Indian Quarterly
NCAI News (National Congress of American Indians)
News from Native California
Wassaja (national newspaper of Indian America)

General Ethnic Studies Periodicals and Journals

Ethnic Affairs

Ethnic and Racial Studies

Ethnic Forum

Explorations in Ethnic Studies

Immigrants and Minorities

Interracial Books for Children Bulletin

Journal of American Ethnic History

Journal of Ethnic Studies

Race & Class

PART II

INDIVIDUAL CHAPTER RESOURCES
FOR *HUMAN SEXUALITY*

Note: For each of the chapters in the textbook, *The Resource Book* includes the following elements:

Chapter Outline
Learning Objectives
Discussion Questions
Activities
Sex and Popular Culture Discussion and Activities
Health Considerations Discussion and Activities
List of Films and Videos
Bibliography
Student Worksheets
Student Handouts
Transparency Masters

CHAPTER 1
PERSPECTIVES ON HUMAN SEXUALITY

CHAPTER OUTLINE

Sexuality, Popular Culture, and the Media
    Media Portrayals of Sexuality
    Television
    Music and Music Videos
    Hollywood Films
    Computer Sex and Dial-a-Porn

Sexuality Across Cultures and Times
    Sexual Impulse
    Sexual Orientation
    Gender

Societal Norms and Sexuality
    Natural Sex
    Normal Sex
    Think About It: My Genes Made Me Do It: Sociobiology, Evolutionary Psychology, and the Mysteries of Love
    Sexual Behavior and Variations
    Think About It: Am I Normal?

LEARNING OBJECTIVES

At the conclusion of Chapter 1, students should be able to:

1. Discuss the dissemination of sexual images through the mass media, including men's and women's magazines and advertising.

2. List the different television genres and describe how each genre portrays sexuality.

3. Describe depictions of sexuality in Hollywood films, including gay/lesbian relationships.

4. Discuss the nature of anonymous sexual interaction facilitated by the Internet and phone pornography.

5. Describe and compare the sexual impulse as seen among the Mangaia, Dani, and Victorian Americans.

6. Discuss same-sex relationships in ancient Greece and among contemporary Sambians as examples of cultural variation.

7. Describe cultural variability of gender concepts, especially in terms of transexuality and two-spirits.

8. Discuss the concepts of "nature" and "natural" sexual behavior in relationship to societal norms.

9. Describe the emergence of the concept of "normal" sexual behavior, including the four criteria used to define it.

10. Explain the concepts of sexual behavior and variations in terms of continuum and nonconformity.

11. Recognize and define the key terms introduced in the chapter.

DISCUSSION QUESTIONS

Textbook Themes. Discuss the main themes of the textbook as described in the Prologue. Ask students their reactions to these themes. The themes are (1) psychosocial orientation, (2) sex as intimacy, (3) gender roles, (4) sexuality and popular culture, (5) normality of gay men and lesbians, (6) significance of ethnicity. Some students may have especially strong feelings about traditional gender roles and gay and lesbian relationships. They may feel uncomfortable about discussing ethnicity because of the taboos surrounding the topic, especially when it is linked to sexuality. The essays on teaching human sexuality, ethnicity, and gay/lesbian relationships in Part One may be useful for you.

Cybersex. Why do people engage in cybersex? Should it be regulated? By whom?

Gender/Orientation/Transsexuality. Discuss the difference between gender, sexual orientation, and transsexuality. Some students mistakenly believe that homosexuality is a form of gender confusion or that gay men or lesbians "want" to be the other sex. Some believe that gay men are "feminine" and lesbians "masculine," mistakenly confusing gender and orientation issues.

Norms. Discuss the relationship between norms and what our culture identifies as natural, normal, and moral. Students often believe that norms are rooted in biology, that there is such a thing as "biologically natural" behavior.

Studying vs. Condoning Sexual Behaviors. Some students mistakenly believe that objectively studying a sexual behavior is the equivalent of advocating the behavior, especially if they have moral objections. Ask students to identify the difference between "studying," "understanding," "advocating," "condoning," "tolerating," and "accepting" diverse sexual activities, values, and orientations.

ACTIVITIES

Using the Textbook. The student handout "Getting to Know Your Textbook: A Self-Guided Tour" located in Part I of the *Study Guide* is a series of exercises that gives students the opportunity to familiarize themselves with the different components of each chapter as well as the components of the textbook as a whole, including the glossary, bibliography, and index.

Discussing "Discussing Sex." Ask students to suggest reasons why it is difficult to discuss sexuality. List the reasons on the blackboard and ask students to prioritize the list. This exercise can also be done in discussion groups.

Sexual Vocabulary. In order to discuss sexuality, it is useful to students to: densensitize the use of words relating to human sexuality. Distribute the student worksheet "Sexual Vocabulary" (Worksheet 1) and ask students to fill it out. After they have completed it, ask them to form small groups to discuss the appropriateness of sexual vocabulary in different situations. As a class, discuss appropriate sexual vocabulary in a class setting.

What Students Want to Learn. Pass out 3 x 5 cards and ask students to anonymously write what they want to learn in the class and why they are taking the class. Collect the cards, then randomly distribute them to groups to discuss; have groups exchange cards every few minutes. Then ask class members to identify what students most want to learn and their reasons for taking the class.

Anonymous-Question Cards. Have students write anonymous questions on 3 x 5 cards, indicating only their gender. Fold them in half and give or pass them to the instructor. Take 5–10 minutes of class time to answer and discuss the questions. You may do this at the end of class or earlier if you need to break up your lecture. This activity can be done at each class session or as time permits. (This is a popular activity that can wake up a sleepy class.)

Normal, Natural, and Moral Sexuality. One of the great inhibitors to objectively studying human sexuality is the tendency to evaluate sexual activities as normal, natural, or moral. To provide insight into underlying beliefs about these judgments, give students the worksheet "Classifying Sexual Behavior" (Worksheet 3). After students complete the worksheet, discuss the reasons students give for classifying different behaviors as normal, natural, or moral.

Class Sexual Attitudes. Use the Self-Assessment "Exploring Your Sexual Attitudes" from the *Study Guide* to create a profile of the class's sexual attitudes by asking students to respond to the assessment using an anonymous Scantron. Collect the Scantrons and post the results. Discuss the results in class or in small groups.

Mehinakan Anthropologists. Ask students to imagine they are Mehinakan anthropologists studying American sexual behavior. What "curious" customs and behaviors might they find? Ask them to provide descriptive names, such as "exchanging saliva" (kissing) and "sex with the hand" (masturbation) described in the textbook.

SEX AND POPULAR CULTURE

Popular Culture Response Paper (Worksheet 2): Sexuality and Your Favorite TV program. Ask students to utilize the student worksheet to analyze their favorite television program. After the students have completed the assignment, make a list of the five most popular TV shows and ask students to comment on their portrayal of sexuality. (This activity can be done either in groups or in the class as a whole.)

Discussion: Ask students to identify current media stories (newspapers, magazines, or TV), talk shows, or specials relating to human sexuality. Relate this to the appropriate chapter in the textbook or lecture. How accurate is the material? This exercise may be done during each class session or occasionally, as time permits.

Discussion: Ask students to describe how sexuality is portrayed in TV, movies, commercials, popular music, and music videos. Are there differences in what is portrayed in different media?

Discussion: Ask students to describe recent portrayals of gay/lesbian relationships on TV or in film. To what degree are the portrayals stereotypical?

Activity: Make a list of recent magazine article titles relating to human sexuality, love, or relationships, with a separate list of the magazines. Ask students to identify which article came from which magazine. On what basis did they make their choices?

Activity: Make a videocassette recording of a music video or commercial in which sexuality plays an important role. Show the recording to the class and ask them to discuss the use of sexuality in the video.

HEALTH CONSIDERATIONS

Discussion: What are some of the sexual issues confronting health care providers in the 1990s, such as the relationship between sexual well-being and health, new reproductive technologies, HIV/AIDS, risk-taking behaviors, and the sexual rights of patients?

Discussion: What is healthy sexual behavior? On what basis is "healthy" decided?

Discussion: Although many people turn to physicians for sexual advice and counseling, physicians often do not have training in human sexuality. In fact, medical schools rarely offer courses in human sexuality. If you were going to design a human sexuality course for physicians, what would be included in the course?

Activity: Have students make a list of healthy and unhealthy sexual behaviors. On what basis did they decide to classify behaviors as healthy or unhealthy?

SUPPORT MATERIAL

Films and Videos

"Before Stonewall: The Making of a Gay and Lesbian Community" (1984, 87 min., VHS, University of Minnesota Film and Video). Using filmed recollections and archival material, this program traces the social, political, and cultural development of the gay and lesbian community.

"Honored by the Moon" (1989, 15 min., VHS, University of Minnesota Film and Video). Describes traditional roles of men and women in Native American society (also cited in Chapter 6).

"Silent Pioneers" (1985, 42 min., VHS and 16mm, University of Minnesota Film and Video). Profiles eight older gay men and lesbians who managed to lead meaningful lives despite living through an era when homosexuality was not tolerated.

"The Diary of Adam and Eve by Mark Twain" (1978, 15 min., VHS and 16mm, Indiana University Audio Visual Center). Retells and embellishes the story of Adam and Eve using separate diaries which comment on the same situations to point out the differences in the sexes.

"Who's Doing It? Sexual Attitudes in America" (1982, 13 min., VHS, Multi-Focus, Inc.). This video explores sexual attitudes in America through illustrations and live interviews with people of all ages.

Bibliography

The books and articles listed below may be helpful for instructors wishing additional background or information on some of the topics covered in this chapter. In addition, the books listed in this chapter's "Suggested Reading" in the textbook may also be useful.

Bullough, V. *Sexual Variance in Society and History.* New York: John Wiley & Sons, 1976.

Buxton, R. "Dr. Ruth Westheimer: Upsetting the Normalcy of the Late-Night Talk Show." *Journal of Homosexuality,* 1991 21(1/2), 139–153.

Dines, G., and Humez, J. *Gender, Race, and Class in the Media.* Thousand Oaks, CA: Sage, 1995.

Goldberg, V. "Testing Limits in a Culture of Excess." *New York Times,* Oct. 29, 1995, 145, (50229), p. 1.

Grady, D. "Sex Test of Champions: Olympic Officials Struggle to Define What Should Be Obvious—Just Who Is a Female Athlete." *Discover: The World of Science,* June 1992, 78–82.

Gregersen, E. "Human Sexuality in Cross-Cultural Perspective." D. Byrne and K. Kelley (eds.). *Alternative Approaches to the Study of Sexual Behavior.* Hillsdale, NJ: Lawrence Erlbaum Associates, 1986.

Lowry, D., and D. Towles. "Prime Time TV Portrayals of Sex, Contraception, and Venereal Disease." *Journalism Quarterly,* June 1989, 66(2), 347–352.

McMahon, K. "The Cosmopolitan Ideology and the Management of Desire." *Journal of Sex Research,* Aug. 1990, 27(3), 381–396.

Moffatt, M. *Coming of Age in New Jersey: College and American Culture.* New Brunswick, NJ: Rutgers University Press, 1989.

Roscoe, W. *The Zuni Man/Woman.* Albuquerque, NM: University of New Mexico Press, 1991.

Russo, V. *The Celluloid Closet.* New York: Harper & Row, 1987.

Sherman, B., and J. Dominick. "Violence and Sex in Music Videos: TV and Rock 'n' Roll." *Journal of Communication,* Dec. 1986, 36(1), 79–93.

Smith, R. W. "What Kind of Sex Is Natural?" V. Bullough (ed.). *The Frontiers of Sex Research.* Buffalo, NY: Prometheus Books, 1979.

Snitow, A. "Mass Market Romance: Pornography for Women is Different." A. Snitow et al. (ed.). *Powers of Desire: The Politics of Sexuality.* New York: Monthly Review Press, 1983.

Wolf, M., and A. Kielwasser. "Introduction: The Body Electric: Human Sexuality and the Mass Media." *Journal of Homosexuality,* 1991, 21(1/2), 7–18, 1991.

Name _____ Section _____ Date _____

WORKSHEET 1

Sexual vocabulary

Make a list of all the words you know for sexual activities (including scientific, slang, and colloquial).

In the boxes below, write the words you would use (1) in class, (2) with boyfriend/girlfriend/partner, (3) with peers, and (4) with parents.

Class

Boyfriend/girlfriend/partner

Peers

Parents

Do you find your vocabulary changes according to situation or person? Why?

Strong/DeVault/Sayad, *Human Sexuality,* 3rd ed. © 1999 Mayfield Publishing Company. Chapter 1

WORKSHEET 2

Popular culture response paper: Sexuality and Your Favorite TV Program

Name of program:

Description of content:

What underlying message or stereotype about sexuality did the program present?

Did it present its message or stereotype visually or verbally? How? Was it effective?

Comments:

Strong/DeVault/Sayad, *Human Sexuality,* 3rd ed. © 1999 Mayfield Publishing Company. Chapter 1

WORKSHEET 3

Classifying sexual behavior

In the boxes below, indicate whether you believe each activity listed is "natural/unnatural," "normal/abnormal," or "moral/immoral."

	Natural/Unnatural	Normal/Abnormal	Moral/Immoral
Sexual Intercourse			
Oral Sex			
Gay/Lesbian Sex			
Masturbation			
Extramarital Sex			
Premarital Sex			
Anal Sex			

What are your criteria for identifying a behavior as "natural" or "unnatural"?

What are your criteria for identifying a behavior as "normal" or "abnormal?"

Strong/DeVault/Sayad, *Human Sexuality,* 3rd ed. © 1999 Mayfield Publishing Company. Chapter 1

What are your criteria for identifying a behavior as "moral" or "immoral"?

Do you use similar or different criteria for "natural," "normal," and "moral"? Why?

CHAPTER 2
STUDYING HUMAN SEXUALITY

CHAPTER OUTLINE

Sex, Advice Columnists, and Pop Psychology
    Information and Advice as Entertainment
    The Use and Abuse of Statistics
    Practically Speaking: Evaluating Pop Psychology

Thinking Critically About Sex
    Value Judgments Versus Objectivity
    Opinions, Biases, and Stereotypes
    Confusing Attitudes and Behavior
    Common Fallacies: Egocentric and Ethnocentric Thinking

Sex Research Methods
    Research Concerns
    Clinical Research
    Survey Research
    Observational Research
    Experimental Research

The Sex Researchers
    Richard von Krafft-Ebing (1840–1902)
    Sigmund Freud (1856–1939)
    Havelock Ellis (1859–1939)
    Alfred Kinsey (1894–1956)
    William Masters and Virginia Johnson
    National Health and Social Life Survey

Emerging Research Perspectives
    Feminist Scholarship
    Gay and Lesbian Research
    Directions for Future Research

Ethnicity and Sexuality
    African Americans
    Latinos
    Asian and Pacific Islander Americans

LEARNING OBJECTIVES

At the conclusion of Chapter 2, students should be able to:

1. Describe the sex information/advice genre, its function as entertainment, and how to evaluate it in conjunction with statistical data.

2. List and describe critical thinking skills, including examples of value judgments and objectivity; opinions, biases, and stereotypes; confusing attitudes and behavior; and egocentric and ethnocentric fallacies.

3. Discuss ethical and sampling issues in sex research.

4. Describe and critique clinical, survey, observational, and experimental methods of sex research.

5. Discuss and critique the contributions of the early sex researchers, including Richard von Krafft-Ebing, Sigmund Freud, and Havelock Ellis.

6. Discuss and critique the contributions of Alfred Kinsey.

7. Discuss and critique the contributions of William Masters and Virginia Johnson.

8. Discuss findings of the 1994 National Health and Social Life Survey.

9. Discuss and critique the contributions of feminist and gay/lesbian scholars, as well as directions for future research.

10. Describe emerging research on African Americans, including socioeconomic status, stereotyping, subculture, and increasing numbers of unmarried adults.

11. Describe emerging research on Latinos, including diversity of subgroups, stereotyping, and assimilation.

12. Discuss emerging research on Asian and Pacific Islander Americans with an emphasis on changing cultural traditions.

13. Recognize and define the key terms introduced in the chapter.

DISCUSSION QUESTIONS

Ethical Considerations in Sex Research. Discuss the ethical issues involved in sex research. Ethical guidelines were issued in 1993 by the Society for the Scientific Study of Sex (see "Society for the Scientific Study of Sex Statement of Ethical Guidelines," *Journal of Sex Research,* 1993, 30[2], pp. 192–198).

Developing Critical Thinking Skills. Ask students to give examples of a value judgment and an objective statement concerning sexuality. Ask for examples of an opinion, a biased statement, and a stereotype regarding sexuality. Discuss how these can be identified in class or group discussions without discouraging individual participation.

Religion and the Study of Human Sexuality. Some students may have to deal with conflicts between their religious beliefs and what they learn about human sexuality. You may want to discuss the differences between religious beliefs and the objective study of human sexuality. The Reverend Sandra Dager, a campus minister, has written a sensitive essay that concerns such conflicts, to accompany this textbook. This essay, which is found at the end of the materials for this chapter, can be copied and distributed to students. A particularly troubling issue for many religious individuals is the issue of homosexuality. (Diverse religious interpretations of homosexuality are discussed in Chapter 17.)

Sex Research Devalued. Why has sex research been devalued in both the academic and scientific community and in society as a whole? What role has statistics played in this process?

Reading a Journal Article. Distribute the student handout "Reading a Journal Article," which can be found in Part V of the *Study Guide,* and discuss the significance of journals in publishing scientific information.

Methodologies. Discuss the advantages/disadvantages of survey, clinical, observational, and experimental studies. Note: Some students have difficulty understanding independent and dependent variables and correlational studies.

Changing Views on Masturbation. Discuss the changing views on masturbation from Krafft-Ebing to Masters and Johnson.

Changing Views of Female Sexuality. Discuss the changing views of female sexuality from Krafft-Ebing to Masters and Johnson. Contrast with feminist perspectives on sexuality.

Changing Views on Homosexuality. Discuss the changing views on homosexuality, including the work of Ulrichs, Kertbeny, Hirschfeld, Ellis, Kinsey, Hooker, and Foucault. Contrast with Krafft-Ebing and Freud.

Age/Ethnicity. As most social science research is done with White middle-class students, discuss the problems of generalizing such research to older men and women and to diverse ethnic groups.

Diversity Among Ethnic Groups. Indicate the significance of socioeconomic status in studying diverse ethnic groups (as well as Whites). Point out that Latinos consist of diverse subgroups (such as Mexican American, Puerto Rican, Cuban American, Guatemalan, Salvadoran, and so on) that may have significantly different experiences and values from each other. Similarly, Asian Americans are divided into numerous subgroups, including Japanese Americans, Chinese Americans, Korean Americans, Hmong, Vietnamese, and so on. Among all groups, the degree of assimilation is also important.

Limited Ethnic Research. Discuss why little research has been conducted with ethnic groups.

Feminist Scholarship. Discuss the validity of the main tenets of feminist research. These include: (1) Gender is significant in all aspects of social life; (2) The female experience of sex has been devalued; (3) Power is a critical element in male/female relationships; (4) Traditional empirical research needs to be combined with qualitative research and interpretative studies; (5) Ethnicity is important. The second and third propositions may generate considerable discussion.

Gay/Lesbian Research. Discuss why current gay/lesbian research has moved away from the "origins" of homosexuality. What are the methodological and political limits on conducting research on homosexuality?

ACTIVITIES

Developing a Survey Instrument. To give students a feel for developing survey instruments, have students develop a 10-item questionnaire on a specific sex research topic such as attitudes toward masturbation, premarital sex and guilt, and so on. Each student should anonymously contribute 3 questions. Distribute the questions to small groups and have the members choose 10 questions for their group's instrument. In selecting questions, have members evaluate questions in terms of ambiguity, bias, options in answering, and so on. In class, discuss problems in developing an accurate survey instrument.

Research Subjects. Following up on the survey instrument, ask students to discuss in class or groups how they would find research subjects, sampling problems, how the survey would be administered (telephone, face-to-face, mail) and advantages or disadvantages. Bring up the issue of ethnicity and sexual orientation in sampling.

Ethnic Stereotypes. Sexual stereotypes often interfere with knowledge about diverse ethnic groups. Because students are often unwilling to begin a discussion of ethnic stereotypes for fear of appearing prejudiced, pass out 3 x 5 cards and ask them to anonymously identify the various ethnic stereotypes regarding sexuality. Discuss the research available regarding the stereotypes and the function these stereotypes play in justifying discrimination.

Looking at Your Values. Located in Chapter 2 of the *Study Guide* is "Looking at Your Values," a survey that students can complete in class and use as an activity to explore personal values and discuss gender differences. To do the latter, have students complete the survey, collect it, and separate male responses from female responses. Redistribute the surveys, giving males' surveys to males and vice versa. Read the questions aloud and have students stand up when the response they are holding is read. Follow up with a discussion on gender differences. (Additional discussion can occur in an electronic discussion group, sponsored and run by the instructor.)

SEX AND POPULAR CULTURE

Popular Culture Response Paper (Worksheet 4): Daytime Talk Shows. Ask students to watch a daytime talk show with a sexual topic and to respond using the student worksheet.

Discussion: Ask students to describe recent talk shows that included a sex expert. What is the role of the expert on the show? What have they learned from talk shows?

Activity: Ask students to bring in clippings from "Dear Abby," "Ann Landers," and other newspaper and magazine advice columnists. Distribute them to students in small groups. What norms are being reinforced by the columnists? How do the columnists utilize social science research?

Activity: Read several questions or letters sent to advice columnists to your class. Ask students to write their own "advice" column in response. Have students read some of their advice aloud to the class. Ask for the basis of their advice.

Activity: Ask students to read a newspaper or magazine about a sexual topic. Then give them a list of relevant journals and ask them to find an article about the same topic. Ask students to compare the two articles in terms of goals, methodology, generalizations, references, and data.

HEALTH CONSIDERATIONS

Discussion: Havelock Ellis argued against nineteenth-century beliefs that masturbation had no ill health effects. Why has morally proscribed behavior—such as masturbation—often been seen to have dangerous health consequences? Today some continue to link morally proscribed behavior to negative health consequences, such as homosexuality and AIDS. From a public health point of view, what are the consequences of viewing health problems as moral problems?

Discussion: In designing research projects, what are special concerns for health care? For example, can conclusions based on data collected from males be applied to females? Similarly, can conclusions based on data collected from middle-class Whites be applied to ethnic groups or to those from a different socioeconomic group?

Activity: In the activity "Developing a Survey Instrument," have students select a health-related topic, such as safer sex practices, alcohol use and sexual behavior, and so on.

GUEST SPEAKERS/PANELS

Researcher Speaker: If another faculty member or graduate student in anthropology, biology, health sciences, psychology, sociology, or women's studies is involved in sex research or is knowledgeable about it, invite him or her to discuss differing approaches, questions, research methods.

Researchers Role-Playing Panel: Ask students to role-play a panel discussion consisting of important sex researchers. The researchers they could portray might include Hirschfeld, Krafft-Ebing, Ellis, Freud, Kinsey, Hooker, Masters, or Johnson. Ask each to make a 3-minute statement of her/his most important research findings. The class can ask questions of the panel.

Religious Panel: Invite a panel of campus or community religious leaders to discuss the relationship between religious values and the scientific study of human sexuality. How does science affect religious thinking? What happens when religious beliefs and scientific conclusions clash? Subjects may include masturbation, premarital sex, gender roles, transsexuality, and homosexuality.

SUPPORT MATERIAL

Films and Videos

"Changing Our Minds: The Story of Dr. Evelyn Hooker" (no date but recent, 75 min., 16mm). A documentary about Dr. Evelyn Hooker, who spoke out against "treating" homosexuals in the 1950s. She conducted a scholarly study comparing the psychological profiles of gay and nongay men, finding that there was no difference between them.

"Sex and the Scientist" (1989, 86 min., VHS, Indiana University Audio Visual Center). Chronicles the life of Alfred Kinsey. Includes interviews with Clyde Martin, Wardell Pomeroy, and Paul Gebhard.

Bibliography

The books and articles listed below may be helpful for instructors wishing additional background or information on some of the topics covered in this chapter. In addition, the books listed in this chapter's "Suggested Reading" in the textbook may also be useful.

Bullough, V. *Science in the Bedroom: A History of Sex Research.* New York: Basic Books. 1994.

Cortese, A. "Subcultural Differences in Human Sexuality: Race, Ethnicity, and Social Class." K. McKinney and S. Sprecher (eds.). *Human Sexuality: The Societal and Interpersonal Context.* Norwood, NJ: Ablex Publishing Corporation, 1989.

Faludi, S. *Backlash: The Undeclared War Against American Women.* New York: Crown, 1991.

Guerrero Pavich, E. "A Chicana Perspective on Mexican Culture and Sexuality." L. Lister (ed.). *Human Sexuality, Ethnoculture, and Social Work.* New York: Haworth Press, 1986.

Harry, J. "Sampling Gay Men." *Journal of Homosexuality,* Feb. 1986, 22(1), 21–34.

Irvine, J. M. *Disorders of Desire.* Philadelphia: Temple University Press, 1991.

Laumann, E., J. Gagnon, M. Robert, and S. Michaels. *The Social Organization of Sexuality.* Chicago: University of Chicago Press, 1994.

Morokoff, P. "Volunteer Bias in the Psychophysiological Study of Female Sexuality." *Journal of Sex Research,* Feb. 1986, 22(1), 35–51.

Parker, R., and Gagnon, J. Conceiving Sexuality: *Approaches to Sex Research in a Postmodern World.* New York: Routledge, 1995.

Pomeroy, W. *Dr. Kinsey and the Kinsey Institute.* New York: Harper and Row, 1972.

Rieff, P. *Freud: The Mind of a Moralist.* Chicago: University of Chicago Press, 1979.

Robinson, P. *The Modernization of Sex.* New York: Harper & Row, 1976.

Staples, R. "The Black American Family." C. Mindel, R. Habenstein, and R. Wright Jr., (eds.). *Ethnic Families in America: Patterns and Variations* (3d ed.). New York: Elsevier North Holland, Inc., 1988.

Tavris, C. *The Mismeasure of Woman.* New York: Norton, 1992.

Vance, C. S., and C. Pollis. "Introduction: Special Issue on Feminist Perspectives on Sexuality." *Journal of Sex Research,* Feb. 1990, 27(1), 1–5.

Weeks, J. *Sexuality.* New York: Tavistock Publications and Ellis Horwood, Ltd., 1986.

WORKSHEET 4

Popular culture response paper: Daytime Talk Shows

Name of program:

Description of content:

What underlying message or stereotype about sexuality did the program present?

Did it present its message or stereotype visually or verbally? How? Was it effective?

Comments:

Strong/DeVault/Sayad, *Human Sexuality,* 3rd ed. © 1999 Mayfield Publishing Company. Chapter 2

SEXUALITY, SCIENCE, AND THE BIBLE: WHEN RELIGIOUS BELIEFS ARE CHALLENGED

Reverend Sandra Dager

Sandra Dager is an ordained minister in the Evangelical Lutheran Church and a campus minister at California Lutheran University. In this essay, Rev. Dager discusses some of the pressures and thought processes experienced by people whose religious beliefs about human sexuality are challenged by science and experience. Reprinted by permission of the author.

John came into my office, looked me straight in the eye, and said, "Do you think God made homosexuals?" I tried not to look surprised, but I *was* surprised. Not so much by the question but by the fact that it was John asking it. John believed the Bible was the literal word of God and the final authority in all matters. He believed that the Bible forbade long hair on men, drinking beer, smoking, swearing, women ministers, masturbation, premarital sex, and viewing R-rated movies. But over Christmas break, John questioned his understanding of the Bible. He had attended a conference on Christianity and sexuality. For the first time in his life, his beliefs about sexuality had been challenged.

At the religion conference, he met men and women who were both gay *and* Christian. He found it very disturbing to learn that sex researchers and therapists thought that homosexuality was something that could not be "cured." He was surprised further to discover that even he did not accept the Bible as literally as he had supposed. He did not consider himself ritually unclean, for example, if he touched his mother or sister during their menstrual periods, as the Bible states in the book of Leviticus (15:24–29). He didn't follow the Bible's teachings against lending money for interest nor believe that the earth was flat. John also shaved his sideburns and wore polyester/cotton shirts—things he would not have been doing if he had been following the Bible to the letter.

John left the conference confused. He felt overwhelmed by scientific information that was leading him to reconsider some of his religious beliefs, such as his beliefs about masturbation, homosexuality, sex-change operations, artificial insemination, and birth control. He feared that by questioning a single biblical sentence that he would question the entire Bible. And if he questioned the literal truth of the Bible, on what would he be able to base his faith?

It takes considerable thought and reflection for a person to come to a mature understanding of human sexuality. But if scientific knowledge conflicts with religious beliefs, the task can be even more difficult, as it was for John. How do people with deeply held religious beliefs come to terms with science and religion, especially in such a value-laden area as sexuality? What do *you* do when your attitudes and beliefs about sexuality, such as premarital sex or homosexuality, are challenged by scientific evidence? Or, vice versa, when scientific knowledge is challenged by religious belief?

There are many ways of dealing with conflicts between religious beliefs and science. One way of dealing with such differences is the "cafeteria approach." In this approach we choose beliefs and facts much as we select food in a cafeteria: We pick only what suits our tastes and ignore the rest. Some of us believe, for example, that the Bible tells us everything there is to know about homosexuality, which we believe to be a "curable" sin. We are reluctant to study any scientific evidence that suggests otherwise. A key issue for us is the authority of the Bible. We do not believe that the word of God could contain any error or inconsistency.

A second method of resolving conflicts between science and religion might be called the "fortress approach." Those of us using this approach never venture into the cafeteria. Instead, we build a fortress around our beliefs and guard them with care. We surround ourselves with people who believe as we do. We attend religious institutions that reinforce our homogeneity of belief. From within our secure walls, questions and ideas that conflict with our beliefs are treated as enemy invaders, which we fire upon as soon as they come into view. We rarely allow enemies or their ideas to get close enough for us to see the "whites of their eyes." There is no chance of dialogue, no exchange of views, as long as our "enemies" can be kept at a safe distance.

Two problems may occur when we construct belief fortresses. The first is that we use a lot of energy constructing and maintaining our fortress—energy that usually has its origin in fear. The second is that we cut ourselves off from the life, thought, and inquiry that go on outside the fortress. In the end, we are often the ones who suffer the most. We end up being prisoners in our fortress, walled in by our fears.

But sometimes even fortresses are penetrated by an indisputable truth, as when Galileo, contrary to the church, argued that the earth revolved around the sun. (It was not until 1992, however, that the Church withdrew its condemnation against him.) Although it took centuries, we no longer believe, as did the early Christians, that sexuality itself was inherently sinful, even within marriage. It will be interesting to see what notions about human sexuality will become "indisputable facts" in the future. It will be even more interesting to see how those of us inside the fortress, who have disbelieved these facts, will respond.

Choosing beliefs cafeteria-style or building fortresses are not the only ways for us to deal with notions about human sexuality. A third way is to attempt to integrate religious beliefs and scientific knowledge. Of the three approaches, this is by far the most demanding. It requires that we examine our religious beliefs and the assumptions which preceded them with a high degree of openness and honesty even though the outcome of such an examination can never be predicted.

It takes considerable courage to reexamine religious beliefs. Scientific data may contradict or disprove certain beliefs, such as the belief that God created the earth in six 24-hour days rather than over a long period of time. What happens in view of such a contradiction? What implications does this have for a person's faith in general? Such questions have the potential for leading us to a deeper understanding of our faith. It may help us separate core religious beliefs from peripheral ones; it can help us separate ignorance or prejudice from genuine religious beliefs.

When we undertake an integrated approach, we need to ask ourselves how well we understand the basic sources of our religious beliefs. If our primary authority is the Bible, we need to understand the social and historical context surrounding a given text. The Bible, for example, forbids women to braid their hair and instructs them to keep silent in church. What is the origin of these beliefs? Are they central or peripheral to our faith?

In today's world, perhaps one of the most important issues facing religion is the Bible's relationship to human sexuality. There are many different views of this relationship. What role should the Bible play in discussions about sexuality? For example, should prohibitions against contraception be reevaluated in the light of the world's population today? And how should we interpret the Bible's silence on such matters as sexual orientation (as opposed to sexual acts), artificial insemination, and pseudohermaphroditism? There are many views about the Bible's relationship to human sexuality. Some are based on sound, faithful thinking whereas others are rooted in prejudice or ignorance. Each of us must seek answers to these complex questions with as much personal integrity and openness to the truth as we can muster.

CRITICAL THINKING (1) What role should the Bible play in discussions about sexuality? (2) What were the reasons for the Bible's original prohibitions? Are they still relevant? (3) Is the Bible supplanted by science, or does it supplant science? (4) Can the two co-exist without either losing its authority? (5) What implications does science have for an individual's faith? How do you respond when there is a conflict between science and faith?

1 Kinsey Heterosexual/Homosexual Scale

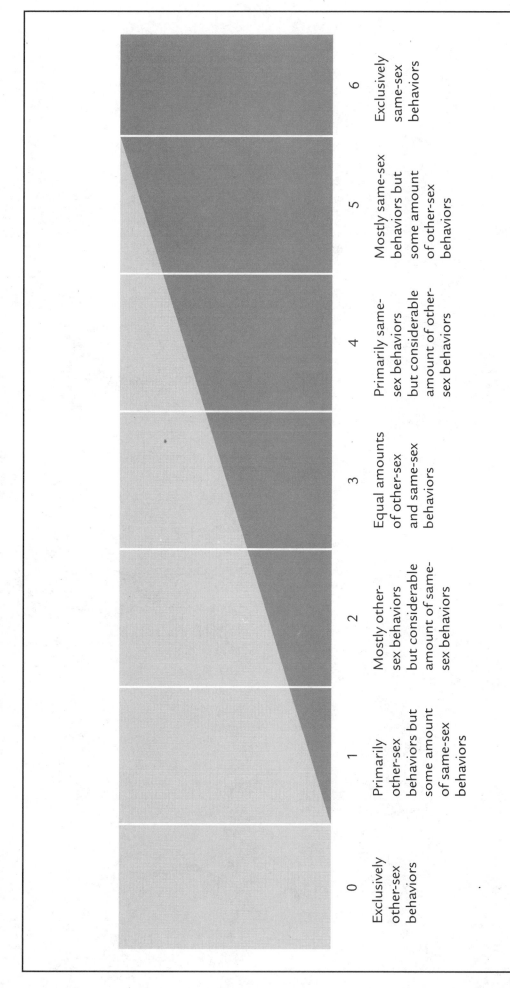

0	1	2	3	4	5	6
Exclusively other-sex behaviors	Primarily other-sex behaviors but some amount of same-sex behaviors	Mostly other-sex behaviors but considerable amount of same-sex behaviors	Equal amounts of other-sex and same-sex behaviors	Primarily same-sex behaviors but considerable amount of other-sex behaviors	Mostly same-sex behaviors but some amount of other-sex behaviors	Exclusively same-sex behaviors

Strong/DeVault/Sayad, *Human Sexuality*, 3rd ed. © 1999 Mayfield Publishing Company

CHAPTER 3

FEMALE SEXUAL ANATOMY, PHYSIOLOGY, AND RESPONSE

CHAPTER OUTLINE

Female Sex Organs: What Are They For?
   External Structures (The Vulva)
   Internal Structures
   Practically Speaking: Vaginal Secretions and Lubrication
   Other Structures
   The Breasts

Female Sexual Physiology
   Reproductive Hormones
   The Ovarian Cycle
   Practically Speaking: Medical Care: What Do Women Need?
   The Menstrual Cycle

Female Sexual Response
   Sexual Response Models
   Desire: Mind or Matter?
   Experiencing Sexual Arousal
   Think About It: The Role of the Orgasm

LEARNING OBJECTIVES

At the conclusion of Chapter 3, students should be able to:

1. List and describe the functions of the external female sexual structure.

2. List and describe the functions of the internal female sexual structures.

3. Describe the structures and processes involved in ovulation.

4. Describe the structure and function of the breasts.

5. List the principal female reproductive hormones.

6. Describe the phases of the ovarian cycle.

7. Describe the phases of the menstrual cycle and its interrelationship with the ovarian cycle.

8. Discuss menstruation, including cultural aspects, physical effects, and possible problems.

9. Compare and contrast Masters and Johnson's and Kaplan's models of the sexual response cycle.

10. Describe the psychological and physiological processes involved in female sexual response, including vaginal secretions and lubrication and the role of orgasm.

11. Identify difficulties women face in having their health-care needs met

12. Recognize and define the key terms introduced in the chapter.

DISCUSSION QUESTIONS

The Misnamed Female Sex Organ. People often mistakenly use the word "vagina" when they actually mean "vulva." In class, read the following statement, asking students to complete it, "Erotically speaking, men have penises and women have _____." The majority of students, including women, will probably respond with "vaginas," but the correct answer is "vulvas." Discuss why people tend to ignore the vulva and clitoris and focus instead on the vagina. Ask why children are taught to use the word "vagina" but not "vulva" or "clitoris." Is it because of the reproductive model of sexuality or ignorance about (or fear of) female eroticism?

Blaming Menstruation. Both men and women sometimes attribute certain behaviors, such as crankiness, irritability, and moodiness, to a woman's menstruating at the time. Discuss whether such attributions are valid. Do men and women have different reasons for attributing behavior to menstruation?

Menarche. Ask women students to recall feelings they had at the time of their menarche. Whom did they tell? What was their family's reaction? Friends? For both men and women, ask how they would teach their children (both girls and boys) about menarche. Are there family or cultural traditions they would pass on?

Uncovering the Breasts in Public. Periodically women complain about laws requiring them to cover their breasts in public, whereas men are not so required. Occasionally women protest such laws, go in public with their breasts uncovered, and are arrested. What is the justification for such laws? Are they discriminatory against women?

ACTIVITIES

Female Reproductive System (Internal/External). Distribute the worksheet on the female reproductive system (Worksheet 5) and ask students to label each part. Note that the same sheet (with answers) appears in the *Study Guide*.

Female Breast. Distribute the worksheet on the female breast (Worksheet 6; also found in the *Study Guide*) and ask students to label each part.

Experience of Desire. Ask students to write descriptions of what "desire" feels like. The descriptions should be anonymous; students should identify whether they are male or female and optionally if they are heterosexual, gay, lesbian, or bisexual. Read the descriptions aloud. Ask students to discuss whether there are male/female or orientation differences in their experience of desire.

The Guessing Game. On 3 x 5 cards, write the names of parts of the female sexual anatomy. (This can also be done for stages of the ovarian cycle and menstrual cycle.) Give students the cards and have them break into small groups. Have students pin one card on each student's back without his or her knowing what the terms are. Then have students try to guess the name on the card on their back by asking others questions that can be answered "yes" or "no." For example, a student might begin by asking "Is it anatomical?" Once the correct answer is made, the student can answer questions of another or pin his or her card on the back of a different student who then can ask questions.

SEX AND POPULAR CULTURE

Popular Culture Response Paper (Worksheet 7): Menstruation and TV. How is menstruation treated in television? What kind of references are made to it? Does sitcom treatment differ from that of talk shows?

Media Breasts. How does the media use breasts to convey certain images of women as sexy, intelligent, or asexual? ("Sexy" women often have large breasts, there may be suggestion of nipples, and so forth). Include how cameras "gaze" at women's bodies, focusing on breasts, often from the male point of view.

Naming. Ask students to identify the different names, including slang and private usage, for the vulva, clitoris, and vagina. (You can also do this exercise anonymously by having students write the names on 3 x 5 cards.) List these on the blackboard or on a transparency. Note the various contexts in which they are used and whether the meanings are positive, negative, or neutral. Also note how words such as "cunt" and "pussy" are used derogatorily.

Vulval/Vaginal Myths. Ask students to identify myths, legends, and humor about the vulva or vagina. Examples might include stories of vaginas containing razor blades, broken glass, or teeth, which are found cross-culturally. Ask what these stories signify.

Menstrual Names/Folklore/Myths/Rituals/Taboos. Ask students to identify the different terms used to describe menstruation, such as "on the rag," "falling off the roof." Rituals can include *mikva;* others involve slapping the girl at first menstruation. Discuss purity concerns in Leviticus (14:19–24) that describe menstruating women as impure. What taboos are associated with menstruation today, such as refraining from sexual intercourse?

HEALTH CONSIDERATIONS

Discussion: If a client came to you to discuss gynecological problems and she used "vagina" when she meant "vulva," would you let the error pass or inform her that she meant "vulva"? What would you say, if anything? Why?

Discussion: If a man experienced sexual difficulties when his partner was menstruating, what would you advise the couple?

SUPPORT MATERIAL

Films and Videos

"Girl to Woman" (1984, 17 min., 16mm, Indiana University Audio Visual Center). Illustrates the changes that occur during the onset of adolescence in girls. Covers the primary sexual changes and secondary changes. Discusses fertilization and menstruation.

"Growing Up Female" (50 min., VHS, New Day). This film shows the socialization of the American woman through a personal look into the lives of six women ranging in age from 4 to 35. We see the forces that shape them—parents, teachers, guidance counselors, advertising, pop music, and marriage.

"The Human Body: Reproductive System" (1980, 16 min., VHS, Kent State University). Animated presentation of the structures of the male and female reproductive systems. Explains bodily changes that occur during maturation, explains the function of hormones, and shows the process of fertilization and development of the embryo.

"Sexual Anatomy and Physiology" (1986, 20 min., VHS, Multi-Focus, Inc.). A lecturer using slides of male and female genitals examines the sexual response capacities, sexual physiology, and structure of the male and female anatomy.

Bibliography

The books and articles listed below may be helpful for instructors wishing additional background or information on some of the topics covered in this chapter. In addition, the books listed in this chapter's "Suggested Reading" in the textbook may also be useful.

Boston Women's Health Book Collective. *The New Our Bodies, Ourselves for the New Century.* New York; Touchstone Books, 1998.

Delaney, J., et al. *The Curse: A Cultural History of Menstruation.* New York: Dutton, 1976.

Gutin, J. C. "Why Bother?" *Discover,* June 1992, 13(6), 32–39.

Hatcher, R., et al. *Contraceptive Technology.* New York: Irvington Publishers, 1993.

Ladas, A. K., B. Whipple, and J. Perry. *The G Spot and Other Recent Discoveries About Human Sexuality.* New York: Holt, Rinehart & Winston, 1982.

Lips, H. *Sex & Gender.* (3d ed.). Mountain View, CA: Mayfield Publishing Co., 1997.

Marieb, E. N. *Human Anatomy and Physiology.* Redwood City, CA: Benjamin/Cummings, 1992.

McCormick, N. *Sexual Salvation: Affirming Women's Sexual Rights and Pleasure.* Westport, CT: Greenwood Publishing, 1994.

Meuwissen, I., and R. Over. "Sexual Arousal across Phases of the Human Menstrual Cycle." *Archives of Sexual Behavior,* 1992, 21(101–119).

Northrup, C. *Women's Bodies, Women's Wisdom.* New York: Bantam, 1994.

Perry, J. D. and B. Whipple. "Pelvis Muscle Strength of Female Ejaculators: Evidence in Support of a New Theory of Orgasm." *Journal of Sex Research,* 1981, 17(1), 22–39.

Rome, E. "Anatomy and Physiology of Sexuality and Reproduction." Boston Women's Health Book Collective, *The New Our Bodies, Ourselves.* New York: Touchstone Books, 1992.

Speroff, L., R. H. Glass, and N. G. Kase. *Clinical Gynecologic Endocrinology and Infertility* (4th ed.). Baltimore: Williams & Wilkins Co., 1989.

Tavris, C. *The Mismeasure of Woman.* New York: Norton, 1992.

WORKSHEET 5

Female reproductive system

Label the parts of the female reproductive system.

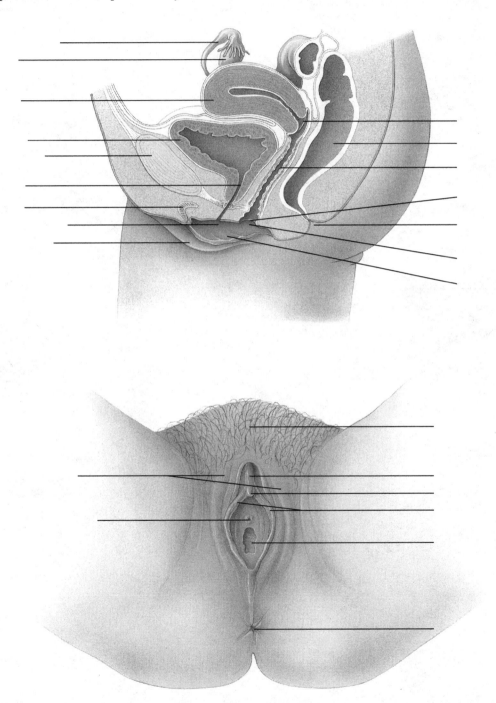

Name _____   Section _____   Date _____

WORKSHEET 6

Female breast

Label the parts of the female breast.

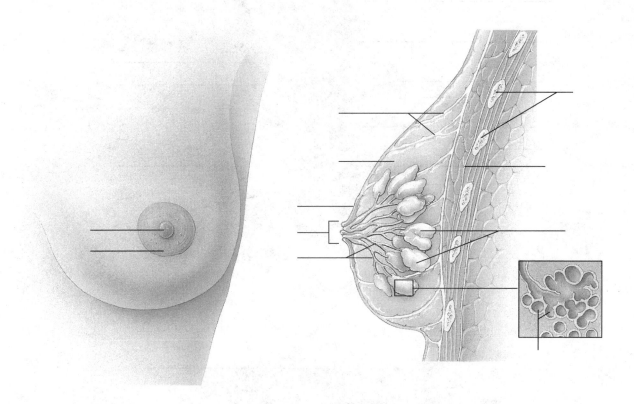

WORKSHEET 7

Popular culture response paper: Menstruation and TV

Name of program:

Description of content:

What underlying message or stereotype about menstruation did the program present?

Did it present its message or stereotype visually or verbally? How? Was it effective?

Comments:

Female Self-Examination

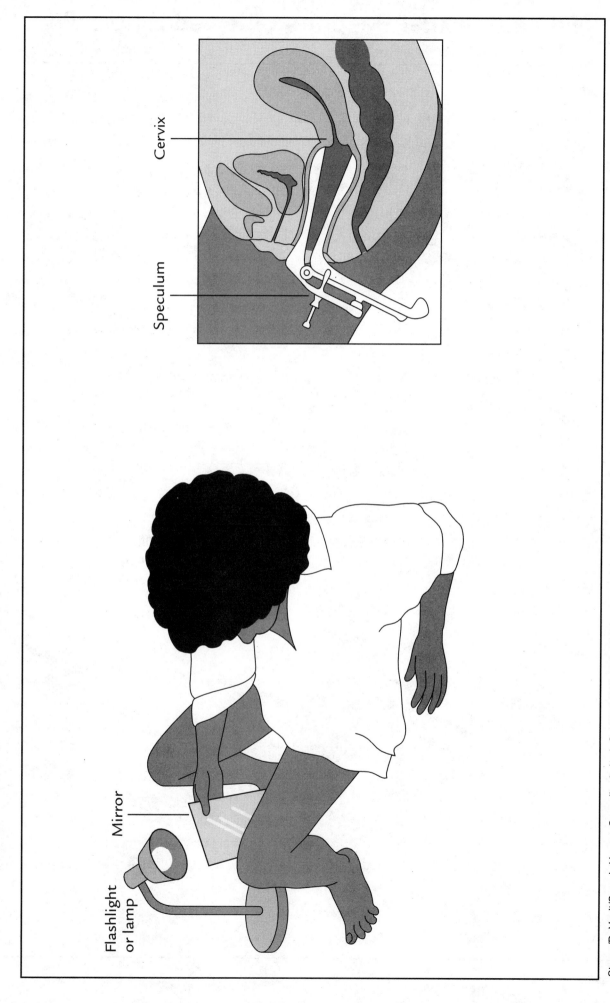

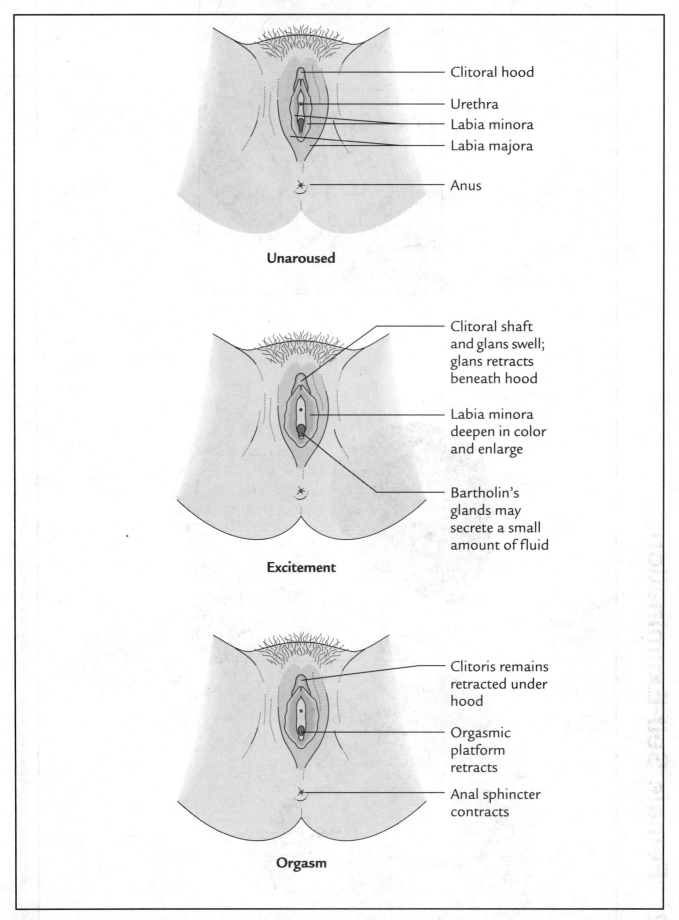

Clitoral hood

Urethra

Labia minora

Labia majora

Anus

Unaroused

Clitoral shaft and glans swell; glans retracts beneath hood

Labia minora deepen in color and enlarge

Bartholin's glands may secrete a small amount of fluid

Excitement

Clitoris remains retracted under hood

Orgasmic platform retracts

Anal sphincter contracts

Orgasm

Strong/DeVault/Sayad, *Human Sexuality*, 3rd ed. © 1999 Mayfield Publishing Company

4 Sexual Differentiation of the Fetus

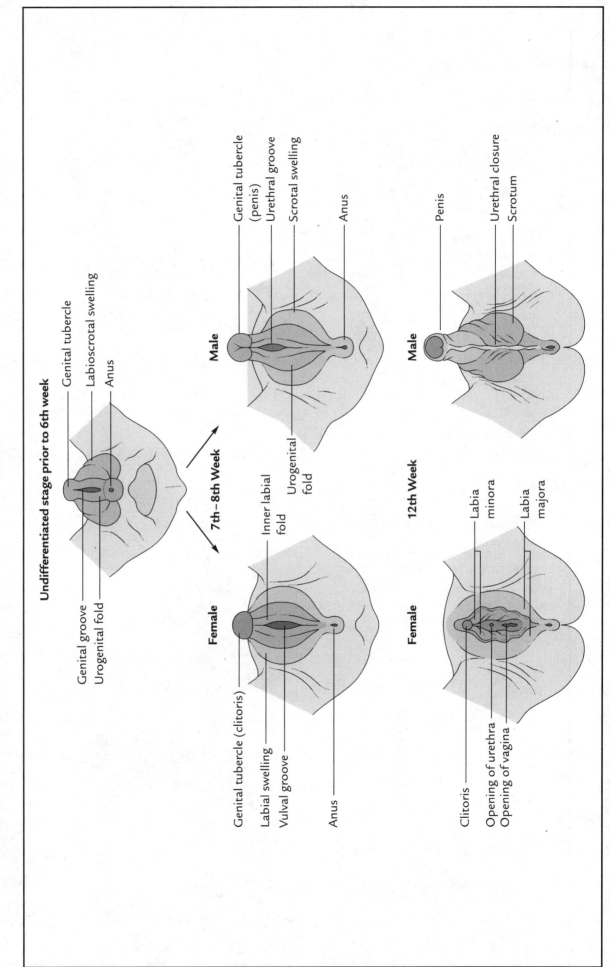

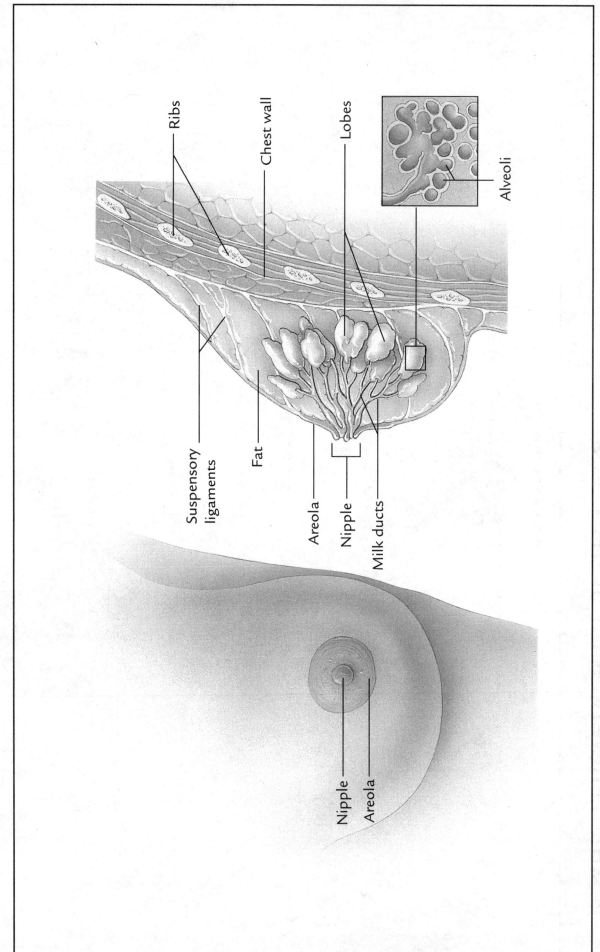

Ribs

Chest wall

Lobes

Alveoli

Suspensory ligaments

Fat

Areola

Nipple

Milk ducts

Nipple

Areola

Strong/DeVault/Sayad, *Human Sexuality*, 3rd ed. © 1999 Mayfield Publishing Company

6 Human Sexual Response Cycles

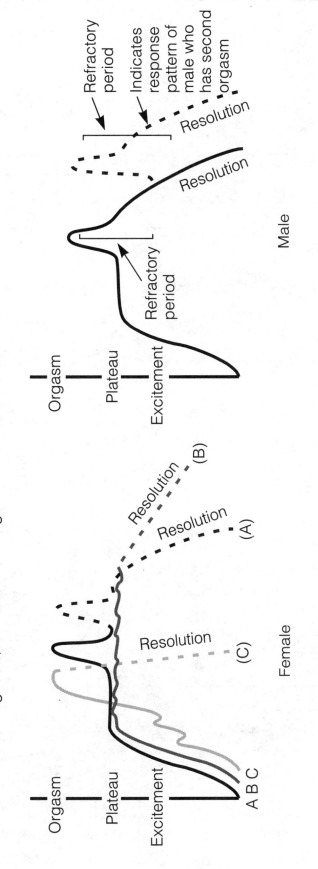

A, B, and C are three different female sexual response patterns, Female C—one orgasm, Female A—two orgasms, Female B—no orgasm.

Orgasm
Plateau
Excitement

Resolution (B)
Resolution (A)
Resolution (C)

A B C

Female

The refractory period represents the last, irregular contractions during which sexual tension rapidly subsides.

Refractory period
Indicates response pattern of male who has second orgasm
Resolution
Resolution

Orgasm
Plateau
Excitement

Refractory period

Male

Source: Human Sexual Response by W. H. Masters and V. E. Johnson, 1966, Boston: Little Brown. Used by permission of Lippincott, William, and Wilkins.

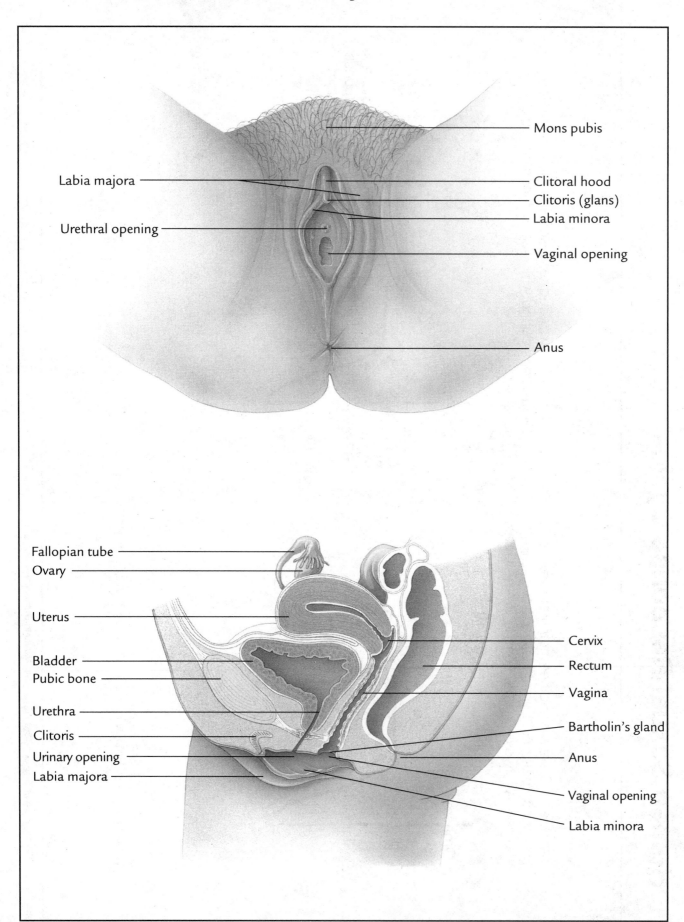

Mons pubis

Labia majora

Clitoral hood

Clitoris (glans)

Labia minora

Urethral opening

Vaginal opening

Anus

Fallopian tube
Ovary

Uterus

Cervix

Bladder
Pubic bone

Rectum

Vagina

Urethra

Clitoris

Bartholin's gland

Urinary opening

Anus

Labia majora

Vaginal opening

Labia minora

8   Internal and External Changes During the Female Sexual Response Cycle

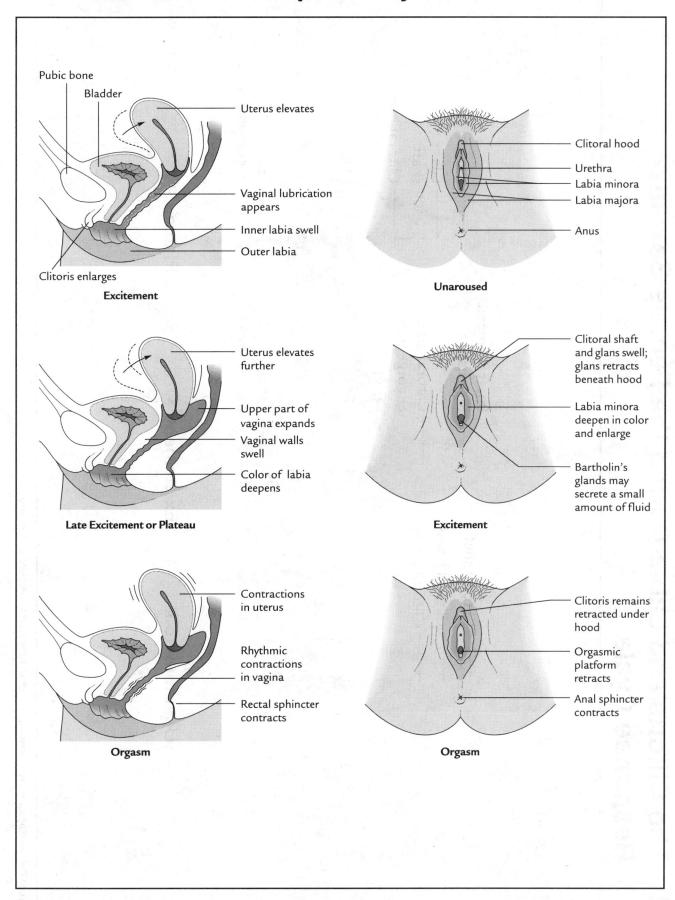

Pubic bone
Bladder
Uterus elevates
Vaginal lubrication appears
Inner labia swell
Outer labia
Clitoris enlarges

Excitement

Clitoral hood
Urethra
Labia minora
Labia majora
Anus

Unaroused

Uterus elevates further
Upper part of vagina expands
Vaginal walls swell
Color of labia deepens

Late Excitement or Plateau

Clitoral shaft and glans swell; glans retracts beneath hood
Labia minora deepen in color and enlarge
Bartholin's glands may secrete a small amount of fluid

Excitement

Contractions in uterus
Rhythmic contractions in vagina
Rectal sphincter contracts

Orgasm

Clitoris remains retracted under hood
Orgasmic platform retracts
Anal sphincter contracts

Orgasm

Strong/DeVault/Sayad, *Human Sexuality,* 3rd ed. © 1999 Mayfield Publishing Company

9   The Clitoris and Labia During the Female Sexual Response Cycle

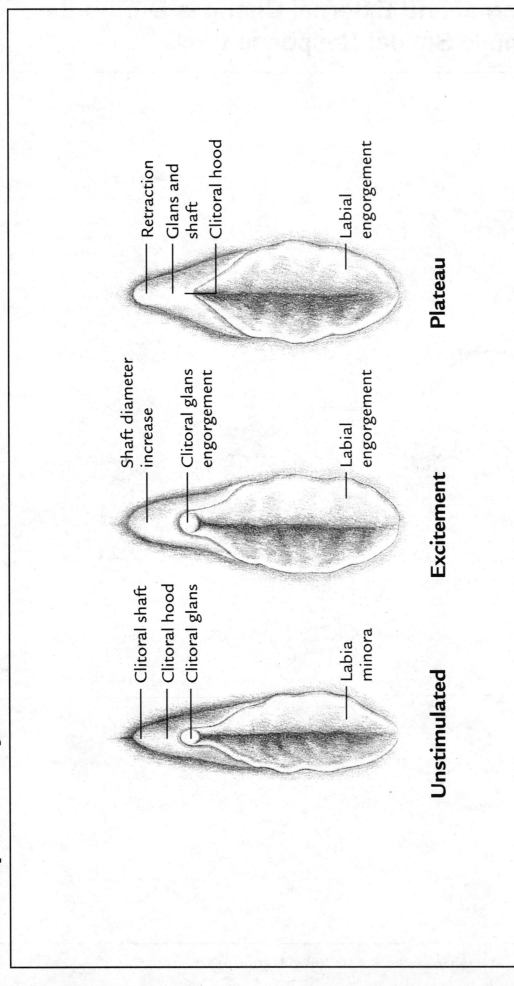

Unstimulated

Clitoral shaft
Clitoral hood
Clitoral glans

Labia minora

Excitement

Shaft diameter increase
Clitoral glans engorgement

Labial engorgement

Plateau

Retraction
Glans and shaft
Clitoral hood

Labial engorgement

Strong/DeVault/Sayad, *Human Sexuality*, 3rd ed. © 1999 Mayfield Publishing Company

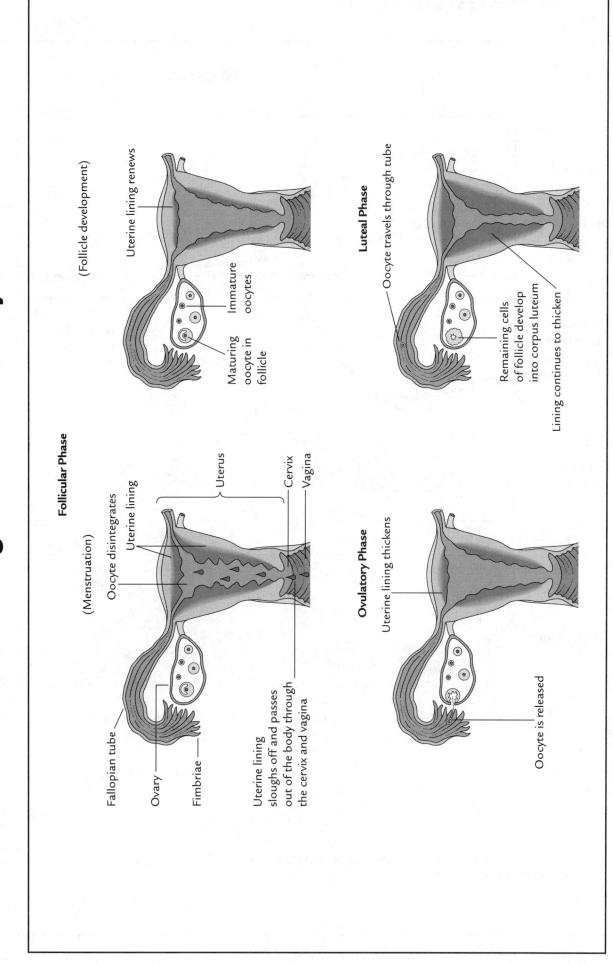

Follicular Phase

(Menstruation)

Oocyte disintegrates

Uterine lining

Uterus

Cervix

Vagina

Fallopian tube

Ovary

Fimbriae

Uterine lining sloughs off and passes out of the body through the cervix and vagina

(Follicle development)

Uterine lining renews

Immature oocytes

Maturing oocyte in follicle

Ovulatory Phase

Uterine lining thickens

Oocyte is released

Luteal Phase

Oocyte travels through tube

Remaining cells of follicle develop into corpus luteum

Lining continues to thicken

11 The Menstrual Cycle

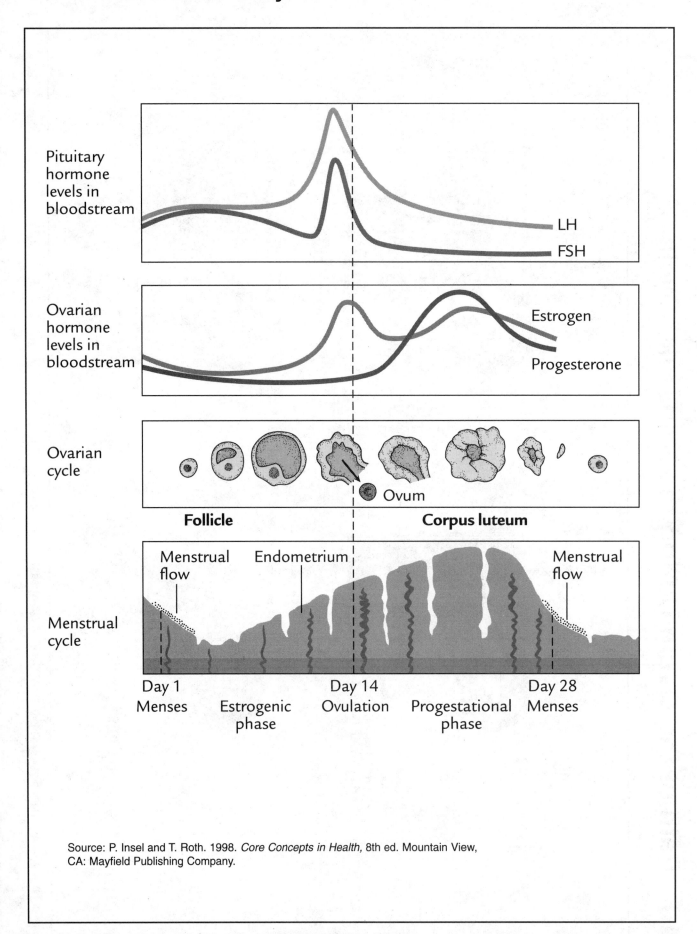

Source: P. Insel and T. Roth. 1998. *Core Concepts in Health,* 8th ed. Mountain View, CA: Mayfield Publishing Company.

12 Female Reproductive Hormones

Hormone	Where Produced	Functions
Estrogen (including estradiol, estrone, estriol)	Ovaries, adrenal glands, placenta (during pregnancy)	Promotes maturation of reproductive organs, development of secondary sex characteristics at puberty, regulates menstral cycle, sustains pregnancy
Progesterone	Ovaries, adrenal glands	Promotes breast development, maintains uterine lining, regulates menstrual cycle, sustains pregnancy
Gonadotropin-releasing hormone (GnRH)	Hypothalamus	Promotes maturation of gonads, regulates menstrual cycle
Follicle-stimulating hormone (FSH)	Pituitary	Regulates ovarian function and maturation of ovarian follicles
Luteinizing hormone (LH)	Pituitary	Assists in production of estrogen and progesterone, regulates maturation of ovarian follicles, triggers ovulation
Human chorionic gonadotropin (HCG)	Embryo and placenta	Helps sustain pregnancy
Testosterone	Ovaries, adrenal glands	Helps stimulate sexual interest
Oxytocin	Hypothalamus	Stimulates uterine contractions during childbirth
Prolactin	Pituitary	Stimulates milk production
Prostaglandins	All body cells	Mediate hormone response, stimulate muscle contractions

Strong/DeVault/Sayad, *Human Sexuality,* 3rd ed. © 1999 Mayfield Publishing Company

CHAPTER 4

MALE SEXUAL ANATOMY, PHYSIOLOGY, AND RESPONSE

CHAPTER OUTLINE

Male Sex Organs: What Are They For?
    External Structures
    Think About It: The Penis: More Than Meets the Eye
    Internal Structures
    The Breasts and Other Structures

Male Sexual Physiology
    Sex Hormones
    Think About It: Does Testosterone Cause Aggression?
    Spermatogenesis
    Semen Production

Male Sexual Response
    Erection
    Practically Speaking: Can An Erection Be Willed?
    Ejaculation and Orgasm
    Emission
    Expulsion
    Orgasm

LEARNING OBJECTIVES

At the conclusion of Chapter 4, students should be able to:

1. List and describe the functions of the external male sexual structures.

2. List and describe the functions of the internal male sexual structures.

3. Discuss our culture's myths about the penis and compare these with myths of other cultures.

4. Discuss the male breasts and other structures that may be involved in sexual activities.

5. Discuss male sexual physiology, including sex hormones and the male cycle.

6. Discuss the role of testosterone in male behavior.

7. Explain the brain-testicular axis and compare it with the ovarian cycle.

8. Describe the process of spermatogenesis, including spermiogenesis and sex determination.

9. Describe semen production.

10. Compare and contrast male and female sexual response.

11. Describe the psychological and physiological processes involved in male sexual response, including erection, ejaculation, and orgasm.

12. Recognize and define the key terms introduced in the chapter.

DISCUSSION QUESTIONS

Naming. Ask students to identify the different names, including slang and private usage, for the penis, testicles, and scrotum. (You can also do this exercise anonymously by having students write the names on 3 x 5 cards.) List these on the blackboard or on a transparency. Note the various contexts in which they are used and whether the meanings are positive, negative, or neutral. Also note how words such as "cock" and "prick" are used derogatorily.

Penis Size. Discuss cross-cultural concern about or interest in penis size. What different meanings may large to gigantic penises signify? Slides of art from ancient Rome, Japan, and Mesoamerica, as well contemporary erotic art, may be used to illustrate the point. What are some myths about penis size? How does the myth that Black men have large penises reinforce ethnic stereotypes?

Male Breasts and Eroticism. Although there are many reports of the male breasts being erotic, their eroticism is rarely discussed. Why? If heterosexual women (as well as gay men) find male breasts erotic, why aren't men required to cover their breasts in public as women are required?

Male/Female Similarities/Differences. Ask students to identify male/female similarities and differences in sexual arousal and orgasm.

ACTIVITIES

Male Reproductive System (Internal/External). Distribute the worksheet on the male reproductive system (Worksheet 8) and ask students to label each part. Note that this same sheet (with answers) is located in the *Study Guide*.

Cross Section of Penis and Testicles. Distribute the worksheet on the cross section of the penis and testicles (Worksheet 9) and ask students to label each part. Note that this same sheet (with answers) is located in the *Study Guide*.

Experience of Orgasm. Ask students to write descriptions of what "orgasm" feels like. The descriptions should be anonymous; students should identify whether they are male or female and optionally if they are heterosexual, gay, lesbian, or bisexual. Read the descriptions aloud. Ask students to discuss whether there are male/female or orientation differences in their experience of desire.

The Guessing Game. On 3 x 5 cards, write the names of parts of the male sexual anatomy. Give students the cards and have them break into small groups. Have students pin one card on each student's back without his or her knowing what the terms are. Then have students try to guess the name on the card on their back by asking others questions that can be answered "yes" or "no." For example, a student might begin by asking "Is it external?" Once the correct answer is made, the student can answer questions of another or pin his or her card on the back of a different student who then can ask questions.

SEX AND POPULAR CULTURE

Discussion: In mainstream films, the penis, whether flaccid or erect, cannot be shown in nude scenes. What "magical" power does the penis possess to cause its depiction to be censored? The state of the penis is important in classifying sexually oriented material as soft-core or hard-core: depictions of the flaccid penis are soft-core, whereas depictions of the erect penis are hard-core. Why is the state of the penis important in such classifications?

Popular Culture Response Paper (Worksheet 10): Crotch Grabbing and Bulges. Ask students to discuss the role of "crotch grabbing" and "bulges" in performers' pants in music videos by performers such as Michael Jackson and Marky Mark. (They may also look in print advertising.) What do these signify?

HEALTH CONSIDERATIONS

Discussion: If a client expressed discomfort or anxiety about the size of his penis, what would you say?

SUPPORT MATERIAL

Films and Videos

"Finding Our Way" (38 min., VHS, New Day). How men view their own sexuality is the subject of this documentary. Gathered together for a weekend retreat to talk about their sexual selves, 12 men of different ages, backgrounds, and sexual orientations participate in candid discussions that question the equation of aggression, domination, and conquest with being male.

"The Human Body: Reproductive System" (1980, 16 min., VHS, Kent State University). Animated presentation of the structures of the male and female reproductive systems. Explains bodily changes that occur during maturation, the function of hormones, and the process of fertilization and development of the embryo.

"Man Oh Man" (18 min., VHS, 16mm, New Day). This film looks at the forces that mold young boys into men. It explores personal definitions of masculinity, intergender communications, self-worth, gender stereotyping, and changing roles.

"Men's Lives" (43 min., VHS, 16mm, New Day). A beautifully done film that discusses the impact society has on defining the roles and responsibilities of being male. It shows the physical as well as the emotional impacts of sex-role typing.

"Physiological Responses of the Sexually Stimulated Male in the Laboratory" (1975, 16 min., 16mm, University of Minnesota Film and Video). Provides visual documentation of physiological changes in males during sexual stimulation.

"Sexual Anatomy and Physiology" (1986, 20 min., VHS, Multi-Focus, Inc.). A lecturer using slides of male and female genitals examines the sexual response capacities, sexual physiology, and structure of the male and female anatomy.

"The Sexual Brain" (28 min., VHS, Films for the Humanities and Sciences, Inc.). Identifies cultural, social, and physiological differences between male and female brains with respect to sexuality.

Bibliography

The books and articles listed below may be helpful for instructors wishing additional background or information on some of the topics covered in this chapter. In addition, the books listed in this chapter's "Suggested Reading" in the textbook may also be useful.

Eisler, R. *Sacred Pleasures: Sex, Myth, and the Politics of the Body.* New York: Harper Collins, 1995.

Gorman, C. "Sizing Up the Sexes." *Time,* Jan. 20, 1992, 42–51.

Gouchie, C., and D. Kimura. "The Relationship Between Testosterone Levels and Cognitive Ability Patterns." *Psychoneuroendocrinology,* 1991, 16, 323–334.

Kaplan, H. S. *The New Sex Therapy.* New York: Bruner/Mazel, 1974.

Marieb, E. N. *Human Anatomy and Physiology.* Redwood City, CA: Benjamin/Cummings, 1992.

Masters, W., and V. Johnson. *Human Sexual Response.* Boston: Little, Brown, 1966.

McAnich, J. "Editorial Comment on the Report of the Task Force on Circumcision." *Pediatrics,* 1989, 84, 667.

Morin, J. *Anal Pleasure and Health: A Guide for Men and Women.* Burlingame, CA: Yes Press, 1986.

Reinisch, J., M. Ziemba-Davis, and S. Sanders. "Hormonal Contributions to Sexually Dimorphic Behavioral Development in Humans." *Psychoneuroendocrinology,* 1991, 16, 213–278.

Strage, M. *The Durable Fig Leaf.* New York: William Morrow and Company, 1980.

Yap, P. M. "Koro—A Culture-Bound Depersonalization." D. N. Suggs and A. W. Miracle (eds.). *Culture and Human Sexuality.* Pacific Grove, CA: Brooks/Cole, 1993.

Zilbergeld, Bernie. *The New Male Sexuality.* New York: Bantam Books, 1992.

WORKSHEET 8

Male reproductive system

Label the parts of the male reproductive system.

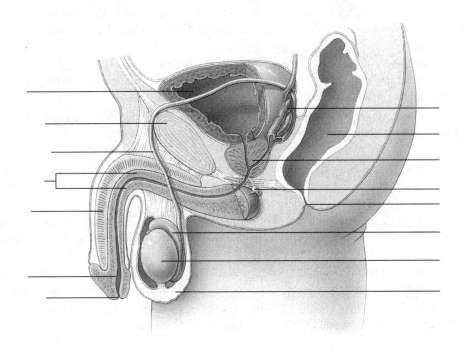

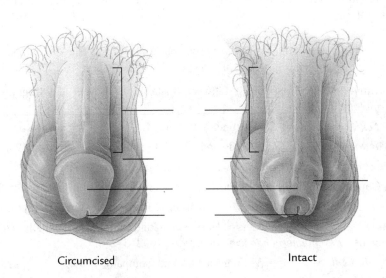

Circumcised   Intact

Strong/DeVault/Sayad, *Human Sexuality,* 3rd ed. © 1999 Mayfield Publishing Company. Chapter 4

WORKSHEET 9

Cross section of the penis and testicles

Label the parts of the penis, testicles, and shaft.

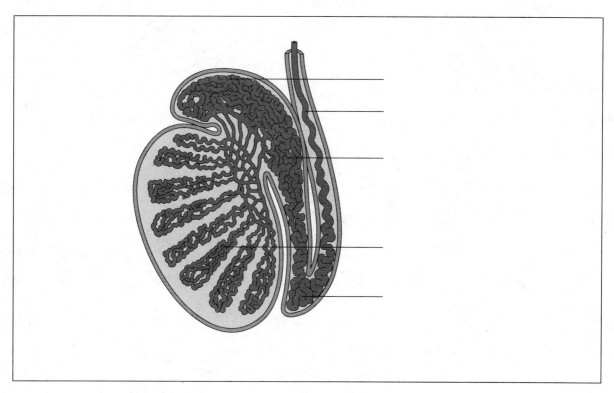

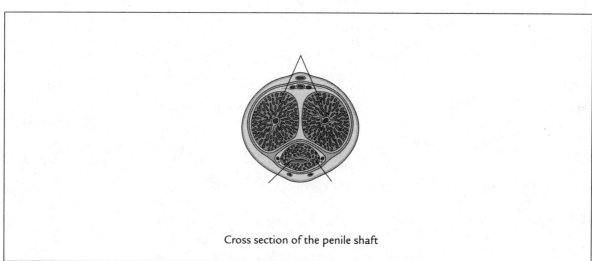

Cross section of the penile shaft

WORKSHEET 10

Popular culture response paper: Crotch Grabbing and Bulges

Name of music video/ad:

Description of content:

What underlying message or stereotype about male sexuality did the video/ad present?

Did it present its message or stereotype visually or verbally? How? Was it effective?

Comments:

Strong/DeVault/Sayad, *Human Sexuality,* 3rd ed. © 1999 Mayfield Publishing Company. Chapter 4

13 Male Sexual Anatomy

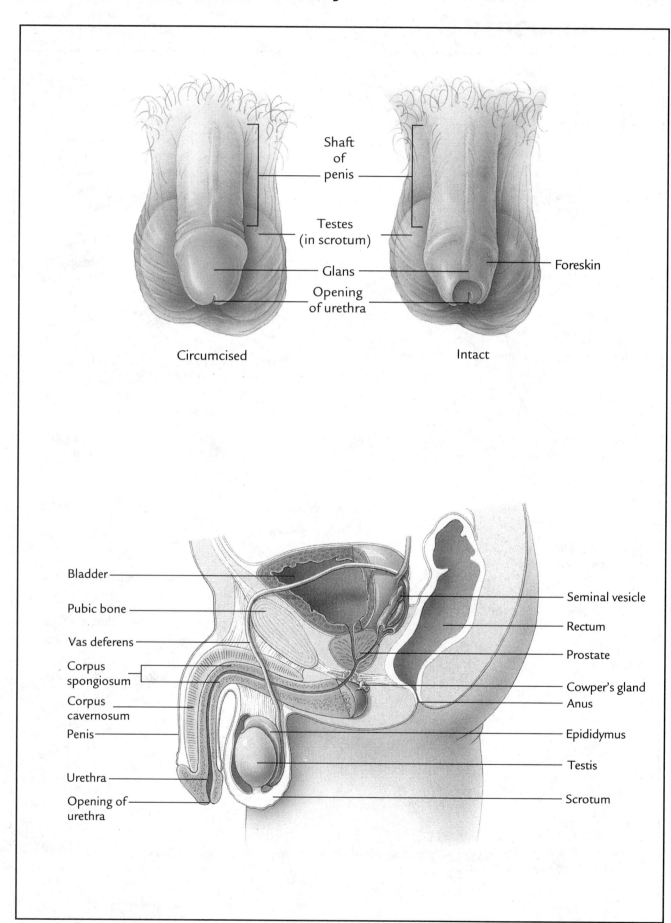

Shaft
of
penis

Testes
(in scrotum)

Glans

Opening
of urethra

Foreskin

Circumcised

Intact

Bladder

Pubic bone

Vas deferens

Corpus
spongiosum

Corpus
cavernosum

Penis

Urethra

Opening of
urethra

Seminal vesicle

Rectum

Prostate

Cowper's gland

Anus

Epididymus

Testis

Scrotum

14 Changes During the Male Sexual Response Cycle

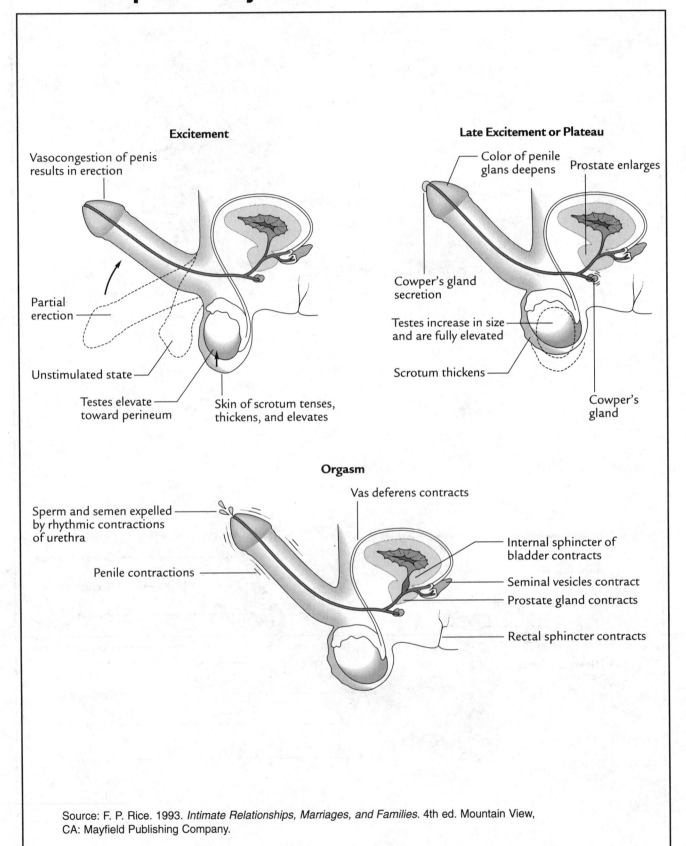

Excitement

Vasocongestion of penis results in erection

Partial erection

Unstimulated state

Testes elevate toward perineum

Skin of scrotum tenses, thickens, and elevates

Late Excitement or Plateau

Color of penile glans deepens

Prostate enlarges

Cowper's gland secretion

Testes increase in size and are fully elevated

Scrotum thickens

Cowper's gland

Orgasm

Vas deferens contracts

Sperm and semen expelled by rhythmic contractions of urethra

Penile contractions

Internal sphincter of bladder contracts

Seminal vesicles contract

Prostate gland contracts

Rectal sphincter contracts

Source: F. P. Rice. 1993. *Intimate Relationships, Marriages, and Families.* 4th ed. Mountain View, CA: Mayfield Publishing Company.

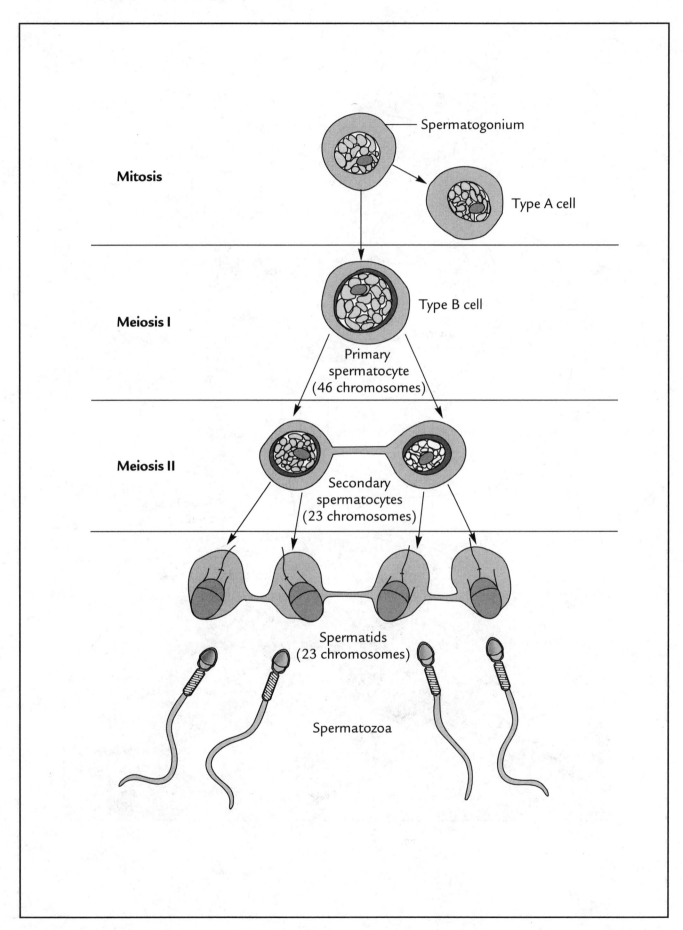

Spermatogonium

Mitosis

Type A cell

Meiosis I

Type B cell

Primary
spermatocyte
(46 chromosomes)

Meiosis II

Secondary
spermatocytes
(23 chromosomes)

Spermatids
(23 chromosomes)

Spermatozoa

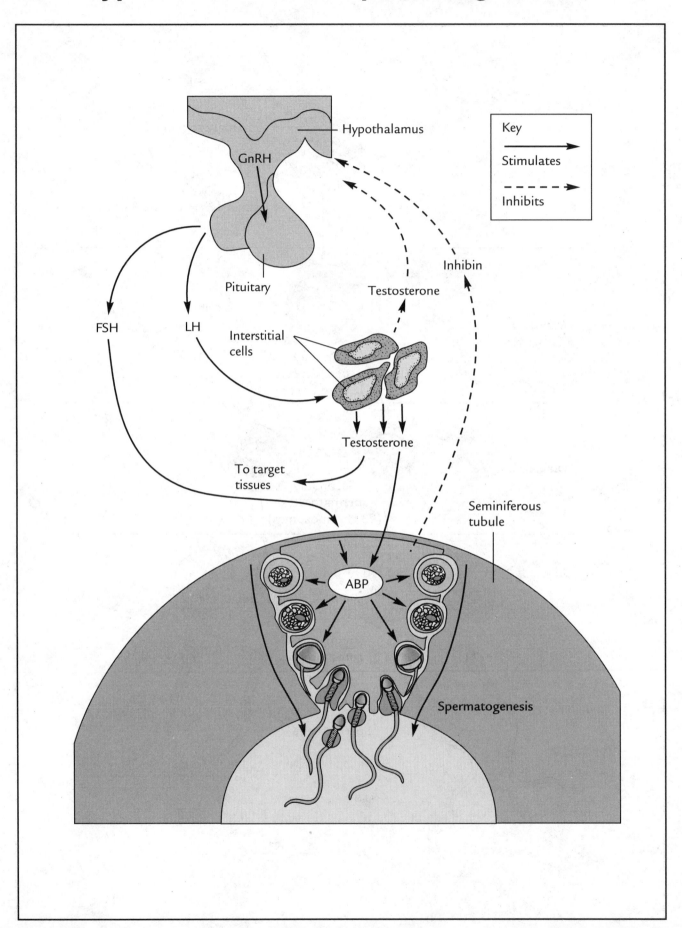

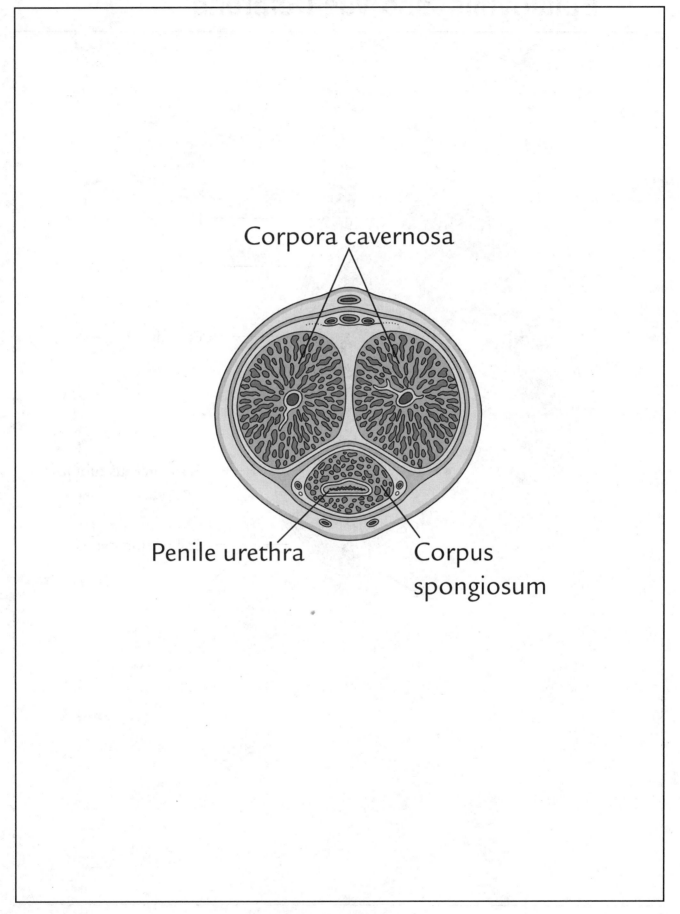

Corpora cavernosa

Penile urethra

Corpus
spongiosum

18 Cross Section of the Testicle, Epididymis, and Vas Deferens

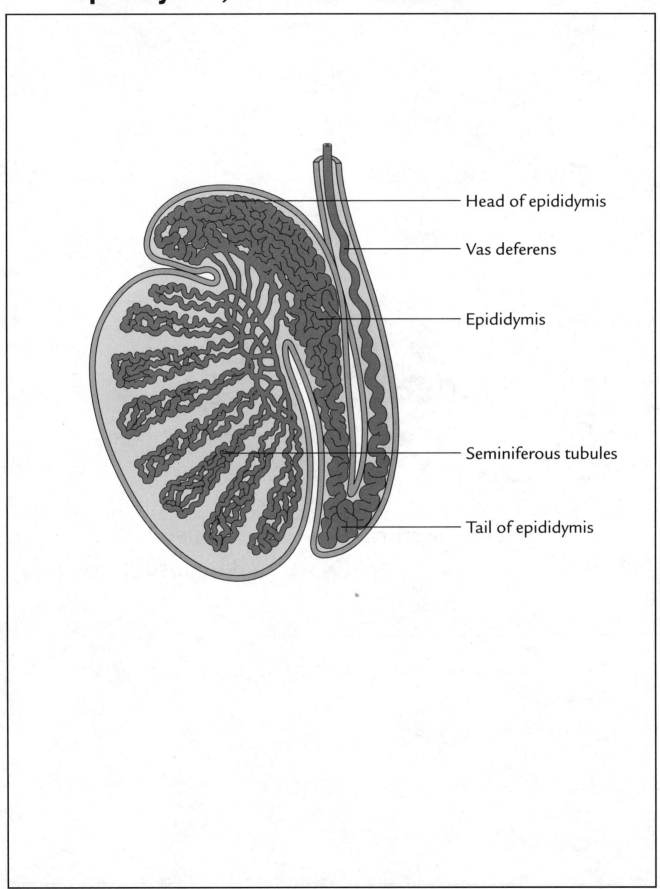

Head of epididymis

Vas deferens

Epididymis

Seminiferous tubules

Tail of epididymis

19   Male Reproductive Hormones

Hormones	Where Produced	Functions
Testosterone	Testes, adrenal glands	Stimulates sperm production in testes, triggers development of secondary sex characteristics, regulates sex drive
GnRH	Hypothalamus	Stimulates pituitary during sperm production
FSH	Pituitary	Stimulates sperm production in testes
ICSH (LH)	Pituitary	Stimulates testosterone production in interstitial cells within testes
Inhibin	Testes	Regulates sperm production by inhibiting release of FSH
Relaxin	Prostate	Increases sperm motility

Strong/DeVault/Sayad, *Human Sexuality,* 3rd ed. © 1999 Mayfield Publishing Company

CHAPTER 5
GENDER AND GENDER ROLES

CHAPTER OUTLINE

Studying Gender and Gender Roles
Sex, Gender, and Gender Roles: What's the Difference?
Sex and Gender Identity
Masculinity and Femininity: Opposites or Similar?
Gender and Sexual Orientation
Perspective 1: Don't Judge a Man by His Lipstick or a Woman by Her Motorcycle Boots
Gender Theory

Gender-Role Learning
Theories of Socialization
Gender-Role Learning in Childhood and Adolescence

Gender Schema: Exaggerating Differences

Contemporary Gender Roles
Traditional Gender Roles
Changing Gender Roles
Androgyny
Androgyny and Health

When Gender is Ambiguous: Intersexuality, Transsexuality, and Transgenderism
Intersexuality: Atypical Chromosomal and Hormonal Conditions
Transsexuality
Transsexual Surgery
The Transgender Phenomenon

New Approach in the Treatment of Sexual Ambiguities

LEARNING OBJECTIVES

At the conclusion of Chapter 5, students should be able to:

1. Define sex, gender, assigned gender, gender identity, gender roles, and sexual orientation and describe their differences from one another.

2. Discuss the evidence and implications for describing males and females as opposite or similar to each other.

3. Describe and critique sociobiology and gender theory and discuss the role of gender schema in creating or exaggerating female/male differences.

4. Explain cognitive social learning theory and cognitive developmental theory.

5. Describe gender-role learning from childhood through adolescence, including the major socialization influences.

6. Discuss traditional male and female gender roles and sexual scripts, including the significance of ethnicity.

7. Identify changes in contemporary gender roles and sexual scripts.

8. Define androgyny and explain how it contributes to psychological and emotional health.

9. Discuss hermaphroditism and list the major chromosomal and hormonal errors and their relationship to gender identity.

10. Discuss gender dysphoria and transsexuality, including causes and transsexual surgery.

11. Recognize and define the key terms introduced in the chapter.

DISCUSSION QUESTIONS

Sexual and Gender Identity Essay. The Student Handout in Part I of this book (also found in the *Study Guide*) is an explanation and format for an essay exploring gender and sexual identity. Take time to discuss how gender identity contributes to sexual expression. Tie this discussion to the paper and encourage students to examine influences (religious, peers, media, etc.) that contributed to their gender-role learning.

Gender-Related Concepts. Because gender-related issues can become heated and confusing, it is important to take a few minutes to help students understand terminology and concepts. To eliminate some of the confused thinking on the topic, make sure students understand the concepts, then ask students to define and give examples of sex, gender, assigned gender, gender identity, gender role, gender-role stereotypes, gender-role behavior, gender-role attitudes, and sexual orientation.

Critical Thinking. As students often use stereotypical images of men and women in discussing gender roles, it is important to remind them about stereotypical thinking. (This might be a good time to review the material on critical thinking in Chapter 2 of the text.) Ask students to list gender-role stereotypes. What evidence is there to support or refute these stereotypes? What are the functions of these stereotypes? How do they affect relationships and sexual interactions?

The Opposite Sex. How does referring to men or women as "the opposite sex" affect our perception of gender differences? "Opposite sex" terminology reflects the concept of bipolar gender roles.

War Between the Sexes. Ask what "war between the sexes" means. How does referring to female/male relationships as a "war between the sexes" reflect the idea that men and women are opposites or have different needs; for example, men want sex, women want love? How does it polarize relationships?

Biological/Social Origins of Gender Roles. An ongoing debate among students (as well as many others) is the origin of gender roles. Do our gender roles reflect an instinctive/biological nature or are they created by society? Ask what kind of data, such as animal or anthropological studies, are needed to support such theories. What are their shortcomings? Ask if male aggression and female nurturance are biological or social in nature—or both. What evidence is there to support assertions?

Gender-Role Learning in Childhood. Ask students to recount what they learned about being a girl or boy. Who or what—parents, peers, teachers, the media—were the most important socializers? Ask what it meant to be a sissy or tomboy, noting that the terms relate to gender rather than gender roles.

Gender-Role Learning in Adolescence. How does gender-role learning change in adolescence? Are there different pressures to conform? How is deviation from the norms handled? Do gay and lesbian adolescents have different or additional gender-role issues?

Ethnicity and Gender Roles. Ask students how ethnicity affects gender roles. Does ethnicity affect female/male gender roles equally?

Negotiating Gender Roles in Relationships. What are gender-role issues in relationships? Ask students how their partners have led them to modify their gender-role attitudes and behaviors and vice versa.

Why Can't a Woman be More Like a Man and Vice Versa. Ask students what gender-role attitudes and behaviors of the other sex they would like to see become more like their own sex's.

The Men's Movement. The new men's movement, spearheaded by Robert Bly, has sought to restore "manhood." Some argue that men are being devalued, that they have become too "feminine." Others describe the movement as a group of whiners who are reacting to women's increasing equality. Ask students to comment.

ACTIVITIES

Sexual Scripts. Ask students to anonymously write on 3 x 5 cards what the sexual scripts are for their gender (they should only identify themselves as female or male). Distribute the cards in small groups for discussion. Have each group create a list of female/male sexual scripts and report their results to the class. Then discuss sexual scripts, noting how female/male scripts facilitate or hamper relationships. Ask how sexual scripts may differ according to sexual orientation.

Gender Roles. Using Worksheet 11, ask students to list characteristics and behaviors they associate with being male and female. Do they find characteristics that apply to them in both male and female lists? What role do they think society plays in determining whether we consider certain behaviors and characteristics male and female?

Gender Schema. Ask students to divide a sheet of paper into two columns, "Masculine" and "Feminine." Ask them to list colors, activities, behavior, feelings, and so on that they consider more appropriate for one gender or the other. Is there general agreement as to whether specified items are masculine or feminine, such as pink being a female color?

Androgyny Self-Assessment. Ask students to complete the self-assessment "Masculinity, Femininity, and Androgyny" located in the *Study Guide*. Discuss how students feel if they share traits traditionally associated with the other sex.

Homosexuality and Gender Role Stereotypes. Using the list of traits in the self-assessment, ask students to identify which traits they associate with gay men and which they associate with lesbians. Do students tend to believe that gay men have more traditionally "feminine" traits then heterosexual men and that lesbians have more traditionally "masculine" traits than heterosexual women? Discuss this in terms of the misconception that homosexuality is a "failure" to fulfill traditional masculine/feminine stereotypes. Discuss whether fear of being labeled gay or lesbian reinforces adherence to traditional gender roles.

Baby X Photo. Ask students to look at the photograph of the baby on page 123. Ask them to guess the child's sex (he's a boy) and describe her or his traits. What cues did they use to guess the child's gender? Or, you could tell some students that the child is a girl and others that the child is a boy and ask them to describe traits.

Adult X. Ask a student to come to class dressed in such a way that others cannot determine gender. (The student should wear a mask that disguises cues to his or her gender.) Ask other students to introduce themselves to Adult X and make small talk How does not knowing the individual's gender affect their interaction? Why does it matter what a person's gender is?

What You Want to Know About the Other Sex. On 3 x 5 cards, have students ask anonymously for information about what they would like to know about the other sex. Distribute randomly to small groups and discuss.

SEX AND POPULAR CULTURE

Discussion: Partner as Transsexual: Ask students to imagine they were involved in a deeply loving relationship with a partner who decided she or he was trapped in the body of the wrong sex and decided to have surgery. Would they continue to love their partner if their partner changed sex? Is love dependent on genitals or does it transcend genitals?

Popular Culture Response Paper (Worksheet 12): Portrayal of Women in Advertising. Ask students to analyze advertising in TV, radio, or print, and then to determine how women are portrayed to sell products such as soft drinks, beer, automobiles, and men's cologne. What images and fantasies about women are being sold to men? Women? What role does female sexuality have in advertising?

Activity: Ask students to make a collage of titles from the covers of men's and women's magazines, such as *Playboy* and *Cosmopolitan*. Paste the women's titles on the men's magazine cover and the men's titles on the women's magazine cover. What does this juxtaposition tell you about gender roles and sexuality?

HEALTH CONSIDERATIONS

Discussion: Traditional gender roles continue to affect the medical and health profession. What kind of reactions do people have to male nurses? Female surgeons? If you are a woman, does it make a difference to you if your gynecologist or health-care worker is male or female? If you are a man, does it matter if a physician performing a testicular or prostate exam is male or female?

Activity: Role playing. An individual feels that he or she is in the wrong body and wants transsexual surgery to correct the "error." There are four roles: the gender dysphoric individual, his or her partner, a psychologist, and a plastic surgeon. The four discuss the problem, the relationship between the transsexual and partner, and the advantages and disadvantages of surgery.

Activity: Role playing. A child has just been born with a chromosomal or hormonal abnormality that has created ambiguous genitals. There are three roles to play: the mother, the father, and the attending physician, nurse, or midwife. The plot: The attendant must tell the parents about the condition and suggest alternatives.

GUEST SPEAKERS/PANELS

Invite an anthropologist to discuss gender roles in cross-cultural context.

Invite a biologist to discuss the biological basis of gender.

Invite a transsexual speaker to discuss gender dysphoria and transsexuality. The Harry Benjamin Gender Dysphoria Association, 900 Welch Road, Suite 402, Palo Alto, CA 94304 may be able to put you into contact with a transsexual in your area.

Form a panel of students from different cultural backgrounds to discuss gender learning in their families. What strengths did they find? Have they experienced conflict within their families regarding gender roles?

SUPPORT MATERIAL

Films and Videos

"The Blank Point: What is Transsexualism?" (1994, 57 min., the Cinema Guild). Examines the gender transition process.

"Brain Sex" (1993, 3 volumes, 150 min. total, Insight Media). A biological look at gender and behavior. Parts of these films can be used to demonstrate gender differences and similarities.

"Cathryn: Making the Transition from Male to Female" (1988, 20 min., VHS, Multi-Focus, Inc.). Cathryn discusses her long and costly sex-change process.

"Conversations with Chris" (1985, 185 min., VHS, University of Minnesota Film and Video). A series of four interviews covering the period of 1971–1985 with Chris, a male to female transsexual, provide a sense of the progression and change in her life as she moves toward presenting herself in her true female identity.

"Discovering Psychology Series: Sex and Gender" (1989, 56 min., VHS, Indiana University Audio Visual Center). Discusses ways in which men and women are psychologically different and similar. Explores how sex roles reflect social values.

"Gender Dysphoria" (1981, 59 min., VHS, University of Minnesota Film and Video). Several theories on the cause and psychological effects of gender dysphoria are examined. The typical procedure for sexual reassignment surgery (including graphic presentations) is provided.

"The Diary of Adam and Eve By Mark Twain" (1978, 15 min., VHS and 16mm, Indiana University Audio Visual Center). Retells and embellishes the story of Adam and Eve using separate diaries which comment on the same situations to point out the differences in the sexes.

"Female Misbehavior" (1992, 26 min. Icarus Films from Indiana University). A candid interview with a female-to-male transsexual and the logistical and personal issues he faces during his transition.

"The Gap Between the Sexes" (1989, 28 min., VHS, Kent State University). Looks at how and why men and women are different. Examines everything from hormones to the environment.

"Gender Socialization" (1993, 60 min., Insight Media). Describes the effects of socialization on feelings, thoughts, and behavior.

"Metamorphosis: Man into Woman" (58 min., VHS, 16mm, Filmakers). Shot over three years, this documentary shows the transformation of a man into a woman. The film follows Gary/Gabi through surgery, hormone therapy, psychological counseling, support groups, and dealing with coworkers.

"The Pinks and the Blues" (1980, 58 min., VHS and 16mm, PCR: Films and Video in the Behavioral Sciences). A study of the socialization process that modifies a child's behavior according to common assumptions about what is "masculine" or "feminine."

"Sex and Money" (50 min. VHS, Filmakers). In this documentary, Dr. John Mondy of Johns Hopkins Hospital shares his ideas on gender identity. He presents his theories on the anatomical and biological factors that steer one toward masculinity or femininity, as well as the historical, cultural, and sociological influences at each stage of a person's gender-identity development.

"What Sex Am I?" (57 min., Facets Multi Media). A documentary that looks at male-female and female-male transsexuals as well as transvestites. Also includes discussions with their partners.

"Woman and Man" (1986, 52 min., VHS, Kent State University). First examines the innate biological and behavioral differences between men and women. Then discusses how society has traditionally reinforced these differences. (From the "Phil Donahue Examines the Human Animal Series").

Bibliography

The books and articles listed below may be helpful for instructors wishing additional background or information on some of the topics covered in this chapter. In addition, the books listed in this chapter's "Suggested Reading" in the textbook may also be useful.

Barbach, L. *For Each Other: Sharing Sexual Intimacy.* Garden City, NY: Doubleday, 1982.

Bergen, D. J. and J. E. Williams. "Sex Stereotypes in the United States Revisited: 1972–1988." *Sex Roles,* 1991, 24(7/8), 413–423.

Binion, V. "Psychological Androgyny: A Black Female Perspective." *Sex Roles,* April 1990, 22(7–8), 487–507.

Bonvillain, N. *Women and Men: Cultural Constructs of Gender* (2nd ed.). New Jersey: Prentice-Hall, 1998.

Bullough, V. "Transvestism: A Reexamination." *Journal of Psychology and Human Sexuality,* 1991, 4(2), 53–67.

Dancey, C. "The Relationship of Instrumentality and Expressivity to Sexual Orientation in Women." *Journal of Homosexuality,* 1992, 23(4), 73–82.

Faderman, L. *Odd Girls and Twilight Lovers.* New York: Penguin Books, 1991.

Fausto-Sterling, A. *Myths of Gender: Biological Theories about Women and Men.* New York: Basic Books, 1985.

Hare-Mustin, R. T. and J. Marecek. (eds.). *Making a Difference: Psychology and the Construction of Gender.* New Haven, CT: Yale University Press, 1990.

Hunter, A. G. and J. E. Davis. "Constructing Gender: An Exploration of Afro-American Men's Conceptualization of Manhood." *Gender and Society,* September 1992, 6(3), 464–479.

Kockott, G. and E. M. Fahrner. "Male-to-Female and Female-to-Male Transsexuals: A Comparison." *Archives of Sexual Behavior,* December 1988, 17(6), 539–546.

Lips, H. *Sex and Gender.* (3d ed.). Mountain View, CA: Mayfield Publishing Co., 1997.

Pauly, J. "Gender Identity Disorders: Evaluation and Treatment." *Journal of Sex Education and Therapy,* 1990, 16(1), 2–24.

Reid, P. and L. Comas-Diaz. "Gender and Ethnicity: Perspectives on Dual Status." *Sex Roles,* April 1990, 22 (7), 397–408.

Tavris, C. and C. Wade. *The Longest War: Sex Differences in Perspective* (2d ed.). New York: Harcourt Brace Jovanovich, 1984.

Zilbergeld, B. *Male Sexuality*. New York: Little, Brown, 1992.

WORKSHEET 11

Gender roles

In the spaces provided below, list ten characteristics and behaviors that you associate with being male and female in our society.

Male	**Female**
1. _____	1. _____
2. _____	2. _____
3. _____	3. _____
4. _____	4. _____
5. _____	5. _____
6. _____	6. _____
7. _____	7. _____
8. _____	8. _____
9. _____	9. _____
10. _____	10. _____

Circle the numbers of ten characteristics from the twenty that you feel best apply to yourself. Did you choose any characteristics from your list for the opposite sex? If so, how many? _____

If you found most of the characteristics you chose for yourself were from your list for your own sex, are there any characteristics from the other list you wish you did have? Do you feel our society's definitions of gender roles are preventing you from behaving or developing in the ways you'd most like to?

Strong/DeVault/Sayad, *Human Sexuality,* 3rd ed. © 1999 Mayfield Publishing Company. Chapter 5

If the characteristics you chose for yourself were a mix of both lists, what do you think your description of yourself indicates about the prevailing ideas about male and female characteristics you described for our society? How valid are they?

WORKSHEET 12

Popular culture response paper: Portrayal of Women in Advertising

Name of Ad:

Description of Content:

What underlying message or stereotype about women did it present?

Did it present its message or stereotype visually or verbally? How? Was it effective?

Comments:

Strong/DeVault/Sayad, *Human Sexuality,* 3rd ed. © 1999 Mayfield Publishing Company. Chapter 5

20 Abnormalities in Prenatal Development

	Chromosomal Sex*	Gonads	Internal Reproductive Structures	External Reproductive Structures	Secondary Sex Characteristics	Gender Identity
Chromosomal Abnormalities						
Turner syndrome	Female (45, XO)	Nonfunctioning or absent ovaries	Normal female except for ovaries	Underdeveloped genitals	No breast development for menstruation at puberty	Female
Klinefelter syndrome	Male (47, XXY)	Testes	Normal male	Small penis and testes	Female secondary sex characteristics develop at puberty	Male, but frequent gender confusion at puberty
Hormonal Abnormalities						
Androgen-insensitivity syndrome	Male (46,XY)	Testes, but body unable to utilize androgen (testosterone)	Shallow vagina, lacks normal male structures	Labia	Female secondary sex characteristics develop at puberty; no menstruation	Female
Cogenital adrenal hyperplasia (pseudo-hermaphroditism)	Female (46,XX)	Ovaries	Normal female	Ambiguous, tending toward male appearance; fused vagina and enlarged clitoris may be mistaken for empty scrotal sac and micropenis	Female secondary sex characteristics develop at puberty	Usually male unless condition discovered at birth and rectified by hormonal therapy
DHT deficiency	Male (46,XY)	Testes undescended until puberty	Partially formed internal structures but no prostate	Ambiguous; clitoral-appearing micropenis; penis enlarges and testes descend at puberty	Male secondary sex characteristics develop at puberty	Female identity until puberty; majority assume male identity later

*Chromosomal sex refers to 46, XX (female) or 46, XY (male). Sometimes a chromosome will be missing, as in 45, XO, or there will be an extra chromosome, as in 47, XXY. In these notations, the number refers to the number of chromosomes (46, in 23 pairs, is normal); the letters X and Y refer to chromosomes and O refers to a missing chromosome.

Strong/DeVault/Sayad, *Human Sexuality*, 3rd ed. © 1999 Mayfield Publishing Company

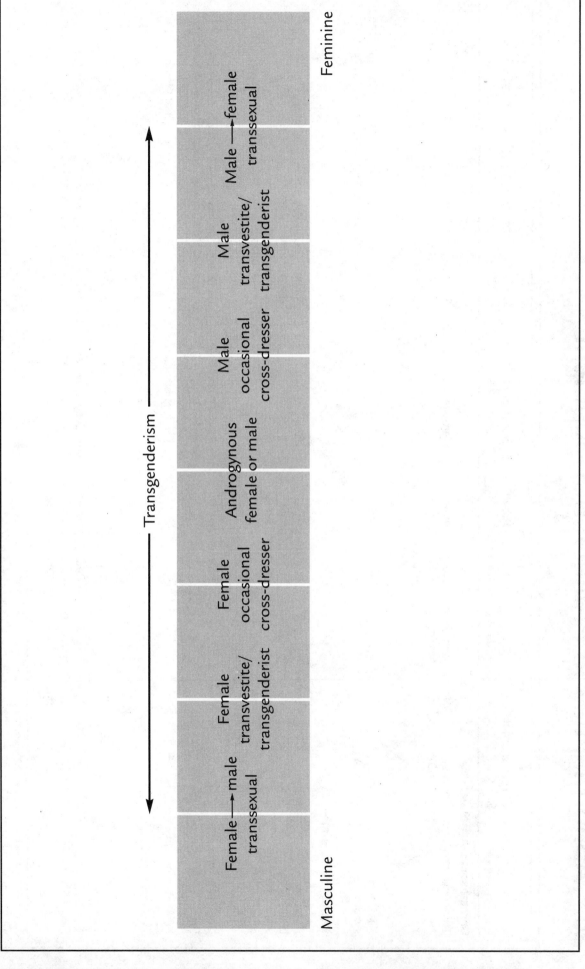

Strong/DeVault/Sayad, *Human Sexuality*, 3rd ed. © 1999 Mayfield Publishing Company

CHAPTER 6
SEXUALITY OVER THE LIFE SPAN

CHAPTER OUTLINE

Sexuality in Infancy and Childhood
Childhood Sexuality
The Family Context

Sexuality in Adolescence
Psychosexual Development
Think About It: The "Origins" of Homosexuality
Adolescent Sexual Behavior
Adolescent Pregnancy
Think About It: Reducing Adolescent Pregnancy
Sex Education
Think About It: Sex Education: A Cross-Cultural Perspective

Sexuality in Early Adulthood
Developmental Concerns
Premarital Sexuality
Establishing Sexual Orientation
Think About It: Bisexuality: The Nature of Dual Attraction
Being Single
Think About It: Common Misconceptions About Homosexuality
Cohabitation

Sexuality in Middle Adulthood
Developmental Concerns
Marital Sexuality
Extramarital Sexuality
Divorce and After

Sexuality in Late Adulthood
Developmental Concerns
Stereotypes of Aging
Sexuality, Partner Availability, and Health
Male and Female Differences
Think About It: What Physicians (and the Rest of Us) Need to Know About Sex and Aging

LEARNING OBJECTIVES

At the conclusion of Chapter 6, students should be able to:

1. Discuss psychosexual development in infancy and childhood, including sexual curiosity, sex play, and masturbation, and the role of the family in teaching children about sexuality.

2. Discuss current research on the "origins" of homosexuality.

3. List and discuss physical changes during puberty for both girls and boys.

4. Discuss influences on adolescent psychosexual development, including parents, peers, and the media.

5. Describe special problems confronted by gay and lesbian adolescents.

6. Discuss adolescent sexual learning, including masturbation, normative behavior sequence, virginity, and first intercourse.

7. Discuss adolescent contraceptive use, including the roles of erotophobia, lack of information, risk taking, and role testing.

8. Describe and critique contemporary sex education.

9. Discuss teenage pregnancy, including causes and motivation and the characteristics and needs of teenage mothers and fathers.

10. Describe the policy components for reducing adolescent pregnancy.

11. Discuss premarital sexuality, including its increasing acceptance and the factors leading to premarital sexual involvement.

12. Describe the process of establishing a gay or lesbian identity and the different forms of bisexuality.

13. Describe cohabitation among heterosexuals, gay men, and lesbians, including advantages and disadvantages and differences between heterosexual and gay/lesbian cohabitation.

14. Discuss marital sexuality, including frequency of sexual interactions, the significance of monogamy, and reproductive legitimacy.

15. Describe extrarelational involvements, including extrarelational sex in dating/cohabitating relationships and extramarital sex in sexually exclusive and sexually nonexclusive marriages.

16. Explain the different factors affecting nonmarital sex for postdivorce individuals and single parents.

17. Describe the stereotypes of aging, male/female and orientation differences in aging, and the significance of health and partner availability.

18. Recognize and define the key terms introduced in the chapter.

DISCUSSION QUESTIONS

Childhood Sexuality. Ask students what they learned about sexuality during childhood from their parents, peers, the media, school, and religion. How were sexual curiosity and sex play treated? What were they taught about sexual pleasure? Encourage them to include these thoughts in their gender/sexual identity paper.

Body Image Transition. As girls and boys begin to physically mature, there may be a discordance between how they feel and how they are perceived by others as increasingly sexual beings. Ask students how they felt about themselves and their body during this transition period between childhood and adolescence.

Parents and Adolescents. What did parents do to encourage or restrain their children's sexual activities during junior high school, high school, and college? How did parents' actions differ during each particular period? Did parental rules differ depending on whether their child was male or female? (These are the kinds of questions that students should ask when preparing the gender/sexual identity paper.)

Ethnicity and First Intercourse. Age of first intercourse tends to differ by ethnicity. Ask the class what cultural factors might be involved in these differences. What stereotypes are used to account for ethnic differences? What are the underlying messages of these stereotypes?

Heterosexuality/Homosexuality. At what age should children be taught about heterosexuality and homosexuality? What should they be told? What do they already know at that age?

Goals of Sex Education. Ask students what they learned about sexuality in their sex education courses in school. Should sex education teach abstinence and the use of condoms to prevent pregnancy and STDs/HIV or only abstinence? Should sex education be expanded beyond pregnancy and disease prevention to include discussions of sexual pleasure? What should be taught about homosexuality?

Causes of Heterosexuality. Ask students to identify the causes of heterosexuality. Are they biological or social? (Most will argue that heterosexuality is rooted in biology.) What evidence do they have? (Usually none except biological inferences.) What is the significance of people expressing great interest in the origins of homosexuality but little in the origins of heterosexuality?

Developmental Issues of Adulthood. Discuss the developmental concerns involved in early adulthood. How is each addressed? Compare those concerns to those of middle adulthood and old age. What ones remain the same? Change? How does breaking up and divorce affect these concerns?

Gay/Lesbian/Heterosexual Identity Process. Compare the developmental process of how a gay/lesbian identity differs from that of a heterosexual identity. Discuss the role of socialization, role models, expectations, dating, and sexual experiences.

Meeting Spots. Have students discuss the various meeting places where men and women find potential partners. Discuss age, orientation, and ethnic considerations that may affect locations. What are the advantages and disadvantages of each place?

Singlehood. Discuss the pros and cons of singlehood during youth, middle age, and old age for men and women. What are the forces pushing individuals toward marriage and those pulling them toward singlehood? For gay men and lesbians, what are the pros and cons of singlehood versus a committed relationship?

Biological versus Social Basis of Homosexuality. What difference does it make whether homosexuality is biological or social in origin?

Stereotypes of the Aged. Ask students if they can imagine older people being sexual. If they cannot, ask at what age they believe individuals stop being sexual. What are the reasons they cannot imagine older adults being sexual?

ACTIVITIES

First Sexual Awareness/Feeling/Activity. Ask students to write, anonymously, on 3 x 5 cards what their earliest sexual feeling/awareness/activity was and how they felt about it. Break into small groups for discussion. Are there common sexual experiences? Feelings about them?

Age and Level of Sexual Activities. Ask students to write, anonymously, on 3 x 5 cards at what age the following sexual activities are acceptable for females and males: kissing, sexual intercourse, oral sex, holding hands, masturbation, petting, anal sex. Then distribute the cards in small groups. Ask each group to arrive at a consensus for each activity. Are some activities never acceptable? Why? Are there different ages for males and females? Is level of commitment or marital status important?

Parent/Child Role-Playing. This activity consists of four sets of role-playing centering around a parent talking with his or her six-year-old child about masturbation. In each case, the parent has inadvertently discovered the child playing with himself or herself. Set 1: Mother/son. Set 2: Mother/daughter. Set 3: Father/son. Set 4: Father/daughter. Does the message differ depending on the gender combination?

Debate on School-Based Health Clinics. Former Surgeon General Jocelyn Elders has been a long-time proponent of school-based health clinics that would provide, among other services, birth control counseling and the availability of condoms to prevent pregnancy and STD/HIV transmission. Debate the pros and cons of providing birth control counseling and condom distribution.

Coming-Out-to-Family Role-Playing. This role-playing consists of four people—mother, father, sibling, and adolescent. The adolescent tells the parents that she or he is lesbian or gay. What happens?

Premarital Sex. Ask students to take a sheet of paper and make three columns, labeling them "Individual," "Relational," and "Environmental." Ask students to list in the appropriate column the factors involved in their last erotic encounter (which may be hand-holding, kissing, sexual intercourse, and so on).

Extrarelational Sex. Ask students to indicate anonymously on 3 x 5 cards whether they have ever been involved in extrarelational sex (including passionate kissing, fondling, oral sex, or sexual intercourse). If they have, ask them to briefly indicate their motivation. Read some or all of the cards and discuss.

Dating Partners. Ask men and women to list anonymously on 3 x 5 cards the five most important qualities they look for in a dating partner. (They should indicate whether they are male or female and, optionally, their sexual orientation.) These cards should be collected, then distributed randomly to small groups for discussion. The groups should try to find a consensus of male/female traits and report to the class.

Coming-Out Role-Playing. Scenario 1: Lesbian or gay man tells best friend that she or he is gay. Scenario 2: Lesbian or gay man tells roommate that she or he is gay.

SEX AND POPULAR CULTURE

Popular Culture Response Paper (Worksheet 14): Child/Adolescent Sexuality. Have students watch their favorite family-oriented sitcom and report on how child and adolescent sexuality are treated.

Discussion: Compare how child and adolescent sexuality are treated in "Boy Meets World," "My So-Called Life," and "Family Matters." What stereotypes are presented about adolescents? Their parents? Does ethnicity have an impact?

Activity: Have students bring in news or magazine clippings or video excerpts on adolescent pregnancy. How does the media treat adolescent pregnancy? Is adolescent pregnancy perceived as a problem? For whom is it a problem? What stereotypes are involved?

Discussion: What are popular myths about adolescent sexuality? Myths may include "raging hormones lead to preoccupation with sex," "girls get pregnant to snag a guy," and so on.

Popular Culture Response Paper (Worksheet 15): Sex and Older Adults. Have students watch "The Golden Girls" or a similar program on television. How is sexuality depicted among older women? Men? How accurate is its depiction?

Discussion: The majority of sexual encounters on television and in movies are between young single men and women or a married person and someone other than his or her partner. What values and ideas are being conveyed? Is premarital sex a media norm? A cultural norm? What messages are being conveyed about marital sexuality or sexuality among older adults who are widowed?

Discussion: Have students compare and contrast the depiction of marital sexuality in "Married with Children," "Roseanne," and "Growing Pains." What messages about marital sexuality are being conveyed in each?

Discussion: Ask students to imagine that all they knew about extramarital sex was based on TV talk shows and soaps. What would they believe about affairs? How widespread would they think extramarital sex is? Because affairs are a dominant theme of much TV, students are likely to overestimate the incidence.

HEALTH CONSIDERATIONS

Discussion: Ask how students would handle a young adolescent with gynecomastia who came to them with his father. The boy is afraid he is becoming a girl. How would they handle such a situation?

Discussion: Ask students to imagine they were working in a school-based health clinic and a girl came in, concerned because she was bleeding from the vagina. She did not know she was having her first period. How would students counsel the girl?

Activity: Role-playing about adolescent pregnancy in a school-based health clinic. Four roles: Health care provider, pregnant adolescent, her partner, and girl's parent. Act out the following scenario: An adolescent who is 6 weeks pregnant comes to the health clinic for help. She is accompanied by her boyfriend and parent. The girl, boyfriend, and parent can't agree on what to do. The health care provider tries to help them sort out their feelings and to support the pregnant adolescent.

Activity: Role-playing about sexual orientation. Three people—health professional or physician, parent, adolescent—act out the following scenario: A distraught parent comes to the health professional after discovering his or her child is gay or lesbian. The parent wants the adolescent to be heterosexual. The adolescent wants the parent to accept his/her orientation.

Discussion: Imagine you have a middle-aged male client who is distressed because his orgasms are no longer the "cosmic" ones of his youth. He is not frustrated, only bothered. What would you advise him?

Discussion: How would you suggest that individuals adjust their sexual activities, expectations, and meanings as they age? What physiological processes must they consider? Health problems?

Discussion: What health concerns would have to be considered for individuals having sex outside their marriage? If they were bisexual and their partner did not know?

Activity: Role-playing a gay man or a lesbian in a heterosexual marriage. In this activity there are three roles: health-care professional, gay man or lesbian, and his or her heterosexual partner; the couple has several children. The scenario: A heterosexual man or woman complains about the decline of sexual interactions in his or her relationship; his or her partner indicates that he or she may be gay or lesbian. The problem: Find the best possible solution for the couple.

Activity: Role-playing with three people: health-care worker, older man and woman in convalescent hospital; the couple, who are unmarried, are involved in a passionate embrace. The health-care professional walks in on them. What happens next?

GUEST SPEAKERS/PANELS

Invite an early childhood educator to discuss childhood sexuality.

Invite a health-care professional to discuss the role of school-based clinics in the public schools.

Invite a panel of pregnant adolescents and adolescent mothers (and if possible their partners) to discuss experiences, myths, problems, and strengths involved in adolescent parenting. (Speakers may be found through social workers or local school programs for pregnant adolescents or mothers.)

Form a panel with students from diverse ethnic backgrounds, if possible, to discuss their childhood learning experiences about sexuality. What messages were given them by their family? Peers? Media?

Invite a supporter and opponent of comprehensive family life education to debate sex education in your community's schools.

Form a panel of students of diverse ages to discuss the significance of sex in their lives at different ages. How does sexuality change as they age?

Form a panel of individuals who are dating, cohabiting, and married to discuss the role of sexuality in their relationships. Does the meaning of sexuality—such as significance, bonding, and procreating—change according to the nature of the relationship?

Invite a panel of gay men and lesbians (including class members if they are out) to discuss their social lives and the role of the gay/lesbian community in supporting them.

Invite a panel of separated, divorced, or widowed individuals to discuss how dating and sexual issues differ from premarital dating and sex. How does being a single parent affect dating? Being widowed?

SUPPORT MATERIAL

Films and Videos

"An Empty Bed" (56 min., Yankee Oriole Company, Kent State University). Reflections and feelings of an older gay man who now experiences loneliness and regret.

"Baby Clock" (1982, 48 min., VHS, Kent State University). Looks at five women who face the issue of whether or not to have children in middle age. Discusses amniocentesis, peer group pressure, single parenthood, and day care issues.

"Before Stonewall: The Making of a Gay and Lesbian Community" (1984, 87 min., VHS, University of Minnesota Film and Video). Using filmed recollections and archival material, this program traces the social, political, and cultural development of the gay and lesbian community.

"Children of Children" (1987, 31 min., VHS, Indiana University Audio Visual Center). Explores the problem of teen pregnancy and presents two programs aimed at prevention.

"Florence and Robin: Lesbian Parenthood" (1994, 52 min., VHS, Films for the Humanities and Sciences). Describes the processes and challenges that two lesbians experience as they become parents.

"Gay Women Speak" (1979, 15 min., VHS and 16mm, Multi-Focus, Inc.). Three professional women active in the lesbian community share anecdotes of childhood, careers, and the experience of being lesbian.

"The Heart Has No Wrinkles" (1991, 15 min., VHS, Carle Medical Communications). Two retirement home residents become romantically involved and provoke strong reactions from the staff. Designed to stimulate discussion on aging and sexuality. (This film received an honorable mention in the 1991 National Council on Family Relations Media Competition.)

"Honored by the Moon" (1989, 15 min., VHS, University of Minnesota Film and Video). Provides examples of traditional roles and beliefs of Native American women and men. Offers introductory information for discussions about homosexuality and particularly homophobia in the Native American community. (Also cited in Chapter 1.)

"Main Street: Growing Up Gay" (1987, 10 min., VHS, University of Minnesota Film and Video). An NBC news report looks at the lives of teenage gays and lesbians through personal interviews with young people.

"Menopause: Living the Change" (1994, 30 min., VHS, Filmmakers Library, from Indiana University). Interviews a variety of women in order to help demystify the process and explore the choices that are available as one ages.

"Not All Parents Are Straight" (1994, 57 min., Cinema Guild, Kent State University). This program examines the dynamics of the parent-child relationship within several different households where children are being raised by gay and lesbian parents.

"On Being Gay: A Conversation with Brian McNaught" (80 min., VHS, ETR Associates). Author and counselor Brian McNaught discusses the fallacies, facts, and feelings of being gay in a straight world. He encourages both gay and non-gay viewers to realize their own potential and to replace self-doubt with self-esteem, self-knowledge, and self-confidence.

"Project Future: Teenage Pregnancy, Childbirth, and Parenting" (1992, 145 min., VHS, Vida Health Communications). Follows 12 young men and women from the third trimester through the third month postpartum. (This film was a winner in the 1992 National Council on Family Relations Media Competition.)

"Rose by Any Other Name" (1979, 15 min., VHS and 16mm, Multi-Focus, Inc. or University of Minnesota Film and Video). A 79-year-old woman faces pressure from her family and the nursing home staff to end her sexual relationship with a man. This film portrays issues of affection, privacy, and sexuality for older people living in nursing facilities.

"Sex After 50" (1991, 90 min., VHS, The Sexuality Library). Explicit interviews with dozens of men and women from age 50 to 90. (No sex is depicted.)

"Sex and Marriage" (1994, 30 min., VHS, Insight Media). Describes diverse cultural traditions as they relate to marriage and sexuality.

"Sex and Society: Everyday Abuses to Children's Emerging Sexuality" (1991, 55 min., VHS, The Glendon Association). Looks at how society and attitudes negatively impact the developing sexuality of children. Men and women describe the negative feelings they have toward sex and their bodies and where these feelings come from. (This film received an honorable mention in the 1991 National Council on Family Relations Media Competition.)

"Sexual Development in Children" (1983, 45 min., VHS, Multi-Focus, Inc.). Examines development from infancy through the teenage years within the context of sexuality. Also explores societal norms and values regarding childhood sexuality.

"Sexual Orientation: Reading Between the Labels" (1992, 29 min., VHS, NEWIST/CESA). Documents a forum for gay and lesbian teens to discuss their experiences of realizing their sexuality, coping with homophobia, and the reactions of their peers and families. (This film received an honorable mention in the 1992 National Council on Family Relations Media Competition.)

"Sexuality and Aging" (1987, 58 min., VHS, Kent State University). Explores the attitudes, myths, and facts concerning sexuality as it relates to senior citizens.

"Sexuality: A Woman's View" (1981, 30 min., VHS and 16mm, Multi-Focus, Inc.). Stefanie Powers explores the world of women's attitudes about human sexuality. Current changes in views on women's sexuality are discussed.

"Silent Pioneers" (1985, 42 min., VHS and 16mm, University of Minnesota Film and Video). Profiles eight older gays and lesbians who managed to lead meaningful lives despite living through an era when homosexuality was not tolerated.

"Variations on a Theme" (1986, 20 min., VHS, Multi-Focus, Inc.). Men and women from diverse backgrounds discuss the social, psychological, and political ramifications of growing up gay and lesbian.

"What if I'm Gay?" (1989, 30 min., VHS, Coronet/MTI). A teenager raises numerous questions after realizing that he is gay. (This film received an honorable mention in the 1989 National Council on Family Relations Media Competition.)

Bibliography

The books and articles listed below may be helpful for instructors wishing additional background or information on some of the topics covered in this chapter. In addition, the books listed in this chapter's "Suggested Reading" in the textbook may also be useful.

Barbach, L. *The Pause.* New York: Signet Books, 1994.

Bell, A., M. Weinberg, and S. Hammersmith. *Sexual Preference: Its Development in Men and Women.* Bloomington, IN: Indiana University Press, 1981.

Billy, J., K. Tanfer, W. R. Grady, and D. H. Klepinger. "The Sexual Behavior of Men in the United States." *Family Planning Perspectives,* Mar. 1993, 25(2), 52–60.

Blumstein, P., and P. Schwartz. *American Couples.* New York: McGraw-Hill, 1985.

Center for Population Options. *Teenage Pregnancy and Too-Early Childbearing: Public Costs, Personal Consequences,* 1992.

Constantine, L., and F. Martinson (eds.). *Children and Sex.* Boston: Little, Brown, 1981.

DiBlasio, F. A., and B. B. Benda. "Gender Differences in Theories of Adolescent Sexual Activity." *Sex Roles,* 1992, 27(5/6), 221–236.

Doress-Wor, P. *The New Ourselves, Growing Older.* New York: Simon & Schuster, 1994.

Dryfoos, J. "What the United States Can Learn about Prevention of Teenage Pregnancy from Other Developed Countries." *SIECUS Report,* November 1985, 14(2), 1–7.

Fine, M. "Sexuality, Schooling, and Adolescent Females: The Missing Discourse of Desire." *Harvard Education Review,* 1988, 58, 29–53.

Franklin, D. L. "The Impact of Early Childbearing on Development Outcomes: The Case of Black Adolescent Parenting." *Family Relations,* 1988, 37, 268–274.

Gagnon, J. "Attitudes and Responses of Parents to Pre-Adolescent Masturbation." *Archives of Sexual Behavior,* 1985, 14(5), 451–466.

Gecas, V., and M. Seff. "Families and Adolescents." A. Booth (ed.). *Contemporary Families: Looking Forward, Looking Back*. Minneapolis, MN: National Council on Family Relations, 1991.

Gochros, J. S. *When Husbands Come Out of the Closet*. New York: Haworth Press, 1989.

Gullotta, T. P., et al. (eds.). *Adolescent Sexuality*. Newbury Park, CA.: Sage Publications, 1993.

Hamer, D., and P. Copeland. *The Science of Desire*. New York: Simon & Schuster, 1994.

Hansen, G. "Extradyadic Relations During Courtship." *Journal of Sex Research,* Aug. 1987, 23(3), 383–390.

Hochhauser, M. "Moral Development and HIV Prevention Among Adolescents." *Family Life Educator,* Mar. 1992, 10(3), 9–12.

Jacoby, A., and J. Williams, "Effects of Premarital Sexual Standards and Behavior on Dating and Marriage Desirability." *Journal of Marriage and the Family,* Nov. 1985, 47(4), 1059–1065.

Loulan, J. *Lesbian Sex*. San Francisco, CA: Spinsters Books, 1984.

Martin, A. *The Lesbian and Gay Parenting Handbook*. New York: HarperCollins, 1993.

Money, J. *Gay, Straight, and In-Between*. New York: Oxford University Press, 1988.

Moultrup, D. J. *Husbands, Wives, and Lovers: The Emotional System of the Extramarital Affair*. New York: Guilford Press, 1990.

Roberts, E. "Childhood Sexual Learning: The Unwritten Curriculum." C. Davis (ed.). *Challenges in Sexual Science*. Philadelphia: Society for the Scientific Study of Sex, 1983.

Robinson, B. *Teenage Fathers*. Lexington, MA: Lexington Books, 1987.

Rubin, A. M., and J. R. Adams. "Outcomes of Sexually Open Marriages." *Journal of Sex Research,* 1986, 22, 311–319.

Savin-Williams, R., and R. G. Rodriguez. "A Developmental, Clinical Perspective on Lesbian, Gay Male, and Bisexual Youths." T. P. Gullotta et al. (eds.). *Adolescent Sexuality*. Newbury Park, CA: Sage Publications, 1993.

Shostak, A. B. "Singlehood." M. Sussman and S. Steinmetz (eds.). *Handbook of Marriage and the Family*. New York: Plenum Press, 1987.

Smith, E. A., and J. R. Udry. "Coital and Non-coital Sexual Behaviors of White and Black Adolescents." *American Journal of Public Health,* 1985, 75, 1200–1203.

Sonenstein, F. L., J. H. Pleck, and L. C. Ku. "Sexual Activity, Condom Use, and AIDS Awareness among Adolescent Males." *Family Planning Perspectives,* July 1989, 21(4), 152–158.

Sprecher, S., and K. McKinney. *Sexuality*. Newbury Park, CA: Sage Publications, 1993.

Staples, R., and L. B. Johnson. *Black Families at the Crossroads: Challenges and Prospects*. San Francisco, CA: Jossey-Bass Publishers, 1993.

Tanfer, K., and L. A. Cubbins. "Coital Frequency Among Single Women: Normative Constraints and Situational Opportunities." *Journal of Sex Research,* May 1992, 29(2), 221-250.

Teachman, J. D., and K. A. Polonko. "Cohabitation and Marital Stability in the United States." *Social Forces,* Sept. 1990, 69(1), 207–220.

Thornton, A. "The Courtship Process and Adolescent Sexuality." *Journal of Family Issues,* September 1990, 11(3), 239–273.

Tuller, N. R. "Couples: The Hidden Segment of the Gay World." J. De Cecco (ed.). *Gay Relationships*. New York: Haworth Press, 1988.

Voydanoff, P., and B. Donnelly. *Adolescent Sexuality and Pregnancy*. Newbury Park, CA.: Sage Publications, 1990.

Weg, R. (ed.). *Sexuality in the Later Years: Roles and Behavior*. New York: Academic Press, 1983.

Weinberg, M., C. Williams, and D. Pryor. *Dual Attraction: Understanding Bisexuality*. New York: Oxford University Press, 1994.

Name _____ Section _____ Date _____

WORKSHEET 13

Rate your family's strengths

This Family Strengths Inventory was developed by researchers who studied the strengths of over 3,000 families. To assess your family (either the family you grew up in or the family you have formed as an adult), circle the number that best reflects how your family rates on each strength. A 1 represents the lowest rating and a 5 represents the highest.

1. Spending time together and doing things with each other	1	2	3	4	5
2. Commitment to each other	1	2	3	4	5
3. Good communication (talking with each other often, listening well, sharing feelings with each other)	1	2	3	4	5
4. Dealing with crises in a positive manner	1	2	3	4	5
5. Expressing appreciation to each other	1	2	3	4	5
6. Spiritual wellness	1	2	3	4	5
7. Closeness of relationship between spouses	1	2	3	4	5
8. Closeness of relationship between parents and children	1	2	3	4	5
9. Happiness of relationship between spouses	1	2	3	4	5
10. Happiness of relationship between parents and children	1	2	3	4	5
11. Extent to which spouses make each other feel good about themselves (self-confident, worthy, competent, and happy)	1	2	3	4	5
12. Extent to which parents help children feel good about themselves	1	2	3	4	5

Scoring   Add the numbers you have circled. A score below 39 indicates below-average family strengths. Scores between 39 and 52 are in the average range. Scores above 53 indicate a strong family. Low scores on individual items identify areas that families can profitably spend time on. High scores are worthy of celebration but shouldn't lead to complacency. Like gardens, families need loving care to remain strong.

What do you think is your family's major strength? What do you like best about your family?

What about your family would you most like to change?

Inventory used with permission. N. Stinnet and J. DeFrain. 1986. *Secrets of Strong Families.* Boston: Little, Brown, pp. 167–169.

Strong/DeVault/Sayad, *Human Sexuality,* 3rd ed. © 1999 Mayfield Publishing Company. Chapter 6

WORKSHEET 14

Popular culture response paper: Child/Adolescent Sexuality

Name of ad:

Description of content:

What underlying message or stereotype about child and adolescent sexuality did the ad present?

Did it present its message or stereotype visually or verbally? How? Was it effective?

Comments:

WORKSHEET 15

Popular culture response paper: Sex and Older Adults

Name of program:

Description of content:

What underlying message or stereotype about sexuality did the program present?

Did it present its message or stereotype visually or verbally? How? Was it effective?

Comments:

Strong/DeVault/Sayad, *Human Sexuality,* 3rd ed. © 1999 Mayfield Publishing Company. Chapter 6

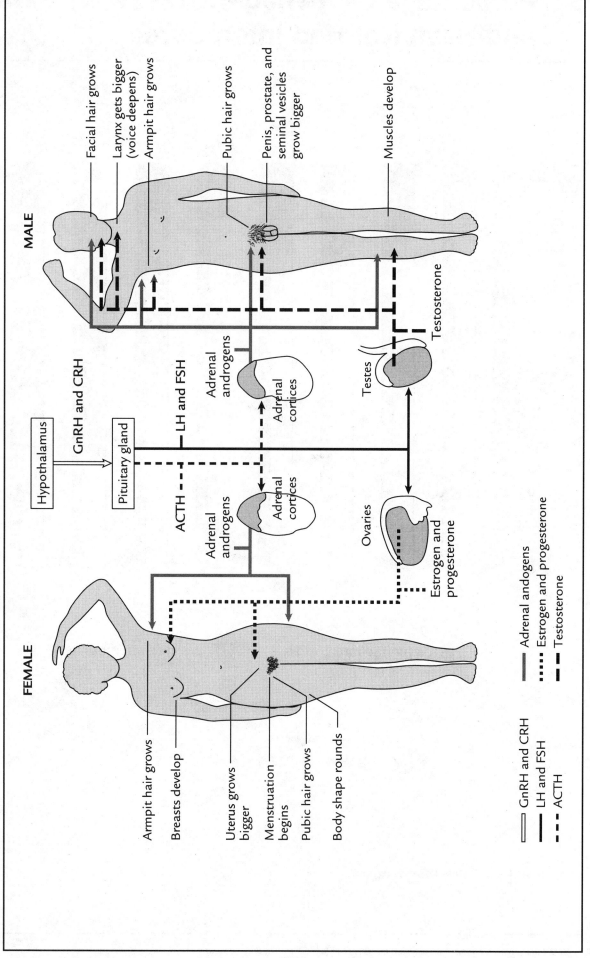

23   Percentage of Teenagers 12–19 Who Have and Have Not Had Intercourse

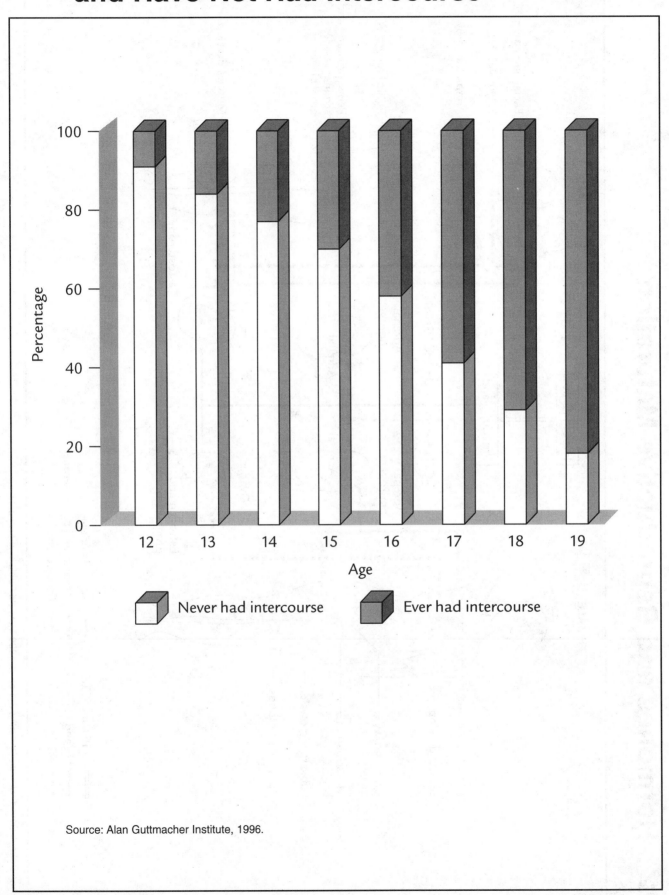

Source: Alan Guttmacher Institute, 1996.

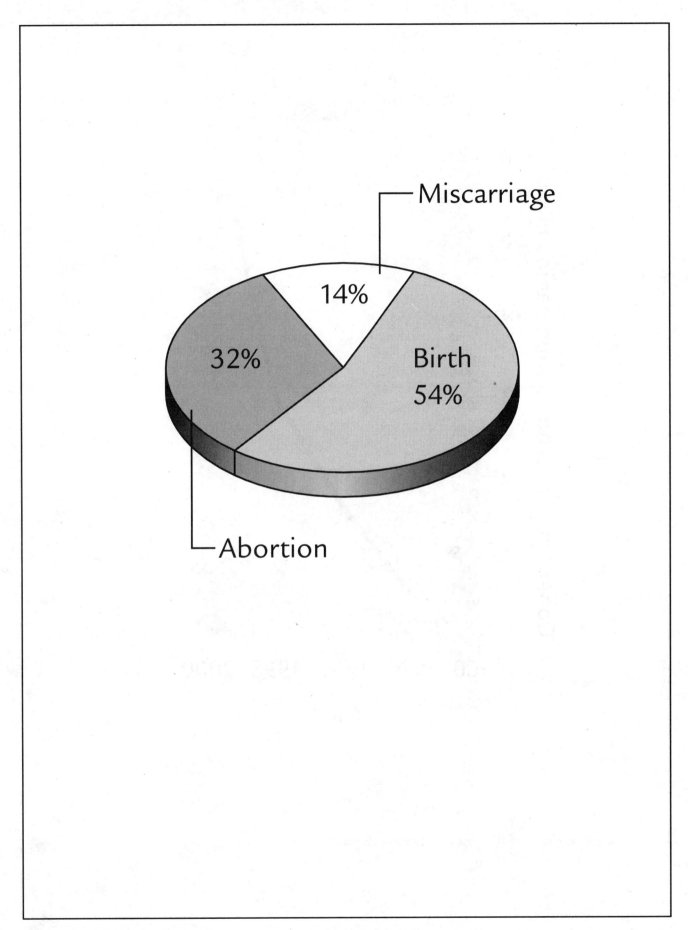

25 Cohabitation: 1960–1996

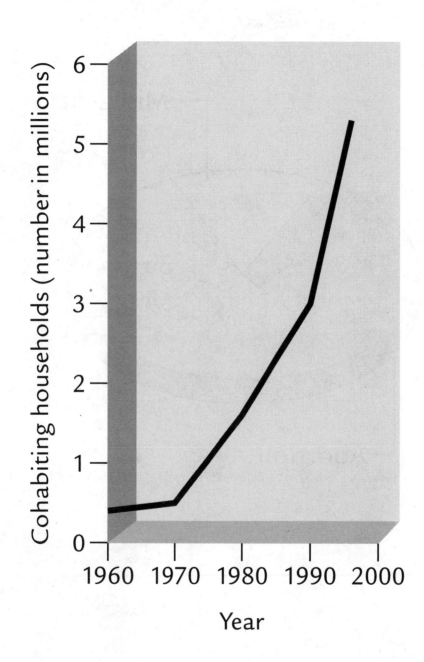

Source: Benokraitis, 1996; U. S. Population Reference Bureau, 1996.

CHAPTER 7
LOVE, INTIMACY, AND SEXUALITY

CHAPTER OUTLINE

Love and Sexuality
    Men, Sex, and Love
    Women, Sex, and Love
    Gay Men, Lesbians, and Love
    Sex Without Love
    Love Without Sex: Celibacy as a Choice

How Do I Love Thee? Approaches and Attitudes Related to Love
    Attitudes and Behaviors Associated with Love
    Styles of Love
    Practically Speaking: Your Style of Love
    The Triangular Theory of Love
    Love as Attachment
    Friendship and Love

Unrequited Love
    Styles of Unrequited Love
    Attachment Theory and Unrequited Love

Jealousy
    What Is Jealousy?
    Think About It: The Web of Deception and How It Affects Relationships
    Managing Jealousy

The Transformation of Love: From Passion to Intimacy
    Think About It: Making Love Last: The Role of Commitment

LEARNING OBJECTIVES

At the conclusion of Chapter 7, students should be able to:

1. Discuss similarities and differences in attitudes toward love by heterosexual men and women and by gay men and lesbians.

2. Discuss sex without emotional attachment and celibacy as a choice.

3. Identify the attitudes and behaviors associated with love.

4. List, describe, and give examples of the different styles of love.

5. List the components of the triangular theory of love and describe how they combine to create different forms of love.

6. Discuss love as a form of attachment, including the different styles of attachment.

7. Discuss the relationship between friendship and love.

8. Discuss jealousy, including psychological dimensions, types of jealousy, and jealousy as a boundary marker.

9. Discuss the role of commitment, caring, and self-disclosure in intimate love.

10. Recognize and define the key terms introduced in the chapter.

DISCUSSION QUESTIONS

What Is Love? How do researchers study love if they can't define it? What are the advantages and disadvantages of using prototypes?

Love, Age, Gender, Ethnicity, and Orientation. Does love differ according to one's age, gender, ethnicity, or orientation? Relate to prototypes of love and attitudes and behaviors associated with love.

Romantic Love. What are the characteristics of romantic love? What is the effect of time on romance? What other factors influence romantic love? What is the course of romance and love in long-term dating relationships, cohabitation, and marriage? What is the relationship between romantic love and intimacy?

Jealousy. How do students feel about jealousy? Do they believe jealousy is reasonable or unreasonable? What is their emotional experience of jealousy? Have they had unreasonably jealous partners? Has jealousy been linked to violence? What are the functions of jealousy?

ACTIVITIES

Prototypes of Love and Sex. Have students make a list of attributes of love and a list of attributes of sex. They should then pick the seven most important from each list and rank them on a scale of 1 through 7 (1 being lowest and 7 highest). They can then make new lists, ranking the attributes in order, and compare love and sex to see if there are common attributes. Suggest they have their partners do the same exercise.

Role-Playing Styles of Love. Ask ten students to role-play one of Lee's styles of love: Eros, Ludus, Storge, Mania, and Pragma. (Two students should play each style.) Then ask them to role-play a romantic relationship in which they are initially matched to others with their own style of love and then with a style different from their own. Be ready for some fun as students ham it up.

Role-Playing Jealousy. Ask two students to play a jealous couple. Create a scenario in which one partner has formed a friendship with a person of the other sex and the other partner is extremely jealous. Have the couple discuss this issue for about 5 minutes. Afterward, each person should describe her or his feelings during the encounter. The class then can discuss jealousy. Is jealousy a natural part of love? You may also repeat this exercise for a gay or lesbian couple, to compare the dynamics.

Analyzing Commitment. Ask students to analyze commitment in a current or past relationship using the ideas in the box titled, "Making Love Last: The Role of Commitment." On a sheet of paper, draw three columns labeled "Balance of Costs to Benefits," "Normative Inputs," and "Structural Constraints." Ask students to identify factors in their relationship in appropriate columns. Then discuss in class the different types of balance of costs to benefits, normative inputs, and structural constraints students experience in their relationships. What are the most important factors in sustaining commitment? Weakening it?

Varying Approaches. Of the different approaches to the study of love, ask students to discuss in small groups which approach they believed was most insightful and why. Have each group report to the class the results of their discussion.

SEX AND POPULAR CULTURE

Popular Culture Response Paper (Worksheet 17): Ask students to report on the development of romantic relationships in an episode of "Beverly Hills 90210." How does the relationship begin, what conflicts exist, and how does the program end? What are the issues involving love and nonmarital sex?

Discussion: Ask students to use Lee's six basic styles of love (those listed above, plus Agape) to analyze love relationships in a soap opera, family program, crime, or action TV program or movie. Which style is most common? Why?

Discussion: Love and sex in the media. Ask students to identify the norms for nonmarital sex in TV crime shows, soap operas, talk shows, and dramas. What is the relationship between love and sex? Sexual attraction and sex?

Activity: Ask students to bring in recordings of their favorite love songs. Listen to the music and discuss what the lyrics tell us about images of love.

Activity: Ask students to bring in copies of their favorite love poetry. Have them read the poems aloud either in small groups or to the class as a whole. Discuss what the poems mean.

HEALTH CONSIDERATIONS

Activity: Role-playing jealousy and violence. Two people: a health-care worker and a person who comes for emergency treatment as the result of her partner's hitting her in a jealous rage. The client downplays the incident as a lover's quarrel. "He wouldn't have hit me unless he loved me. Jealousy is a sign of how much he cares." This scenario may be replayed several times with the client being a heterosexual male, a gay male, and a lesbian to see how such factors affect the health-care worker's response.

Discussion: Chronic illness can deeply strain a loving relationship. What would you advise for a patient and his or her partner who feel their love stressed by illness?

Discussion: Caring health professionals may have clients transferring love and affection from their partners to them. How can professionals deal with such transference issues? What special issues arise if the client is single?

GUEST SPEAKERS/PANELS

Invite a marriage and family counselor or family life educator to discuss how love relationships can be maintained and enhanced.

Invite a social worker who works in domestic violence to discuss the role of jealousy in domestic abuse.

Form a student panel to discuss how members have formed, maintained, and enhanced intimate relationships. Include gay men, lesbians, and students of diverse cultural groups.

Form a student panel to discuss how jealousy has affected members' relationships. Include gay men, lesbians, and students of diverse cultural groups.

SUPPORT MATERIAL

Films and Videos

"As You Like It" (1978, 150 min., VHS, Kent State University). This Shakespeare play develops four different views of love ranging from the sentimental to the realistic against a backdrop of the corruption of city/court life and the benefits of country/forest living.

"The Heart Has No Wrinkles" (1991, 15 min., VHS, Carle Medical Communications). Two retirement home residents become romantically involved and provoke strong reactions from the staff. Designed to stimulate discussion on aging and sexuality. (This film received an honorable mention in the 1991 National Council on Family Relations Media Competition.)

"Love and Sex" (52 min., VHS, Films for Humanities). Falling in love, having sex, making babies—these are easy. Understanding human sexuality is much harder. Love, monogamy, hetero- and homosexuality are among the topics covered in this video hosted by Phil Donahue. Consultants are Dr. William Masters of the Masters & Johnson Institute and Dr. June Reinisch of the Kinsey Institute.

"Obsession" (28 min., VHS, Films for the Humanities and Sciences, Inc.). Adapted from a Phil Donahue program, this video focuses on the problems that arise when love turns into obsession.

Bibliography

The books and articles listed below may be helpful for instructors wishing additional background or information on some of the topics covered in this chapter. In addition, the books listed in this chapter's "Suggested Reading" in the textbook may also be useful.

Ackerman, D. *A Natural History of Love.* New York: Random House, 1994.

Adler, N., S. Hendrick, and C. Hendrick. "Male Sexual Preference and Attitudes toward Love and Sexuality." *Journal of Sex Education and Therapy*, Sept. 1989, 12(2), 27–30.

Aron, A., and E. Aron. "Love and Sexuality." K. McKinney and S. Sprecher (eds.). *Sexuality in Close Relationships.* Hillsdale, NJ: Erlbaum, 1991.

Blumstein, P., and P. Schwartz. *American Couples.* New York: McGraw-Hill, 1985.

Bringle, R., and B. Buunk. "Extradyadic Relationships and Sexual Jealousy." K. McKinney and Susan Sprecher (eds.). *Sexuality in Close Relationships.* Hillsdale, NJ: Lawrence Erlbaum Associates, 1991.

Byrne, D., and K. Murnen. "Maintaining Love Relationships." In R. Sternberg and M. Barnes (eds.). *The Psychology of Love.* New Haven, CT: Yale University Press, 1988.

Fehr, B. "Prototype Analysis of the Concepts of Love and Commitment." *Journal of Personality and Social Psychology,* 1988, 55(4), 557–579.

Hansen, G. "Dating Jealousy Among College Students." *Sex Roles*, April 1985, 12(7–8), 713–721.

Hatfield, E., and G. W. Walster. *A New Look at Love.* Reading, MA: Addison-Wesley, 1981.

Isensee, R. *Love Between Men: Enhancing Intimacy and Keeping Your Relationship Alive.* New York: Prentice-Hall Press, 1990.

Kelley, H. "Love and Commitment." H. Kelley et al. (eds.). *Close Relationships.* San Francisco, CA: Freeman, 1983.

McIntosh, E. "An Investigation of Romantic Jealousy among Black Undergraduates." *Social Behavior and Personality,* 1989, 17(2), 135–141.

Reiss, I. *Journey into Sexuality: An Exploratory Voyage.* Inglewood Cliffs, NJ: Prentice-Hall, 1986.

Shaver, P., C. Hazan, and D. Bradshaw. "Love as Attachment." In R. Sternberg and M. Barnes (eds.). *The Psychology of Love.* New Haven, CT: Yale University Press, 1988.

Sternberg, R. "A Triangular Theory of Love." *Psychological Review,* 1986, 93, 119–135.

Testa, R. J., B. N. Kinder, and G. Ironson. "Heterosexual Bias in the Perception of Loving Relationships of Gay Males and Lesbians." *Journal of Sex Research,* May 1987, 23(2), 163–172.

Weber, A., and J. Harvey (eds.). *Perspectives on Close Relationships.* Boston: Allyn & Bacon, 1994.

WORKSHEET 16

How compatible are you and your prospective partner?

Both you and your partner should take the quiz below and then compare your answers. This quiz is not meant to be a valid scientific measure of your compatibility; it was put together to get you thinking about situations that can be difficult and cause stress in a relationship. It's perfectly OK to have some disagreement—provided you're able to compromise or, at least, agree to disagree. Suggestions for each of the issues mentioned follow the quiz.

Both you and your partner should take the quiz below and then compare your answers. This quiz is not meant to be a valid scientific measure of your compatibility; it was put together to get you thinking about situations that can be difficult and cause stress in a relationship. It's perfectly OK to have some disagreement—provided you're able to compromise or, at least, agree to disagree. Suggestions for each of the issues mentioned follow the quiz.

1. How many of the 10 items on this list do you have in common with your prospective mate: religion, career, same home town or neighborhood, friends, education level, income level, cultural pastimes, sports/recreation activities, travel, physical attraction?

2. Would you prefer a relationship that is
   a. Male-dominated.
   b. Female-dominated.
   c. A partnership.

3. What banking arrangement sounds best after marriage?
   a. Separate accounts.
   b. Joint account.
   c. oint account but some cash for each of you to spend as you please with no accounting.

4. If you share an account, whose responsibility should it be to balance the checkbook and pay bills?
   a. The man in the family.
   b. The woman in the family.
   c. Whoever is better at math and details.

5. If you inherited $10,000, would you prefer it to be:
   a. Saved toward a major purchase.

   b. Spent on something you could enjoy together, such as a vacation.
   c. Spent on luxury items you could enjoy individually, such as a fur coat or golf clubs.

6. Where do you think you should spend major holidays?
   a. With his family.
   b. With her family.
   c. Alternating with his or her family.

7. How frequently do you want to see your in-laws if they live in the same town?
   a. Only on special occasions and holidays.
   b. Twice a month.
   c. At least once a week.

8. How frequently do you enjoy talking with your parents?
   a. Every day.
   b. Once a week.
   c. Once a month or less.

9. If you both have careers, what will be your priority?
   a. Marriage before career.
   b. Marriage equally important to career.
   c. Career before marriage; my spouse is going to have to be understanding.

10. If you are offered a career promotion with a hefty raise making your income much more than your spouse's but involving a move out of state, would
   a. Expect your mate to be agreeable to relocation.
   b. Try a commuter marriage; only seeing each other weekends or occasionally.
   c. Say no rather than move; money isn't everything.

11. If you new spouse sets aside one evening a week to go out with a friend or friends of his or her same sex, would you feel

    a. Jealous of the time away from you.

    b. Happy that he or she has friends.

    c. This should not go on; let your feelings be known.

12. If you've had a bad day at the office and come home feeling moody, would you prefer that your mate

    a. Back off, get out of the way.

    b. Act sympathetic, be a good listener.

    c. Discuss the events that led to your mood, perhaps offering some alternative suggestions for dealing with the people or problems that made you unhappy.

13. If your mate does something that makes you extremely angry, are you most likely to

    a. Forgive and forget it.

    b. Hurl insults.

    c. Mention you are angry at an appropriate time, preferably when the anger is first felt, and explain why without making derogatory accusations.

14. If you can't stand his or her friends and he or she can't stand yours, how will you deal with this after marriage? (You may choose more than one.)

    a. Cultivate new friends that you both can enjoy.

    b. See your friends by yourself; let him or her do the same.

    c. Phase out the friends you knew before marriage; expect your partner to do the same.

15. If you and your spouse-to-be are different religions, would you expect to

    a. Convert before marriage.

    b. Have him or her convert before marriage.

    c. Take turns attending each other's place of worship.

    d. Observe religious days separately.

    e. Not worry about it; religion is not an issue in your relationship.

16. When do you want to start a family?

    a. As soon as possible.

    b. After you have spent a few years enjoying your relationship as a couple.

    c. As soon as careers are firmly established.

    d. Never.

17. What is your attitude about housework? (You may check more than one.)

    a. It is unmasculine for a man to do it. A woman should do all of it even if she chooses to have a career.

    b. It is fine for a man to help, but only with certain tasks, such as mowing the lawn or taking out the trash.

    c. If a woman works outside the home, cleaning should be shared.

    d. Even if a woman does not work outside the home, cleaning should be shared.

18. Before marriage, you go out as a couple several times a week. A few months after marriage, you realize that you are going out a lot less. Would you consider this

    a. OK. The pace was exhausting.

    b. Dull. You worry that you are being taken for granted.

    c. Not OK. You and your mate should make plans for some evenings out or evenings at home with friends.

19. You need to buy a new suit. Your spouse wants to come along. Would you see this as a sign of

    a. Interest in spending time with you.

    b. Crowding your relationship.

    c. Watch-dogging your taste or pocketbook.

20. How would you prefer to spend your annual vacation? (Choose as many as apply.)

    a. On a trip by yourself.

    b. On a trip with your mate.

    c. On a trip with your mate and another couple.

    d. Visiting your relatives or in-laws at their homes.

    e. At a beach relaxing.

    f. Engaged in an active sport such as skiing, tennis camp, or hiking/camping.

    g. Traveling to another city for sightseeing/shopping.

    h. At home catching up on repairs, appointments, books, visits with friends.

    i. I would rather take a vacation less frequently than once a year and spend this money on rent or mortgage, enabling us to live in a more convenient or prestigious neighborhood.

21. If you were hunting for a place to live, would you prefer being in

    a. The country.

    b. The suburbs.

    c. The city.

22. If your spouse-to-be had many loves before he or she met you, would you prefer that he or she

    a. Keep the details to himself or herself.

    b. Tell you everything.

    c. Answer truthfully but only the questions you ask, such as what broke up each relationship.

23. If your new spouse is in a romantic mood and you are not, how would you be most likely to respond?

    a. Communicate your mood; suggest another time.

    b. Pretend you are feeling romantic.

    c. Invent an excuse rather than communicate your mood.

Once you and your prospective partner have completed the questionnaire, compare your answers with the following commentary in mind.

1. The more you have in common, the more of your life you can share and enjoy together.

2. Research and experiences of many couples have shown that the equal relationship is most successful.

3 and 4. There is not one right answer. Decide what works best for you and creates the least tension in your relationship.

5. You need to understand your priorities and be able to communicate them to your partner. Without this, you can find yourself in great financial conflict and tension.

6. Be able to compromise on this one.

7 and 8. Let your spouse know that he or she comes first before parents and in-laws regardless of how often relatives will be seen.

9. Talk about career and marriage priorities. Can you accept your spouse's choice if he or she considers time spent on work more important right now than time spent with you?

10. There is not one right answer. Decide what works best for you and creates the least tension in your relationship.

11. It's healthy to have friends. You can't realistically expect your mate to spend 24 hours around the clock with you. If you or your mate go off for a time with friends, it wouldn't be too mushy to kiss, hug, or otherwise reassure your mate by words or actions that he or she is still first in your life.

12. There are times when each answer would be best. Be sensitive to your mate's mood. If you are the one in the bad mood, don't expect your mate to read your mind as to whether you need space, sympathy, or discussion. Clue him or her in.

13. Answer C is best. You must learn how to express anger constructively.

14. Be careful here. If you make his or her old friends feel left out or unimportant, they could work on your prospective mate to break up your relationship.

15. If you have major differences on this one, you may want to consider terminating the relationship instead of committing to marriage.

16. It's impossible to have half a child. Compromise won't work on this one, so it is best to speak your mind before marriage.

17. The most successful marriages are the ones in which men and women do not limit themselves in the traditional masculine-feminine roles. The sharing of responsibility heightens a sense of trust, caring, and cooperation.

18. Sometimes the pace during dating is frantic. It is nice to calm down, but not nice to settle down to the point that each of you is taking the other for granted. Marriage requires continual work if you are going to keep adventure and interest in the relationship.

19. Whether you see it as interest, crowding, or distrust, communicate your feelings to your mate. If you'd rather shop alone, let that be known too.

20. Agree upon your needs in advance of the annual vacation, or what should be a time of relaxation away from the daily grind will turn into a source of tension and arguments. There is nothing wrong with separate vacations if one of you wants to fish on the lake and the other enjoys sightseeing.

21. If you are set on a particular style of living and not willing to change it after marriage, speak up before you say, "I do."

22. In general, it is not a good idea to go into great detail about past relationships because they are not totally relevant to your current one. However, trust and honesty are very important. If your partner asks a question, answer honestly but think very carefully. If you are the one doing the questioning, ask yourself, "Do I really want to hear this?"

23. There are times in your relationship when you may not want to go along with your spouse's romantic feelings, but it is generally best to communicate in a nice way without making him or her feel rejected or unloved because you simply are not in the mood. Do suggest another time.

WORKSHEET 17

Popular culture response paper: Beverly Hills 90210

Description of content:

What underlying message or stereotype about sexuality and romance did the episode present?

Did it present its message or stereotype visually or verbally? How? Was it effective?

Comments:

Strong/DeVault/Sayad, *Human Sexuality,* 3rd ed. © 1999 Mayfield Publishing Company. Chapter 7

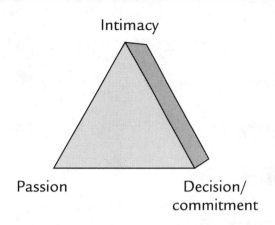

Intimacy

Passion   Decision/
                commitment

Sternberg's Triangle of Love

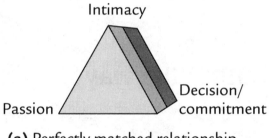

Intimacy

Passion   Decision/
                commitment

(a) Perfectly matched relationship

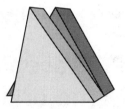

(b) Closely matched relationship

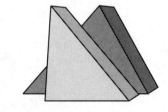

(c) Moderately mismatched
relationship

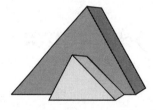

(d) Severely mismatched
relationship

 Self   Other

**Sternberg's Triangle in Different
Types of Relationships**

1. **Trust**

2. **Caring**

3. **Honesty**

4. **Friendship**

5. **Respect**

6. **Concern for other's well-being**

7. **Commitment**

8. **Loyalty**

9. **Acceptance of the other the way he or she is**

10. **Supportiveness**

11. **Wanting to be with the other**

12. **Interest in the other**

Source: Beverly Fehr. (1988). "Prototype Analysis of the Concepts of Love and Commitment." *Journal of Personality and Social Psychology 55*(4), 557–559.

Emotional	Physical	Consequential
1. Caring	1. Intensity	1. Pregnancy
2. Closeness	2. Excitement	2. Pain
3. Expression of feelings	3. Pleasure	3. Violence
4. Specialness	4. Desire	4. Danger
5. Communication	5. Hot/sweaty	5. Diseases
6. Love	6. Sensuality	
7. Relationship	7. Lust	
8. Happiness	8. Satisfaction	
9. Commitment	9. Enjoyment	
10. Emotions	10. Different positions	

Source: Aron and Strong. (1993). "Prototypes of Love and Sexuality."

Eros: Love of beauty.

Mania: Obsessive love.

Ludus: Playful love.

Storge: Companionate love.

Agape: Altruistic love.

Pragma: Practical love.

Attachment

- Attachment bond's formation and quality depend on attachment object's (AO) responsiveness and sensitivity.

- When AO is present, infant is happier.

- Infant shares toys, discoveries, objects with AO.

- Infant coos, talks baby talk, "sings."

- Feelings of oneness with AO.

Romantic love

- Feelings of love are related to lover's interest and reciprocation.

- When lover is present, person feels happier.

- Lovers share experience and goods; give gifts.

- Lovers coo, sing, and talk baby talk.

- Feelings of oneness with lover.

Strong/DeVault/Sayad, *Human Sexuality,* 3rd ed. © 1999 Mayfield Publishing Company

CHAPTER 8

COMMUNICATING ABOUT SEX

CHAPTER OUTLINE

The Nature of Communication
    The Cultural Context
    The Social Context
    The Psychological Context
    Nonverbal Communication
    Practically Speaking: Touch: Overcoming Differences

Sexual Communication
    Sexual Communication in Beginning Relationships
    Think About It: Negotiating Safer Sex
    Sexual Communication in Established Relationships

Developing Communication Skills
    Developing Self-Awareness
    Think About It; Communication Patterns and Marital Satisfaction
    Talking About Sex
    Think About It: Ten Rules for Avoiding Intimacy

Conflict and Intimacy
    Sexual Conflicts
    Practically Speaking: Guidelines for Giving Effective Feedback
    Conflict Resolution

LEARNING OBJECTIVES

At the conclusion of Chapter 8, students should be able to:

1. Discuss the cultural, social, and psychological contexts of communication with examples of each.

2. Identify the role of proximity, eye contact, and touching in nonverbal communication.

3. Describe communication in beginning and established relationships, including the halo effect, interest and opening lines, the first move, initiating and directing sexual activity, and gay and lesbian relationships.

4. Discuss "safe sex" including disclosure of lifestyle and STD information to potential partners.

5. List and give examples of communication patterns in satisfied relationships and discuss gender differences in marital communication.

6. Discuss the obstacles and problems with sexual vocabulary in talking about sex.

7. Describe and give examples of the keys to good sexual communication, including self-disclosure, trust, and feedback.

8. List the guidelines for effective feedback with examples of each.

9. Discuss types of conflicts and the nature and sources of power in intimate relationships, including the power of love.

10. Describe sexual conflicts, including sex and power issues, the characteristics of conflict resolution in happy and unhappy couples, and strategies for resolving conflicts.

11. Recognize and define the key terms introduced in the chapter.

DISCUSSION QUESTIONS

Communication Contexts. Have students give examples of each of the communication contexts from their personal experience: cultural, social, and psychological.

Halo Effect. Ask students if they have assumed something positive about a person because of his or her appearance, such as intelligence, sexiness, sense of fun. What was it about the appearance that gave the impression? Did the student ever discover an error in judgment later?

Misunderstandings in Sexual Communication. Discuss the types of miscommunication about sexuality that may occur between individuals. What can be done to communicate more clearly?

Verbal Consent for Each Stage of Sexual Contact. In 1993, Antioch University issued sexual consent guidelines that required verbal consent from both parties as they moved to each new level of sexual activity. Ask students to discuss the problem of verbal consent in light of the ambiguity most individuals use in sexual encounters.

Communication Issues in Gay/Lesbian Relationships. What are special communication issues in gay or lesbian relationships? Would gay or lesbian communication patterns be different if homosexuality were accepted by society at large?

Ethnicity and Sexual Communication. How does ethnicity affect communication processes, interactions, and symbols? Sexual communication? The ability to initiate and refuse sexual interactions?

Communication in Beginning and Established Relationships. Discuss how the ability to negotiate sexual interactions differs in beginning and established relationships. Discuss development of shared scripts and vocabulary.

Self-Disclosure, Trust, and Feedback. Ask students to give examples of self-disclosure, trust, and feedback and how they have affected relationships. Is it possible to have good relationships without each of these factors present? What if there was no trust? Self-disclosure? Feedback?

Power. Ask students if it is possible for power to be an element in love relationships. Who has more power: men or women? Discuss the role of power in intimate relationships. Give examples of the exercise of different types of power. What happens in relationships with equal power? Unequal power?

Obstacles to Intimacy. Have students complete Worksheet 18 (Obstacles to Intimacy). Can they identify any attitudes or behaviors they would like to change? What are some ways they could begin making these changes?

What's Your Gender Communications Quotient? Have the students complete Worksheet 19 (What's Your Gender Communications Quotient?) and discuss the results.

ACTIVITIES

Small Group Activity: Ask students to write anonymously on 3 x 5 cards: (1) How they initiate sexual interactions; (2) How they refuse sexual interactions; and (3) How they negotiate sexual interactions. (Students should indicate their gender.) Collect the cards and distribute them randomly to small groups. Ask each group to discuss which methods are effective or ineffective and why.

Small Group Activity: Have students anonymously list on 3 x 5 cards the three most difficult topics in discussing sexuality with a partner. (Indicate male or female.) Distribute the cards to students to determine if there are common problems and to suggest solutions. Report findings to the class.

Role-Playing: To discuss opening lines, have two students role-play meeting each other for the first time. Have students write opening lines they have used or had used on them on 3 x 5 cards. Give random opening lines to students to act out. Be prepared for some laughter. Were some lines more appropriate for females or males to use? Which ones were effective? Ineffective? Why?

Small Group Activity: As an alternative to opening-line role-playing, have students anonymously write opening lines they have used or had used on them on 3 x 5 cards. Distribute the cards in small groups for discussion. Are some lines more appropriate for females or males? Which ones are effective? Ineffective? Why?

Role-Playing: Have two students role-play a situation in which the nonverbal message is incongruent with the verbal message, as in one person saying to the other "I love you" while her or his body language indicates distance.

Small Group Activity: Have students anonymously write on 3 x 5 cards "first moves" they have made (or been the recipients of) to initiate a sexual interaction. Distribute the cards in small groups for discussion and suggestions. Are there gender differences? Ethnic differences? Differences based on sexual orientation?

Role-Playing: Using guidelines for dialogue and feedback, have students role-play a dating, cohabiting, or married couple trying to resolve a sexual conflict. (Remind students of the significance of nonverbal as well as verbal communication.) Do issues or conflict resolution process or solution differ according to type of relationship? (Remind students that the less committed the relationship, the easier it is to dissolve if the conflict is basic and cannot be resolved.)

Role-Playing: Have students role-play a conflict over one partner wanting to change the relationship from exclusive to nonexclusive. (Remind students of the significance of nonverbal as well as verbal communication.) In one role-playing session, have students illustrate relative love and need theory; in the second, illustrate the principle of least interest. The couples may be heterosexual, gay, lesbian, or bisexual.

Small Group Discussion: Ask students to give examples of each feedback element described in the box titled the "Guidelines for Giving Effective Feedback." Students should make suggestions for increasing the effectiveness of feedback.

SEX AND POPULAR CULTURE

Popular Culture Response Paper (Worksheet 20): Initiating and Refusing Sex. Ask students to note the different ways sexual activity is initiated and refused in the media. What are typical scenarios? How well do they depict real-life situations?

Discussion: How do individuals communicate about sex in the media? What nonverbal signals are given? Verbal cues?

HEALTH CONSIDERATIONS

Discussion: In hospital and other institutional settings it may be very difficult for couples to communicate. What can health professionals do to facilitate intimate communication in such settings?

Discussion: Touch is an important element in communication and personal well-being, but patients may be deprived of reassuring tactile contact. Talking with patients is also important; they may sometimes go an entire day without talking to anyone until their health-care professional comes into their room. In what ways can physicians and other health-care professionals be encouraged to touch their patients in a caring manner to assist their healing? How can conversations with patients be encouraged at the same time that health-care professionals are pressed for time because of work overload or administration demands for "efficiency"?

Activity: Ask students to imagine themselves working in an institutional setting. Ask them to anonymously list on 3 x 5 cards the three most important communication ideas, principles, or concepts they have learned that may be applied to their interactions with patients. Collect the cards and randomly distribute them to small groups for discussion.

GUEST SPEAKERS/PANELS

Invite a therapist to discuss communication processes and issues in relationships.

Invite a psychology or communications instructor to discuss gender differences in communication.

Form a panel of students to discuss initiating, refusing, and negotiating sexual interactions in casual, dating, cohabiting, and marital relationships. Include gay men and lesbians.

SUPPORT MATERIAL

Films and Videos

"Intimacy" (1981, 34 min., VHS, Multi-Focus, Inc.). A taping of Roger Mellot's seminars on "pyramid theory"—a progression of physical behaviors and touch. Mellot stresses going through the pyramid in different ways, rediscovering the pleasure in hand-holding and kissing. Recommended for exploring methods of enhancing relationships.

"Men and Women: Talking Together" (1993, 58 min., VHS, Insight Media). A stimulating discussion between Deborah Tannen and Robert Bly on patterns in communication and use of power.

Bibliography

The books and articles listed below may be helpful for instructors wishing additional background or information on some of the topics covered in this chapter. In addition, the books listed in this chapter's" Suggested Reading" in the textbook may also be useful.

Blumstein, P., and P. Schwartz. *American Couples*. New York: McGraw-Hill, 1985.

Byers, E. S., and L. Heinlein. "Predicting Initiations and Refusals of Sexual Activities in Married and Cohabiting Heterosexual Couples." *Journal of Sex Research*, 1989, 26 (210–231).

Christopher, F. S., and M. M. Frandsen. "Strategies of Influence in Sex and Dating." *Journal of Social and Personal Relationships*, 7, 89–105, 1990.

Cornog, M. "Naming Sexual Body Parts: Preliminary Patterns and Implications." *Journal of Sex Research*, Aug. 1986, 22(3), 399–408.

Cupach, W. R., and J. Comstock. "Satisfaction with Sexual Communication in Marriage." *Journal of Social and Personal Relationships*, 1990, 7, 179-186.

Cupach, W., and S. Metts. "Sexuality and Communication in Close Relationships." K. McKinney and Susan Sprecher (eds.). *Sexuality in Close Relationships*. Hillsdale, NJ: Lawrence Erlbaum Associates, 1991.

Hatfield, E., and S. Sprecher. *Mirror, Mirror: The Importance of Looks in Everyday Life*. New York: State University of New York, 1986.

Isensee, R. *Love Between Men: Enhancing Intimacy and Keeping Your Relationship Alive*. New York: Prentice-Hall Press, 1990.

Mays, V. M., S. D. Cochran, G. Bellinger, and R. G. Smith. "The Language of Black Gay Men's Sexual Behavior: Implications for AIDS Risk Reduction." *Journal of Sex Research*, Aug. 1992, 29(3), 425–434.

Metts, S., and W. Cupach. "The Role of Communication in Human Sexuality." K. McKinney and S. Sprecher (eds.). *Human Sexuality: The Social and Interpersonal Context*. Norwood, NJ: Ablex Publishing Co., 1989.

Murnen, S. K., A. Perot, and D. Byrne. "Coping with Unwanted Sexual Activity: Normative Responses, Situational Determinants, and Individual Differences." *Journal of Sex Research*, 1989, 26, 85–106.

O'Sullivan, L., and E. S. Byers. "College Students' Incorporation of Initiator and Restrictor Roles in Sexual Dating Interactions." *Journal of Sex Research*, Aug. 1992, 29(3), 435–446.

Sanders, J., and W. Robinson. "Talking and Not Talking About Sex: Male and Female Vocabulary." *Journal of Communication*, 1979, 29(2), 22–30.

Satir, V. *The New Peoplemaking* (Rev. ed.). Palo Alto, CA: Science and Behavior Books, 1988.

Ting-Toomey, S., and F. Korzenny (eds.). *Cross-Cultural Interpersonal Communication*. Newbury Park, CA: Sage Publications, 1991.

Wheeless, L. R., V. E. Wheeless, and R. Baus. "Sexual Communication, Communication Satisfaction, and Solidarity in the Developmental Stages of Intimate Relationships." *Western Journal of Speech Communication*, 1984, 48, 217–230.

WORKSHEET 18

Obstacles to intimacy

Read through the following list of statements relating to your ability to begin and maintain interpersonal relationships. From your responses, can you identify any attitudes or behaviors you'd like to change? How would you go about making these changes?

Yes	No		
____	____	1.	It's easy for me to compliment or give recognition to others.
____	____	2.	I enjoy being touched and touching others.
____	____	3.	I have close friends.
____	____	4.	It's easy for me to express concern, warmth, and affection.
____	____	5.	I talk over disagreements with others rather than silently worry about them.
____	____	6.	I enjoy meeting new people and talking with new acquaintances.
____	____	7.	I enjoy pleasing others.
____	____	8.	I can express my innermost thoughts and feelings to close friends.
____	____	9.	I can put myself in another person's place and experience his or her emotions.
____	____	10.	I think most people can be trusted.
____	____	11.	I am concerned about social problems even when they don't affect me personally.
____	____	12.	I get along well with salesclerks, waiters and waitresses, service-station attendants, etc.
____	____	13.	I can discuss sex in mixed company without feeling uncomfortable.
____	____	14.	I can express affection physically as well as verbally.
____	____	15.	I can express thanks or appreciation for a gift or a favor without feeling uneasy.
____	____	16.	I am aware of my feelings.
____	____	17.	I enjoy an occasional evening alone.
____	____	18.	I can communicate easily with members of the opposite sex.
____	____	19.	In general, I love myself.
____	____	20.	I am happier now than I have been in the past.
____	____	21.	I do not feel rejected if a person I love wants to preserve his or her independence.
____	____	22.	I can accept the fact that my partner has loved others before me and I do not worry about how I compare with them.
____	____	23.	I can accept the anger of a loved one while still believing he or she loves me.
____	____	24.	I try to always keep communication open and honest.

Strong/DeVault/Sayad, *Human Sexuality,* 3rd ed. © 1999 Mayfield Publishing Company. Chapter 8

Name _____   Section _____   Date _____

WORKSHEET 19

What's your gender communications quotient?

How much do you know about how men and women communicate with one another? The 20 items in this questionnaire are based on research conducted in classrooms, private homes, businesses, offices, hospitals—the places where people commonly work and socialize. The answers are at the end of this quiz.

		True	**False**
1.	Men talk more than women.	_____	_____
2.	Men are more likely to interrupt women than they are to interrupt other men.	_____	_____
3.	There are approximately ten times as many sexual terms for males as females in the English language.	_____	_____
4.	During conversations, women spend more time gazing at their partner than men do.	_____	_____
5.	Nonverbal messages carry more weight than verbal messages.	_____	_____
6.	Female managers communicate with more emotional openness and drama than male managers.	_____	_____
7.	Men not only control the content of conversations, but they also work harder in keeping conversations going.	_____	_____
8.	When people hear generic words such as "mankind" and "he," they respond inclusively, indicating that the terms apply to both sexes.	_____	_____
9.	Women are more likely to touch others than men are.	_____	_____
10.	In classroom communications, male students receive more reprimands and criticism than female students.	_____	_____
11.	Women are more likely than men to disclose information on intimate personal concerns.	_____	_____
12.	Female speakers are more animated in their conversational style than are male speakers.	_____	_____
13.	Women use less personal space than men.	_____	_____
14.	When a male speaks, he is listened to more carefully than a female speaker, even when she makes the identical presentation.	_____	_____
15.	In general, women speak in a more tentative style than do men.	_____	_____
16.	Women are more likely to answer questions that are not addressed to them.	_____	_____

Strong/DeVault/Sayad, *Human Sexuality*, 3rd ed. © 1999 Mayfield Publishing Company. Chapter 8

17. There is widespread sex segregation in schools, and it hinders effective classroom communication.   _____   _____

18. Female managers are seen by both male and female subordinates as better communicators than male managers.   _____   _____

19. In classroom communications, teachers are more likely to give verbal praise to females than to male students.   _____   _____

20. In general, men smile more often than women.   _____   _____

1. T; 2. T; 3. F; 4. T; 5. T; 6-9. F; 10-15. T; 16. F; 17. T; 18. T; 19 & 20. F.

Source: Hazel R. Rozema, Ph.D., and John W. Gray, Ph.D., Department of Communication, University of Arkansas, Little Rock.

WORKSHEET 20

Popular culture response paper: Initiating and Refusing Sex

Name of program/film/song/ad/etc.:

Description of content:

What underlying message or stereotype about sexuality did the material present?

Did it present its message or stereotype visually or verbally? How? Was it effective?

Comments:

Strong/DeVault/Sayad, *Human Sexuality,* 3rd ed. © 1999 Mayfield Publishing Company. Chapter 8

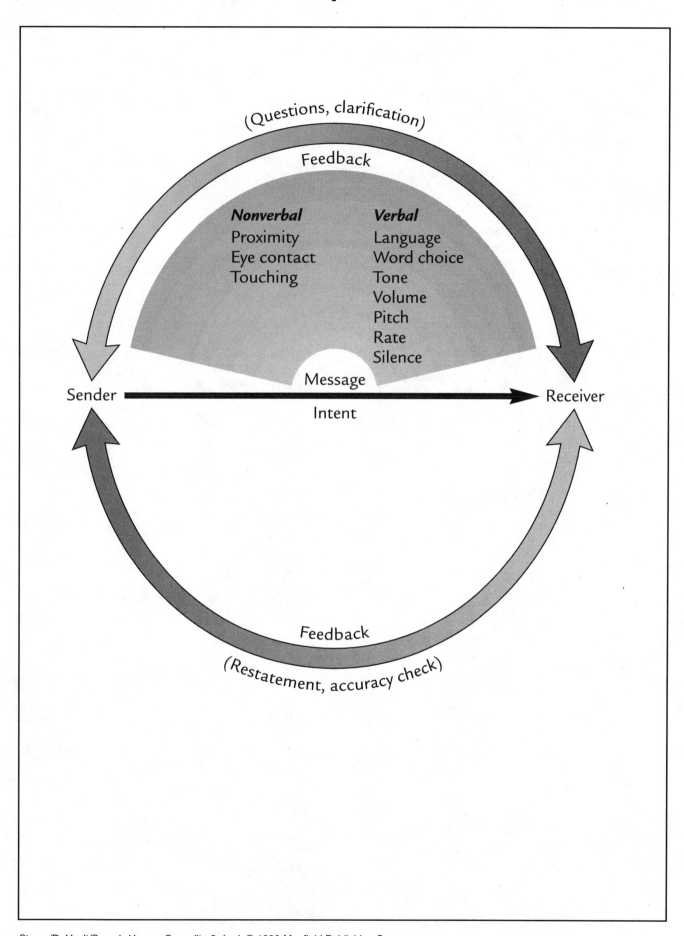

CHAPTER 9
SEXUAL EXPRESSION

CHAPTER OUTLINE

Sexual Attractiveness
    A Cross-Cultural Analysis
    The Halo Effect Revisited
    Sexual Desire
    Practically Speaking: Sexual Desire: When Appetites Differ

Sexual Scripts
    Cultural Scripting
    Intrapersonal Scripting
    Interpersonal Scripting

Autoeroticism
    Sexual Fantasies and Dreams
    Masturbation
    Think About It: Masturbation: From Sin to Insanity

Interpersonal Sexuality
    Touching
    Think About It: Chimps Do It, Humans Do It: Cross-Species Sexual Behavior
    Kissing
    Oral-Genital Sex
    Sexual Intercourse
    Anal Eroticism

LEARNING OBJECTIVES

At the conclusion of Chapter 9, students should be able to:

1. Describe the elements of sexual attractiveness along gender and orientation lines and discuss the impact of the halo effect.

2. Discuss sexual attraction including differences in sexual desire.

3. Explain sexual scripts, including cultural, interpersonal, and intrapersonal scripts with examples of each.

4. Describe the role and function of autoeroticism, including sexual fantasies, dreams, and masturbation through the life cycle.

5. Identify various types of sensuous touching and their role in sexuality.

6. Describe the various meanings associated with kissing and its role as a form of sexual behavior.

7. Discuss oral-genital sex, including cunnilingus and fellatio, changing attitudes toward it, and varying incidence by ethnicity.

8. Discuss the incidence and types of sexual intercourse.

9. Discuss anal eroticism, varying incidence by orientation and ethnicity, and health concerns.

10. Recognize and define key terms introduced in the chapter.

DISCUSSION QUESTIONS

Cultural Scripts. Discuss cultural scripts, asking students what their cultural scripts are. (They may need some help, as cultural scripts are often invisible.) How do cultural scripts differ by ethnicity, such as sequence of behaviors and types of preferred behaviors?

Changing Attitudes Toward Masturbation and Sexual Intercourse. Discuss changing attitudes toward masturbation and sexual intercourse from the nineteenth century to the present. Ask students whether they would have been able to discern the cultural values and taboos concerning masturbation and sexual intercourse taboos if they had lived in the nineteenth century. How can they evaluate the cultural values underlying contemporary attitudes toward masturbation and sexual intercourse?

Sharing Sexual Fantasies. How do students feel about sharing sexual fantasies with their partners? What kind are they most likely to share? To keep secret? Would they tell their partner if they had fantasies about someone else while engaged in sexual activities with their partner? What is threatening about sharing fantasies?

Excessive Masturbation. Is there such a thing as "excessive" masturbation? What current myths and taboos continue about masturbation today? (Students may believe "excessive masturbation" is a sign of "sexual addiction," which is discussed in Chapter 10.)

Sexual Behavior and Orientation. Some students believe that certain sexual behaviors are gay or lesbian, such as oral sex or anal sex. Discuss differences between sexual behaviors and orientation.

Ethnicity and Sexual Behavior. Observe that incidence of masturbation, oral sex, and anal sex differ by ethnicity. Point out that differences do not reflect morality or immorality but differing cultural patterns.

ACTIVITIES

Small Group Activity: Ask students to write, anonymously, on a 3 x 5 card (1) What they find most sexually attractive about others; (2) What they believe others find most sexually attractive about their gender. (Students should indicate whether male or female and, optionally, their sexual orientation.) What do students find most attractive in others? Did women correctly guess what men found attractive about women and vice versa? Discuss.

Small Group Activity: Using 3 x 5 cards, have students anonymously prioritize masturbation, fellatio, sexual intercourse, cunnilingus, kissing, and anal sex in order of acceptability for self. Distribute cards randomly in groups for discussion. Is there agreement in order of priority? Discuss reasons for differences.

Small Group Activity: Have students anonymously write on 3 x 5 cards sexual behaviors in which they would like to engage but that they would be afraid to bring up with their partner. Randomly distribute cards to different groups. Discuss and make suggestions.

Class Activity: Ask students to anonymously describe their own experiences of sexual desire, indicating their gender and, as an option, their sexual orientation. Read aloud in class, asking students to identify whether a description was written by a female or a male and, if available, whether that person is heterosexual, lesbian, or gay.

SEX AND POPULAR CULTURE

Popular Culture Response Paper (Worksheet 21): Masturbation. How is masturbation treated on TV or in the movies? (Is it treated as a sign of immaturity?)

Discussion: When we were young, we often learned how to kiss by watching television or movies. What did you learn about kissing when you were young, including appropriate situations, techniques, and feelings about kissing?

Discussion: What types of sexual behavior are described, depicted, or alluded to in rap? Heavy metal? Rock? Pop? Country? How are these behaviors and context treated differently according to music genre?

Activity: Have students bring short sexual advice articles or columns from newspapers or magazines such as *Playboy* and *Cosmopolitan*. Distribute material in small groups and let individuals read for 5 minutes. Then begin group discussion: What kinds of problems are typical? Are the responses normative? Based on norms, pop psychology, or research? Are the responses helpful?

HEALTH CONSIDERATIONS

Discussion: What sexual behaviors do you regard as risky from a health perspective? Why? What could be done to reduce or eliminate the risks? If a client was engaged in what you considered risky behavior, what would you advise him or her?

Discussion: If you walked into a patient's room and discovered him or her masturbating, what would you do? How would you feel?

SUPPORT MATERIAL

Films and Videos

"Embracing Our Sexuality: Women Talk About Sex" (45 min., VHS, New Day Films). A diverse group of women talk honestly abut their feelings, fantasies, and behaviors.

"Finding Our Way: Men Talk About Their Sexuality" (38 min., VHS, New Day Films). A diverse group of men talk openly about their feelings, fantasies, and behaviors. (Winner of the "Video of the Year" at the 1995 Conference on Sexuality.)

"Intimacy" (1981, 34 min., VHS, Multi-Focus, Inc.). A taping of Roger Mellot's seminars on "pyramid theory"—a progression of physical behaviors and touch. Mellot stresses going through the pyramid in different ways, rediscovering the pleasure in hand-holding and kissing. Recommended for exploring methods of enhancing relationships.

"Love and Sex" (1986, 52 min., VHS, Kent State University). Discusses differences between male and female sexual behavior. Analyzes attitudes toward sex in our society. (From the "Phil Donahue Examines the Human Animal Series")

Bibliography

The books and articles listed below may be helpful for instructors wishing additional background or information on some of the topics covered in this chapter. In addition, the books listed in this chapter's "Suggested Reading" in the textbook may also be useful.

Billy, J., K. Tanfer, W. R. Grady, and D. H. Klepinger. "The Sexual Behavior of Men in the United States." *Family Planning Perspectives,* Mar. 1993, 25(2), 52–60.

Blumstein, P., and P. Schwartz. *American Couples.* New York: McGraw-Hill, 1985.

Fisher, W. A., et al. "Erotophobia-Erotophilia as a Dimension of Personality." *Journal of Sex Research,* 1988, 25(1), 123–151.

Gagnon, J., and W. Simon. *Sexual Conduct: The Social Sources of Human Sexuality.* Chicago: Aldine Publishing Co., 1973.

Kroll, K., and E. L. Klein. *Enabling Romance: A Guide to Love, Sex, and Relationships for the Disabled.* New York: Harmony Books, 1992.

Levine, S. "More on the Nature of Desire." *Journal of Sex and Marital Therapy,* Mar. 1987, 13(1), 35–44.

Love, P., and J. Robinson. *Hot Monogamy.* New York: Dutton, 1994.

Price, J. H., and P. A. Miller. "Sexual Fantasies of Black and White College Students." *Psychological Reports,* 1984, 54, 1007–1014.

Rubin, L. *Erotic Wars.* New York: Farrar, Straus, and Giroux, 1990.

Sprecher, S., et al. "Sexual Relationships." In K. McKinney and S. Sprecher (eds.). *Human Sexuality: The Societal and Interpersonal Context.* Norwood, NJ: Ablex Publishing Corporation, 1989.

Stelzer, C., S. M. Desmond, and J. H. Price. "Physical Attractiveness and Sexual Activity of College Students." *Psychological Reports,* 1987, 60, 567–573.

Sue, D. "Erotic Fantasies of College Students During Coitus." *Journal of Sex Research,* 1979, 15, 299–305.

Wilson, P. "Black Culture and Sexuality." *Journal of Social Work and Human Sexuality,* Mar. 1986, 4(3), 29–46.

Wilson, S. M., and N. P. Medoro. "Gender Comparisons of College Students' Attitudes toward Sexual Behavior." *Adolescence,* 1990, 25, 615–627.

Wyatt, G., et al. "Kinsey Revisited II: Comparisons of the Sexual Socialization and Sexual Behavior of Black Women over 33 Years." *Archives of Sexual Behavior,* Aug. 1988, 17(4), 289–332.

WORKSHEET 21

Popular culture response paper: Masturbation

Name of program/film:

Description of content:

What underlying message or stereotype about masturbation did the program/film present?

Did it present its message or stereotype visually or verbally? How? Was it effective?

Comments:

Strong/DeVault/Sayad, *Human Sexuality*, 3rd ed. © 1999 Mayfield Publishing Company. Chapter 8

32   Frequency of Masturbation by Ethnicity

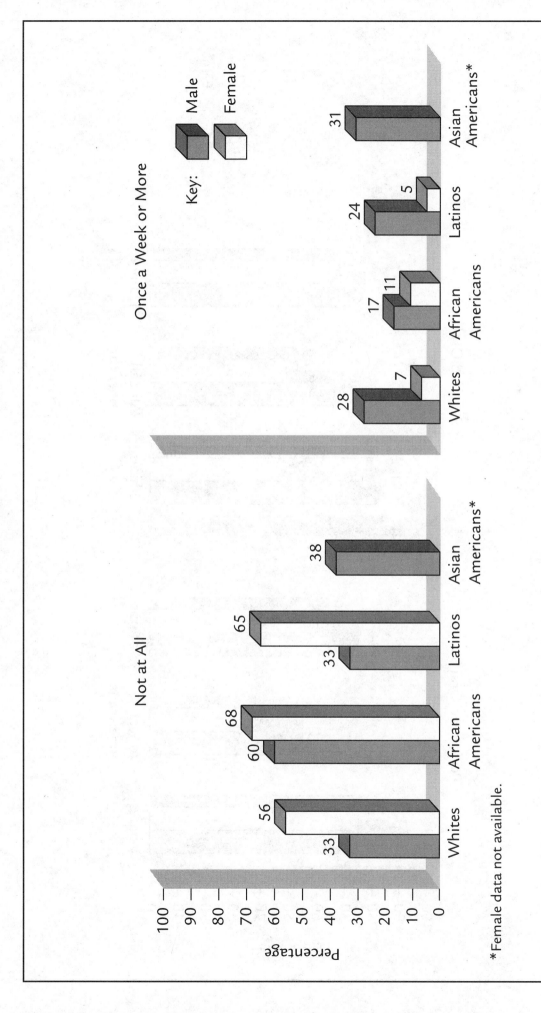

*Female data not available.

Strong/DeVault/Sayad, *Human Sexuality*, 3rd ed. © 1999 Mayfield Publishing Company

33 Oral-Genital Sex by Ethnicity

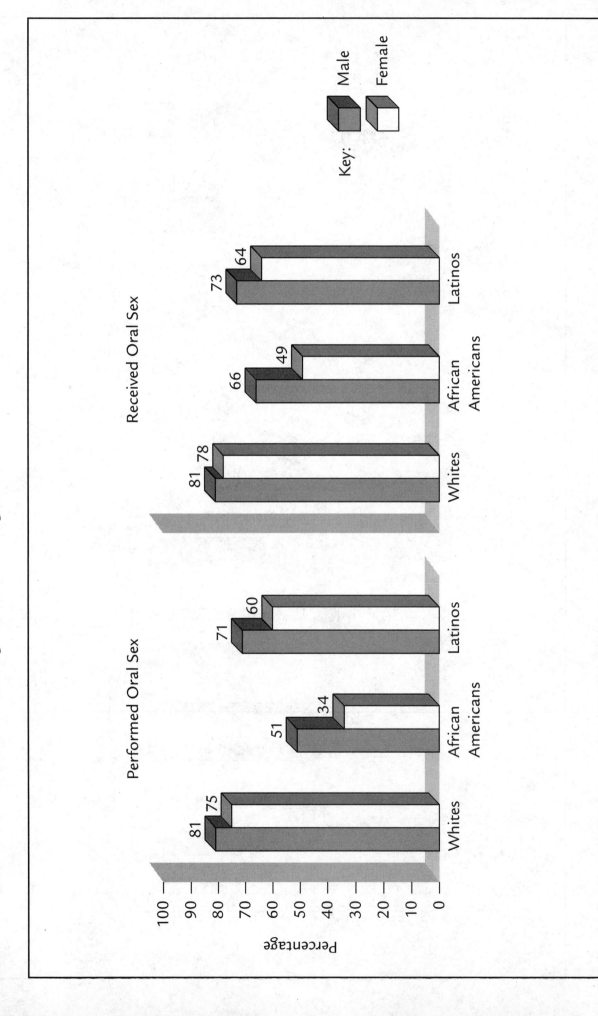

Strong/DeVault/Sayad, *Human Sexuality*, 3rd ed. © 1999 Mayfield Publishing Company

CHAPTER 10

ATYPICAL AND PARAPHILIC SEXUAL BEHAVIOR

CHAPTER OUTLINE

Atypical Versus Paraphilic Behavior
  Think About It: The Myth of Sexual Addiction

Atypical Sexual Behaviors
  Incidence of Atypical Sexual Behaviors
  Domination and Submission
  Think About It: Body Play: Tattooing and Piercing

The Paraphilias

Noncoercive Paraphilias
  Fetishism
  Transvestism
  Think About It: Cross Dressing: What's in a Name?

Coercive Paraphilias
  Zoophilia
  Voyeurism
  Exhibitionism
  Telephone Scatalogia
  Practically Speaking: Dealing with Obscene Phone Calls
  Frotteurism
  Necrophilia
  Pedophilia
  Sexual Sadism and Sexual Masochism

LEARNING OBJECTIVES

At the conclusion of Chapter 10, students should be able to:

1. Compare and contrast atypical and paraphilic sexual behavior.

2. Discuss cross-dressing in popular and gay culture and as a form of "gender relaxation."

3. Discuss domination and submission as atypical behavior, including bondage, the domination and submission subculture, and body piercing and tattooing.

4. Describe briefly the characteristics of paraphiliacs.

5. Describe and characterize the noncoercive paraphilias, including fetishism and transvestism.

6. Describe and characterize the coercive paraphilias, including zoophilia, voyeurism, exhibitionism, telephone scatalogia and frotteurism, and necrophilia.

7. Describe pedophilia, including types of pedophiles, cross-sex and same-sex pedophilia, and female pedophilia.

8. Discuss sexual sadism and sexual masochism, including autoerotic asphyxia.

9. Recognize and define key terms introduced in the chapter.

DISCUSSION QUESTIONS

Changing Perceptions of Pathology. Refer back to Chapter 1's discussion of what is normal/moral/healthy behavior. Discuss how pathology often reflects societal norms, using examples of masturbation and excessive sexual intercourse. Ask if there are some behaviors that can be inherently pathological or whether pathology fundamentally reflects societal norms. Use sexual sadism to argue the inherently pathological position. Use homosexuality to argue the societal norms position, citing the 1972 APA decision to remove homosexuality from the list of mental disorders.

Sexual Continuum. On the blackboard, draw a line representing the sexual continuum for sexualization of inanimate objects (or domination and submission, cross-dressing, voyeurism, exhibitionism, or other atypical behavior). Label one pole "paraphilic" and the other "acceptable." Ask students to suggest behaviors and where to place them on the continuum. Such behaviors might be "kissing a partner's photo," "smelling a partner's perfumed shirt or blouse," "keeping a lock of a partner's hair," "masturbating to a partner's photo," or "masturbating with his or her shirt or blouse." At what point on the continuum does a behavior become a fetish? Should someone engaged in fetishism seek professional help if it does not bother him or her?

Discuss differences between domination and submission and sexual sadism and sexual masochism; differences between cross-dressing and transvestism. What makes one behavior atypical but the other paraphilic? What underlying standards are being applied? Note also that these standards change: Masturbation was once considered pathological.

Cross-dressing, Effeminacy, and Butchness. Discuss differences between cross-dressing and effeminate and butch roles (discussed in Chapter 5) in gay/lesbian subculture.

Halloween and Carnival. Ask students about the types of unusual or atypical behaviors or dress they have seen during Halloween and Carnival. What is the function of relaxing norms during these periods? What kinds of boundaries can be trespassed? Why are some behaviors permitted during Halloween and Carnival but not at other times?

Camp. Ask students to discuss camp. When they call something "campy," what do they mean? What kind of humor is camp? How is it distinguished from other humor?

Pedophilia and Child Sexual Abuse. Discuss the differing dynamics between pedophilia and child sexual abuse (discussed in Chapter 17). Not all child sexual abusers are primarily sexually motivated, whereas pedophiles are.

ACTIVITIES

Taboo Topics. Have students anonymously write on 3 x 5 cards what topics they feel are taboo. When students have turned in the cards, read them (or a sampling) aloud and discuss why the topics are taboo.

Nymphomania and Satyriasis. Have students anonymously write on 3 x 5 cards their criteria for identifying someone as being a nymphomaniac or satyriasiac. Distribute the cards randomly in small groups. Do the terms have scientific value? Are different criteria used for women and men? What kinds of values are reflected in these terms?

SEX AND POPULAR CULTURE

Popular Culture Response Paper (Worksheet 22): Crime TV Shows. Atypical and paraphilic behaviors are often found in crime TV shows. Ask students to describe their role in one program.

Discussion: Ask students to imagine they were involved in a deeply loving relationship and later discovered their partner was cross-dressed, that he or she was not the gender they believed. (You might utilize examples from the film "The Crying Game" and the play/film "M. Butterfly.") Would they continue to love their partner after the discovery? Is love dependent on gender or does it transcend gender?

Discussion: Ask students to compare the various cross-dressing characters in "The Birdcage," "Some Like It Hot,"

"Tootsie," "Torch Song Trilogy," and "The Crying Game." Ask students what they think are the characters' different motives and how they think the men feel when dressed as women. You might ask students to rent a video of any one (or more) of these films a week or so before discussing them.

Discussion: We often casually use the terms "voyeuristic" and "exhibitionistic," "voyeur" and "exhibitionist," to describe activities and people. What are some examples of such usage? What do we mean when we use these terms? What is their relationship, if any, to actual paraphilias?

Discussion: Why has sexual addiction become a popular topic in the media? What evidence is there to support it? What underlying attitudes does the addiction metaphor suggest about atypical or unconventional sexuality?

Discussion: Talk shows often have pedophilia as a topic because it evokes powerful emotions. Because of the strong emotions involved, are the shows able to accurately portray pedophilia?

Activity: Show Madonna's music video "Justify Your Love," which involves cross-dressing. (MTV refused to show it.) Ask students to discuss the use of cross-dressing in the video as an artistic device and as a means of "gender bending." Would the video have been as effective if the cross-dressing elements were missing?

Activity: RuPaul is a popular cross-dresser who appears on cable TV as a guest and performer (see Guy Trebay. "Cross-Dresser Dreams," *The New Yorker,* Mar. 22, 1993, pp. 49–56). Play a song from his recording "Supermodel of the World" about the world of cross-dressing or show one of his music videos. How do people respond to him?

Activity: On 3 x 5 cards, identifying only gender, have class members note if they have cross-dressed on Halloween; during skits, plays, or parties; or on other occasions or at home. Have them briefly describe their feelings. Randomly distribute the cards to small groups of students and discuss the role of cross-dressing in our culture.

HEALTH CONSIDERATIONS

Discussion: If a client sought counseling because he or she was a cross-dresser, would you work to have your client accept or change his or her behavior? Why? How would you counsel the individual's partner?

Discussion: If a client were referred to you for treatment as a pedophile, what would your feelings be? Would you be able to treat him or her? Why?

Activity: Role-play a therapist and a sexually troubled client. Begin role-playing with the client describing himself or herself as a "sex addict."

SUPPORT MATERIAL

Films and Videos

"Sexual Addiction" (28 min., VHS, Films for the Humanities and Sciences, Inc.). This video has been adapted from a Phil Donahue program and shows individuals so compulsively driven by sexual appetite that their dependency is comparable to that of alcoholics or compulsive gamblers.

Bibliography

The books and articles listed below may be helpful for instructors wishing additional background or information on some of the topics covered in this chapter. In addition, the books listed in this chapter's "Suggested Reading" in the textbook may also be useful.

Arndt, W. B., Jr. *Gender Disorders and the Paraphilias.* Madison, CT: International Universities Press, 1991.

Favazza, A. R. *Bodies Under Siege: Self-Mutilation and Body Modification in Culture and Psychiatry* (2nd ed.). Baltimore: Johns Hopkins University Press, 1996.

Freund, K., R. Watson, and R. Dickey. "Does Sexual Abuse in Childhood Cause Pedophilia: An Exploratory Study." *Archives of Sexual Behavior,* Dec. 1990, 19(6), 557–568.

Freund, K., R. Watson, R. Dickey, and D. Rienzo. "Erotic Gender Differentiation in Pedophilia." *Archives of Sexual Behavior,* Dec. 1991, 20(6), 555–566.

Garber, M. *Vested Interests: Cross-Dressing and Cultural Anxiety.* New York: Routledge, 1992.

Levine, M., and R. Troiden. "The Myth of Sexual Compulsivity." *Journal of Sex Research,* Aug. 1988, 25(3), 347–363.

Levine, S. B., C. B. Risen, and Althof, A. E. "Essay on the Diagnosis and Nature of Paraphilia." *Journal of Sex and Marital Therapy,* June 1990, 16(2), 89–102.

Moser, C. "Sadomasochism." D. Dailey (ed.). *The Sexually Unusual.* New York: Harrington Park Press, 1988.

Nestle, J. "The Fem Question." C. Vance (ed.). *Pleasure and Danger.* New York: Routledge and Keagan Paul, 1983.

Okami, P. "Self-Reports of 'Positive' Childhood and Adolescent Sexual Contacts with Older Persons: An Exploratory Study." *Archives of Sexual Behavior,* 1991, 20(5), 437–457.

Person, E. S., N. Terestman, W. A. Myers, and E. L. Goldberg. "Gender Differences in Sexual Behaviors and Fantasies in a College Population." *Journal of Sex and Marital Therapy,* Sept. 1989, 15(3), 187–214.

Saunders, E. "Life-Threatening Autoerotic Behavior: A Challenge for Sex Educators and Therapists." *Journal of Sex Education and Therapy,* June 1989, 15(2), 77–81.

Templeman, T., and R. Stinnett. "Patterns of Sexual Arousal and History in a 'Normal' Sample of Young Men." *Archives of Sexual Behavior,* April 1991, 20(2), 137–150.

Weinberg, T., and G. W. L. Kamel (eds.). *S and M: Studies in Sadomasochism.* Buffalo, NY: Prometheus Books, 1983.

Wise, T. N., and J. K. Meyer. "The Border Area Between Transvestism and Gender Dysphoria: Transvestitic Applicants for Sex Reassignment." *Archives of Sexual Behavior,* 1980, 9, 327–342.

WORKSHEET 22

Popular culture response paper: Crime TV Shows

Name of program:

Description of content:

What underlying message or stereotype about sexuality did the program present?

Did it present its message or stereotype visually or verbally? How? Was it effective?

Comments:

Strong/DeVault/Sayad, *Human Sexuality,* 3rd ed. © 1999 Mayfield Publishing Company. Chapter 10

CHAPTER 11
CONTRACEPTION AND BIRTH CONTROL

CHAPTER OUTLINE

Risk and Responsibility
  Think About It: The Psychology of Risk Taking
  Women, Men, and Birth Control: Who Is Responsible?
  Preventing Sexually Transmitted Diseases

Methods of Contraception and Birth Control
  Birth Control and Contraception: What's the Difference?
  Choosing a Method
  Practically Speaking: Guidelines for Choosing a Contraceptive Method
  Sexual Abstinence and Outercourse
  Hormonal Methods: The Pill and Implants
  Think About It: Unreliable and Mythical Methods of Contraception
  Barrier Methods: The Condom, Female Condom, Diaphragm, and Cervical Cap
  Practically Speaking: Hints for Effective Condom Use
  Spermicides
  The IUD (Intrauterine Device)
  Fertility Awareness Methods
  Sterilization
  Practically Speaking: Is Sterilization the Right Choice for You?
  Emergency Contraception

Abortion
  Methods of Abortion
  A Decline in the Prevalence of Abortion
  Women and Abortion
  Men and Abortion
  The Abortion Debate

Research Issues

LEARNING OBJECTIVES

At the conclusion of Chapter 11, students should be able to:

1. Explain the psychology of contraceptive risk taking and discuss the issues involved in choosing a reliable method.

2. List and describe hormonal methods of contraception (including oral contraceptives, implants, and injections) and their effectiveness, advantages, and possible problems.

3. List and describe barrier methods of contraception (including condoms, diaphragm, cervical cap, and female condoms), their effectiveness, advantages, and possible problems.

4. Describe spermicides (including contraceptive foam, film, creams, and jellies), their effectiveness, advantages, and possible problems.

5. Describe the IUD (intrauterine device), its effectiveness, advantages, and possible problems.

6. List and describe fertility awareness methods (including calendar, BBT, cervical mucus method, and sympto-thermal), their effectiveness, advantages, and possible problems.

7. List and describe forms of sterilization, their effectiveness, advantages, and possible problems.

8. Discuss emergency contraception methods (including the emergency contraceptive pill, suction method, and mifepristone with misoprostol), their effectiveness, advantages and possible problems.

9. Discuss abortion, including methods, prevalence, characteristics of women having abortions and their reasons, and men and abortion, and delineate the arguments in the abortion debate.

10. Discuss reasons that research into new contraceptive methods has been limited.

11. Recognize and define key terms introduced in the chapter.

DISCUSSION QUESTIONS

Psychology of Contraceptive Risk Taking. Ask students to indicate what "costs" are at work to prevent people from (1) acknowledging contraception, (2) obtaining contraception, and (3) planning and continuing contraception. Are the anticipated benefits of pregnancy as strong a factor as the costs in discouraging contraceptive use?

Mifepristone with Misoprostol. Discuss whether mifepristone with misoprostol (RU-486) should be made available on demand in the United States. What impact would its availability have on women's access to abortion?

Morality and the Study of Abortion. Because abortion is an emotionally charged issue, many find it difficult to study scientifically. Ask students to approach the issue as objectively as they can, regardless of their beliefs. (You may want to ask students to review the section on critical thinking in Chapter 2.) Next, ask students to discuss the relationship, if any, between scientific findings and moral stands on abortion. For example, what is the moral significance, if any, of the empirical findings that most women express relief following abortion? Does this finding have any bearing on the belief that abortion is murder?

Demographic and Socioeconomic Factors Associated with Abortion. Discuss: What is the relationship between ethnicity and abortion rates? What are the reasons for different abortion rates? What is the significance of socioeconomic status?

Psychology and Abortion. Why do women have abortions? What are the psychological consequences for women?

Morality and the Abortion Debate. Attitudes and beliefs, whether pro-life or pro-choice, tend to be very stable. Debates about the morality of abortion seldom change minds in either direction. Ask students what information or experiences, if any, would cause them to reconsider or change their moral beliefs concerning abortion. Is it possible to believe one set of principles abstractly yet act differently if one becomes pregnant, either not having or having an abortion? What factors would cause one to act differently from one's beliefs?

Responsibility for Birth Control. Discuss whose responsibility it is in a new relationship to initiate discussion about birth control. Who should ultimately take responsibility for this issue?

Governmental Intervention. What role should the government have in the types of contraception that are available in this country?

Human Rights? Should men and women continue to be allowed to sue contraceptive manufacturers when their device causes health problems? What effect has this type of litigation had on the availability of devices currently on the market?

ACTIVITIES

Condom Buying. Require students to purchase a condom. In a one-page, anonymous response paper, ask them to briefly describe the experience and their feelings about doing so. (You may have them write their name on a cover sheet that is removed from the paper when they hand in the assignment.) Ask students to discuss their experiences in small groups. (This may be one of the most popular and talked-about assignments in your class.)

Contraceptive Risk Taking. Ask students, if they are involved (or have been) in sexual intercourse, to indicate anonymously on 3 x 5 cards the last time that they did not use contraception. Ask them to describe why. If students have not been involved in sexual intercourse, ask them to indicate factors that might discourage them from using contraception.

Sharing Contraceptive Responsibility. In small groups, discuss who is responsible for contraception in a single encounter, in an ongoing relationship, in marriage. Distinguish between what happens in reality and "how it ought to be."

Choosing a Contraceptive Method. Have students complete "Facts About Contraception" (Worksheet 23) and "Which Contraceptive Method Is Right for You and Your Partner?" (Worksheet 24) and discuss in small groups the reasoning behind choosing the best method for yourself and your partner. Does the length or type of relationship matter? (Note that Worksheet 23 is also in the *Study Guide*.)

Thinking About Abortion. Have students complete Worksheets 25 (Facts About Methods of Abortion) and 26 (Your Position on the Legality and Morality of Abortion). Note that Worksheet 26 is also in the *Study Guide*.

SEX AND POPULAR CULTURE

Discussion: How is contraception treated in soap operas? On "Beverly Hills 90210"? In television movies? In films? Is a connection made between pregnancy and failure to use contraception?

Discussion: Have students describe myths about contraception, such as douching with Coca-Cola. What impact do these myths have?

Discussion: How is abortion handled in television dramas and shows? Is the media pro-life or pro-choice? Give examples.

HEALTH CONSIDERATIONS

Discussion: Birth control and STD/HIV prevention. How is the choice of contraceptive method influenced by STD/HIV concerns?

Discussion: Imagine that a man or woman comes to you for contraception. In the course of the conversation, you discover the person is bisexual. What form of contraception would you recommend? Why?

Activity: Role-playing of health-care worker and sexually active couple. The scenario: A new couple wants an effective contraceptive method. They have been sexually involved with others over the past few months and do not know their HIV status. The health-care worker brings up STD/HIV issues and suggests using condoms. The woman wants to use condoms; the man does not.

Activity: Role-play two scenes: Health-care worker advising a 20-year-old man or woman about sterilization and then advising a 35-year-old man or woman. Your unmarried 20-year-old client states that he or she wants to be sterilized because he or she never wants children. What advice would you give? Replay the scenario with a 35-year-old. (Note whether it makes a difference if the client is male or female in terms of traditional gender-role expectations that a woman have children.)

GUEST SPEAKERS/PANELS

Invite a health-care worker from the college health clinic or local Planned Parenthood to demonstrate on a pelvic model and discuss birth control methods and services available in your community.

Invite a panel of females and males to discuss their personal experiences with abortion, focusing on the decision-making process, their feelings, and consequences. (The panel may come from the student health service, Planned Parenthood, or other reproductive health organizations that tend to emphasize positive outcomes. To achieve balance, you might also try Birthright or conservative religious groups, which oppose abortion; they tend to emphasize negative outcomes for women.)

SUPPORT MATERIAL

Films and Videos

"Abortion" (56 min., VHS, Films for Humanities). This *48 Hours* program looks at women who want to terminate their pregnancies and at the effects of the controversy over abortion on women, health care professionals, law enforcement, and the judicial system.

"Abortion: A Different Light" (1982, 29 min., VHS, Kent State University). Abortion issues as seen from a pro-choice position. Pro-choice advocates are interviewed.

"Abortion: Personal Portraits" (26 min., VHS, Films for Humanities). This program profiles a teenager who chose abortion; a woman who backed out of an abortion after seeing an image of the fetus on a monitor; one who chose to abort a fatally handicapped fetus; one who chose abortion rather than raise a child in poverty; and a woman who, divorced and pregnant, put her fourth child up for adoption.

"Are You Listening?" (1985, 28 min., VHS, Kent State University). A group of men and women discuss their change from being against abortion to advocating a moral option to safe abortion for all women.

"Birth Control—Myths and Methods" (26 min., VHS, SVE/Churchill). This video describes the devices and methods available either by prescription or over the counter. It tells how they are used and details the advantages and disadvantages and possible side effects of each.

"Bob's Vasectomy" (1977, 12 min., VHS and 16mm, Multi-Focus, Inc.). Bob, 47, describes his reasons for having a vasectomy. This film clearly depicts both the surgery and the feelings involved.

"Condoms: More Than Birth Control" (11 min., VHS, Polymorph). This video focuses on condom use: why it is important to use condoms, how they should be used, how to minimize the risk of failure. The video presents women with a number of ways they can persuade reluctant partners to participate in using a condom for mutual protection.

"Contraception: The Stalled Revolution" (58 min., VHS, Cinema Guild). Hosted by Linda Ellerbee, this documentary examines the state of contraception in the United States today and why Americans are not getting the family planning options they want. There are interviews with women at a health clinic, a class learning the rhythm method, Congressional representatives, and spokespeople for and against contraception and abortion rights.

"Hope . . . Is Not a Method" (4th ed.) (21 min., VHS, Altschul). This video, produced by Planned Parenthood of Syracuse, features two teen hosts describing contraceptive methods. As they introduce each method, they show the item. Diagrams illustrate the correct way to use each item, and the hosts cover the effectiveness, advantages, and side effects of prescription and over-the-counter methods. The hosts also stress that abstinence is the only method that works 100%.

"How to Use a Condom: Condom & Lubricant" (1988, 15 min., VHS, Multi-Focus, Inc.). Using an acrylic model of a penis, Dr. Clark Taylor demonstrates the correct and incorrect ways to put condoms on and take them off. This video is also available in Spanish.

"It Happens to Us" (32 min., VHS, New Day). First released in 1972, this film remains a classic plea for legal abortion as a choice. The personal stories of a wide range of women and medical descriptions by a physician remind people of the consequences of making abortion illegal and what life was like before the *Roe v. Wade* 1973 Supreme Court decision.

"The Pill: A Young Woman's Guide" (11 min, VHS, Polymorph). This video focuses on the birth control pill: the advantages and disadvantages, contraindications for use, how and when it should be taken, what to do if you forget to take one, why not to share pills, and warning signs that require seeing a physician.

"The Sovereign Self: Right to Live, Right to Die" (1984, 60 min., VHS, Kent State University). Personal freedoms and privacy are balanced against state intervention and societal rights in a discussion that touches on abortion, "Baby Doe" cases, and the right to die.

"Taking Charge" (22 min., VHS, Fanlight). This video looks at the myths and misconceptions many teens told about birth control and contraception, as well as the complex realities they face in dealing with this new and confusing aspect of their lives. Study guide available.

Bibliography

The books and articles listed below may be helpful for instructors wishing additional background or information on some of the topics covered in this chapter. In addition, the books listed in this chapter's "Suggested Reading" in the textbook may also be useful.

Armsworth, M. W. "Psychological Responses to Abortion." *Journal of Counseling and Development,* Mar-Apr, 1991, 69, 377–379.

Boland, R. "Selected Legal Developments in Reproductive Health in 1991." *Family Planning Perspectives*, July 1992, 24(4), 178–185.

Fathalla, M. F. "Reproductive Health in the World: Two Decades of Progress and the Challenge Ahead." *World Health Organization, Reproductive Health (Biennial Report 1990–1991).* Geneva, Switzerland: World Health Organization, 1992.

Hankinson, S. E., G. A. Colditz, D. J. Hunter, T. L. Spencer, B. Rosner, and M. J. Stampflau. "A Quantitative Assessment of Oral Contraceptive Use and Risk of Ovarian Cancer." *Obstetrics and Gynecology,* Oct. 1992, 80(4), 708–714.

Hatcher, R., et al. *Contraceptive Technology.* New York: Irvington Publishers, 1993.

Petchesky, R. P. *Abortion and Woman's Choice: The State, Sexuality, and Reproductive Freedom* (rev. ed.). Boston: Northeastern University Press, 1990.

Tribe, L. *Abortion: Clash of Absolutes.* New York: Norton, 1990.

Trussell, J., R. A. Hatcher, W. Cates, F. H. Stewart, and K. Kost. "Contraceptive Failure in the United States: An Update." *Studies in Family Planning,* 1990, 21(1), Table 1.

Trussell, J., F. Stewart, F. Guest, and R. A. Hatcher. "Emergency Contraceptive Pills: A Simple Proposal to Reduce Unintended Pregnancies." *Family Planning Perspectives,* (1992), 24, 269–73.

Winikoff, B., and S. Wymelenberg. *The Whole Truth About Contraception.* Washington, DC: National Academy of Sciences, 1997.

WORKSHEET 23

Facts about contraception

To help you choose the best method of contraception for you and your partner, you must first be familiar with the advantages, disadvantages, and effectiveness ratings of the different methods. Fill in the boxes below with the appropriate comments, using your text if necessary.

Method	Advantages	Disadvantages	Effectiveness
Oral contraceptives			
Norplant implants			
DMPA (Depo-Provera injections)			
IUD • Copper T-380A • Progestasert IUD			
Male Condom			
Female condom			

Strong/DeVault/Sayad, *Human Sexuality,* 3rd ed. © 1999 Mayfield Publishing Company. Chapter 11

Method	Advantages	Disadvantages	Effectiveness
Diaphragm with spermicide			
Cervical cap			
Vaginal spermicides			
Fertility awareness method			
Withdrawal			
Male sterilization			
Female sterilization			

Name _____   Section _____   Date _____

WORKSHEET 24

Which contraceptive method is right for you and your partner?

If you are sexually active, you need to use the contraceptive method that will work best for you. A number of factors may be involved in your decision. The following questions will help you sort out these factors and choose an appropriate method. Answer yes (Y) or no (N) for each statement as it applies to you and, if appropriate, your partner.

1. I like sexual spontaneity and don't want to be bothered with contraception at the time of sexual intercourse.

2. I need a contraceptive immediately.

3. It is very important that I do not become pregnant now.

4. I want a contraceptive method that will protect me and my partner against sexually transmitted diseases.

5. I prefer a contraceptive method that requires the cooperation and involvement of both partners.

6. I have sexual intercourse frequently.

7. I have sexual intercourse infrequently.

8. I am forgetful or have a variable daily routine.

9. I have more than one sexual partner.

10. I have heavy periods with cramps.

11. I prefer a method that requires little or no action or bother on my part.

12. I am a nursing mother.

13. I want the option of conceiving immediately after discontinuing contraception.

14. I want a contraceptive method with few or no side effects.

If you answered "yes" to the statements listed on the left, the method on the right might be a good choice for you.

1, 3, 6, 10, 11	Oral contraceptives
1, 3, 6, 8, 10, 11	Norplant
1, 3, 6, 8, 10, 11, 12	DMPA (Depo-Provera)
1, 3, 6, 8, 11, 12, 13	IUD
2, 4, 5, 7, 8, 9, 12, 13, 14	Condoms (male and female)
5, 7, 12, 13, 14	Diaphragm and spermicide
5, 7, 12, 13, 14	Cervical cap
2, 5, 7, 8, 12, 13, 14	Vaginal spermicides
5, 7, 13, 14	Fertility awareness methods

Your answers may indicate that more than one method would be appropriate for you. To help narrow your choices, circle the numbers of the statements that are *most* important for you. Before you make a final choice, talk with your partner(s) and your physician. Consider your own lifestyle and preferences as well as characteristics of each method (effectiveness, side effects, costs, and so on). For maximum protection against pregnancy and STDs, you might want to consider combining two methods.

Strong/DeVault/Sayad, *Human Sexuality*, 3rd ed. © 1999 Mayfield Publishing Company. Chapter 11

Name _____ Section _____ Date _____

WORKSHEET 25

Facts about methods of abortion

Familiarize yourself with the different methods of abortion by completing the chart below. Refer to your textbook if necessary.

Method	Description of Procedure	Potential Side Effects	Time in Pregnancy When Used
Mifepristone with misoprostol (RU-486)			
Emergency contraception (postcoital birth control)			
Vacuum aspiration			
Suction method (D&C)			
Dilation and evacuation (D&E)			
Hysterotomy			

Strong/DeVault/Sayad, *Human Sexuality,* 3rd ed. © 1999 Mayfield Publishing Company. Chapter 11

Name _____ Section _____ Date _____

WORKSHEET 26

Your position on the legality and morality of abortion

	Agree	Disagree
1. The fertilized egg is a human being from the moment of conception.	_____	_____
2. The rights of the fetus at any stage take precedence over any decision a woman might want to make regarding her pregnancy.	_____	_____
3. The rights of the fetus depend upon its gestational age: further along in the pregnancy, the fetus has more rights.	_____	_____
4. Each individual woman should have final say over decisions regarding her health and body; politicians should not be allowed to decide.	_____	_____
5. In cases of teenagers seeking an abortion, parental consent should be required.	_____	_____
6. In cases of married women seeking an abortion, spousal consent should be required.	_____	_____
7. In cases of late abortion, tests should be done to determine the viability of the fetus.	_____	_____
8. The federal government should provide public funding for abortion to ensure equal access to abortion for all women.	_____	_____
9. The federal government should not allow states to pass their own abortion laws; there should be uniform laws for the entire country.	_____	_____

10. Does a woman's right to choose whether or not to have an abortion depend upon the circumstances surrounding conception or the situation of the mother? In which of the following situations, if any, would you support a woman's right to choose to have an abortion (check where appropriate)?

_____ An abortion is necessary to maintain the woman's life or health.

_____ The pregnancy is a result of rape or incest.

_____ A serious birth defect has been detected in the fetus through amniocentesis or chorionic villus sampling.

_____ The pregnancy is a result of the failure of a contraceptive method or device.

_____ The pregnancy occurred when no contraceptive method was in use.

_____ A single mother, pregnant for the fifth time, wants an abortion because she feels she cannot support another child.

_____ A pregnant 15-year-old high school student feels having a child would prove to be too great a disruption in her life and keep her from reaching her goals for the future.

_____ A pregnant 19-year-old college student does not want to interrupt her education.

_____ The father of the child has stated he will provide no support and is not interested in helping raise the child.

_____ Parents of two boys wish to terminate the mother's pregnancy because the fetus is male rather than female.

On the basis of your answers, write out your position on abortion. Should it be legal or illegal? Are there certain circumstances in which it should or should not be allowed? What sorts of rules should govern when it can be performed?

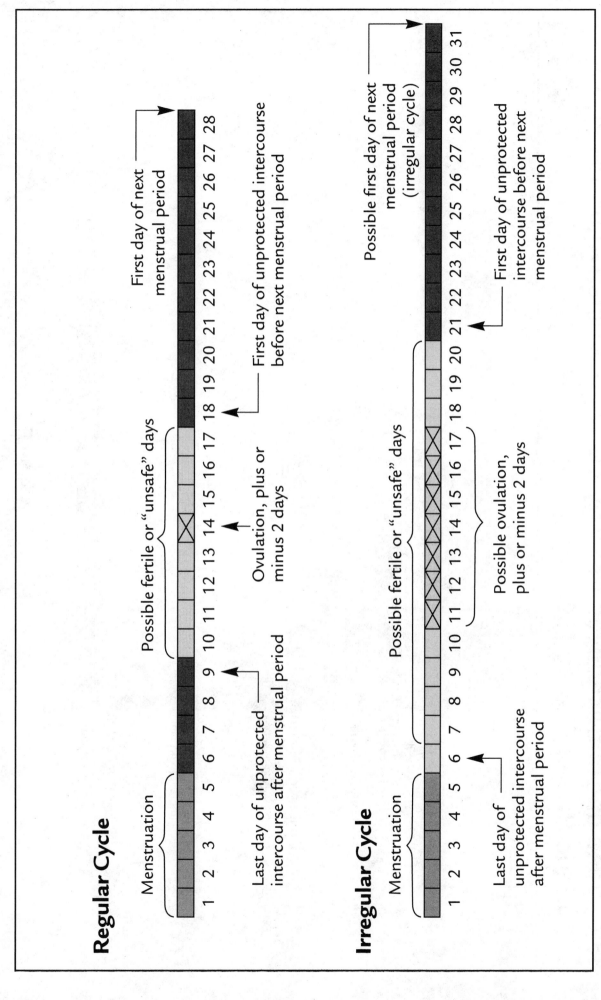

35 Types of Contraceptives Used by Men and Women Ages 15–44 in the United States, 1995

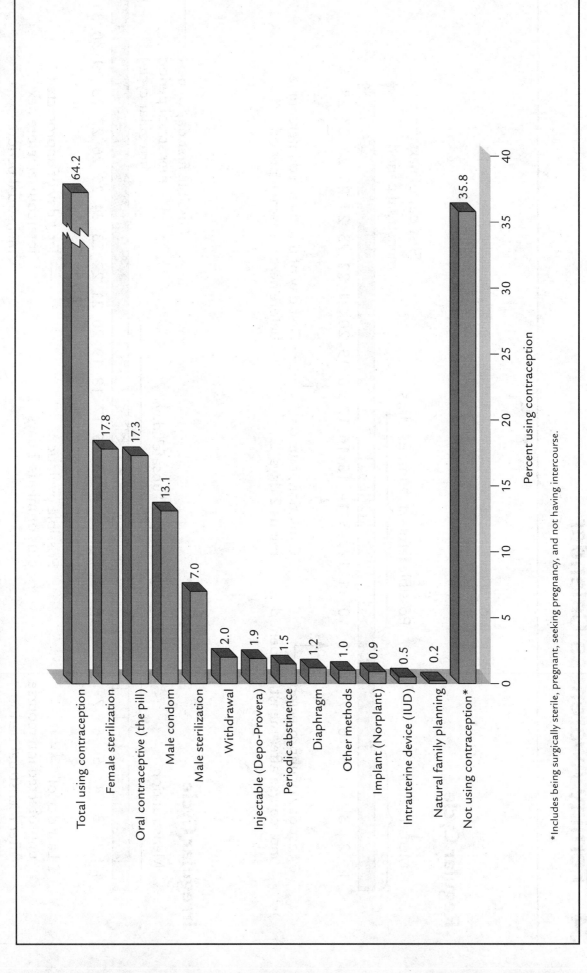

Percent using contraception

Total using contraception	64.2
Female sterilization	17.8
Oral contraceptive (the pill)	17.3
Male condom	13.1
Male sterilization	7.0
Withdrawal	2.0
Injectable (Depo-Provera)	1.9
Periodic abstinence	1.5
Diaphragm	1.2
Other methods	1.0
Implant (Norplant)	0.9
Intrauterine device (IUD)	0.5
Natural family planning	0.2
Not using contraception*	35.8

*Includes being surgically sterile, pregnant, seeking pregnancy, and not having intercourse.

Strong/DeVault/Sayad, *Human Sexuality*, 3rd ed. © 1999 Mayfield Publishing Company

Effectiveness Rates of Various Contraceptive Methods During the First Year of Use

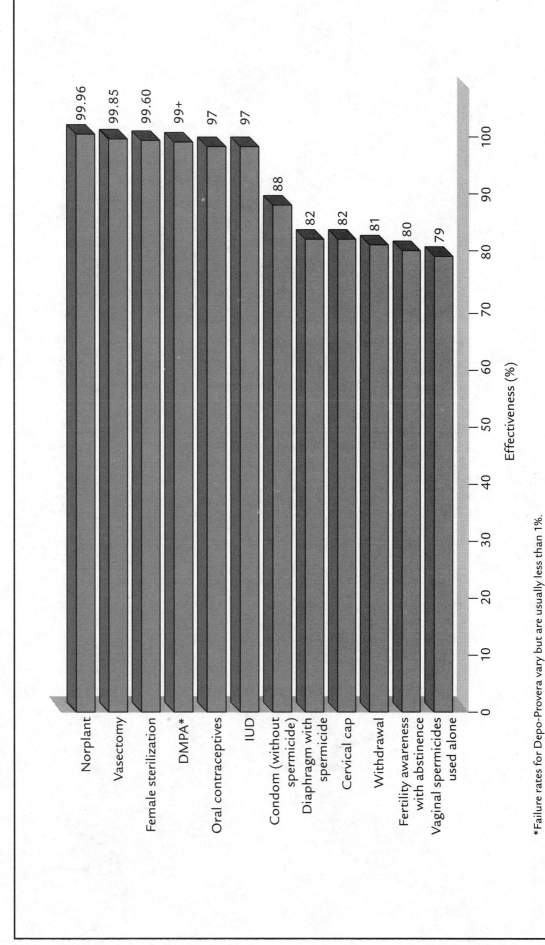

Method	Effectiveness (%)
Norplant	99.96
Vasectomy	99.85
Female sterilization	99.60
DMPA*	99+
Oral contraceptives	97
IUD	97
Condom (without spermicide)	88
Diaphragm with spermicide	82
Cervical cap	82
Withdrawal	81
Fertility awareness with abstinence	80
Vaginal spermicides used alone	79

Effectiveness (%)

*Failure rates for Depo-Provera vary but are usually less than 1%.

Strong/DeVault/Sayad, *Human Sexuality*, 3rd ed. © 1999 Mayfield Publishing Company

Vasectomy and Tubal Ligation

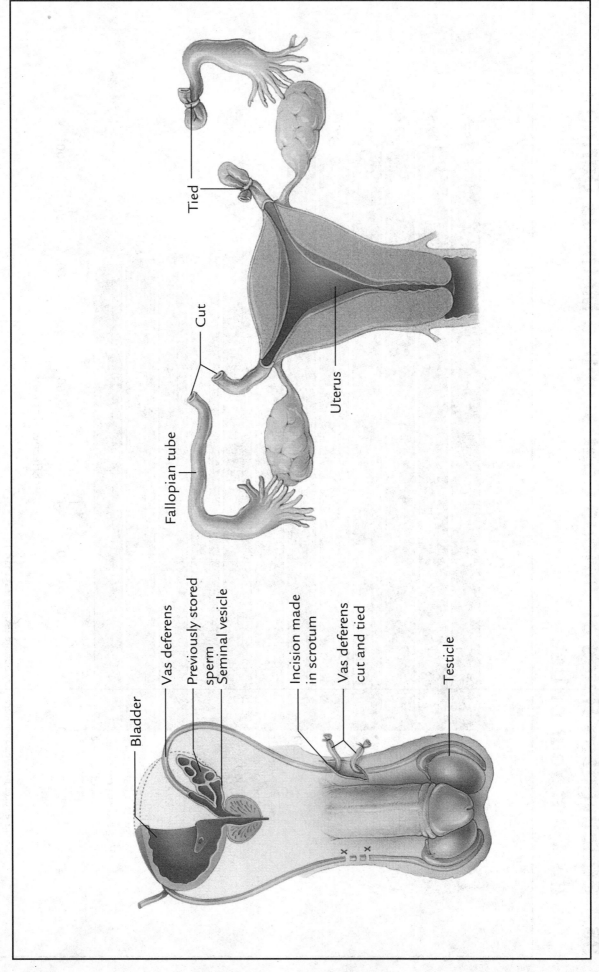

Tied

Cut

Fallopian tube

Uterus

Bladder

Vas deferens

Previously stored
sperm

Seminal vesicle

Incision made
in scrotum

Vas deferens
cut and tied

Testicle

Strong/DeVault/Sayad, *Human Sexuality*, 3rd ed. © 1999 Mayfield Publishing Company

CHAPTER 12

CONCEPTION, PREGNANCY, AND CHILDBIRTH

CHAPTER OUTLINE

Fertilization and Fetal Development
    The Fertilization Process
    Development of the Conceptus

Being Pregnant
    Pregnancy Tests
    Changes That Occur During Pregnancy
    Think About It: Sexuality During Pregnancy
    Complications of Pregnancy and Dangers to the Fetus
    Think About It: Pregnancy and Drugs Don't Mix
    Diagnosing Abnormalities of the Fetus
    Pregnancy Loss

Infertility
    Female Infertility
    Male Infertility
    Emotional Responses to Infertility
    Infertility Treatment
    Think About It: The Ethics of Reproductive Technology
    Surrogate Motherhood

Giving Birth
    Labor and Delivery
    Choices in Childbirth
    Think About It: The Question of Circumcision
    Breast-feeding
    Practically Speaking: Breast Versus Bottle: Which Is Best for You and Your Child

Becoming a Parent
    Think About It: Gay and Lesbian Parents

LEARNING OBJECTIVES

At the conclusion of Chapter 12, students should be able to:

1. Describe the fertilization process and development of the conceptus.

2. Discuss the pregnant woman's relationship to her partner and sexuality during pregnancy.

3. List and describe the possible complications of pregnancy, including teratogens, diseases, conditions, low birth weight, and fetal diagnosis.

4. Discuss pregnancy loss, including spontaneous abortion, infant mortality rates, and coping with loss.

5. List the principal causes of male and female infertility, and discuss emotional responses to infertility, treatments, surrogate motherhood, and ethical issues.

6. Describe the stages of labor and delivery.

7. Discuss childbirth choices, including hospital births, C-sections, prepared childbirth, birthing rooms and centers, and home births.

8. Discuss the question of circumcision including religious, cultural, and health considerations.

9. Discuss breast-feeding, including the physiology, benefits, and issues involved in choosing to breast-feed.

10. Discuss becoming a parent, including the postpartum period, parental roles, gay/lesbian parenting, and coping with stress.

11. Recognize and define key terms introduced in the chapter.

DISCUSSION QUESTIONS

Pregnancy and Marriage. More than 20 percent of women are pregnant at the time they marry. What is the role of pregnancy in marital decisions?

Deciding to Have a Child. What factors go into the decision to have or not have a child? Discuss the role of gender expectations, relationship considerations, economics, societal pressures, and so on. What influences does one's ethnicity have on the decision?

Developmental Tasks of Expectant Parents. Discuss the developmental tasks of an expectant mother and father.

Birth Choices. What factors would influence your choice for hospital birth? Home birth with midwife? Prepared childbirth?

C-sections. With the alarming rate of C-sections, what can individuals do to avoid surgical intervention in their births?

Ethics of Reproductive Technology. Discuss the ethics of reproductive technology as explored in the box titled "The Ethics of Reproductive Technology."

Breast Feeding. What considerations, such as bonding and economic considerations, would go into a decision whether to breast-feed?

Transition to Parenthood. What kinds of stress do new mothers and fathers tend to experience in the transition to parenthood?

ACTIVITIES

Fetus in Uterus. Distribute the worksheet on the fetus in uterus (Worksheet 27) and ask students to label each part. Note that this same sheet (with answers) is in the *Study Guide*.

Birth Class. Have students visit a childbirth preparation class at a local hospital, birth center, or YWCA. They should get permission from the instructor to observe the class or participate in it. Afterwards, they might interview an expectant couple about their choices for birth and their feelings, hopes, anxieties, and so on. They may present their findings in a paper or panel discussion.

Interview: Have students interview their parents about their own births or their grandparents about their parents' births. They may ask such questions as: Where did the birth take place? Who was in attendance? How were they prepared for the birth? What procedures or medications were involved? How did they feel about the experience?

Thinking About Parenthood. Distribute Worksheet 28 (Assessing Your Readiness to Become a Parent). Ask students to complete and then discuss in small groups. Are there factors they had not previously identified? Which factors do they think are most critical?

Facts About Pregnancy and Childbirth. Have students complete Worksheet 29 (Facts About Pregnancy and Childbirth) if review is needed.

SEX AND POPULAR CULTURE

Discussion: How are gay and lesbian parents viewed in the media? How does this contrast with societal views?

Activity: Make a collage of photographs of pregnant women from newspapers and magazines. What images are being presented of pregnancy, such as the radiant mother-to-be?

HEALTH CONSIDERATIONS

Discussion: Imagine that you work in a fertility clinic that provides artificial insemination. What would your response be if a couple asked to have a third party inseminated with the man's semen because his partner had had a hysterectomy? If a lesbian couple in a long-standing relationship wanted one of the partners to be inseminated?

Discussion: How would you counsel a grieving woman who has miscarried? Whose infant was stillborn? What about her partner?

Activity: Role-play a health-care professional working out a birth plan with a pregnant woman and her partner. Next, role-play working out a birth plan with a single pregnant adolescent without a partner. How would her birth plan differ from the couple's?

GUEST SPEAKERS/PANELS

Invite a midwife to talk about the current state of childbirth and options available to expectant mothers and their partners in your community.

Invite a speaker from RESOLVE or another support group for infertile couples to discuss infertility issues these couples must face and ways of coping with them.

Invite a pregnant couple and new parents to discuss the impact of pregnancy and the transition to parenthood on their lives and relationships.

SUPPORT MATERIAL

Films and Videos

"Birth" (8 min., VHS, HRM). Physical processes from conception to birth.

"Birth: How Life Begins" (23 min., 16mm, Encyclopedia Britannica). A factual look at the total birth cycle, from conception to birth to postnatal care. This film examines alternative birth techniques, the importance of proper postnatal care, and the adjustment that parents and siblings must make.

"Birth Stories" (30 min., VHS, Cinema Guild). In a series of funny and frank interviews, women tell their personal stories of pregnancy and birth intercut with black and white footage of actual births. The program captures the full range of women's emotional responses and provides amusing but illuminating insights into this experience.

"Children of Children" (1987, 31 min., VHS, Indiana University Audio Visual Center). Explores the problem of teen pregnancy and presents two programs aimed at prevention.

"Coping with Miscarriage and Stillbirth" (1994, 24 min., VHS, Films for the Humanities and Sciences). A London-based program that helps parents cope with a pregnancy loss.

"Everyday Miracle: Birth" (40 min., VHS, Films Incorporated). Witness the miracle of conception, development, and birth in this astounding documentary. Advanced techniques in microphotography give viewers extraordinary, close-up pictures of a child from the moment of conception to birth.

"The Family of Man. Birth" (1970, 52 min., 16mm, Kent State University). Tells how women from different cultures react to pregnancy and birth, and examines why women in less developed societies seem to have babies so much more easily.

"Five Women: Five Births" (1978, 28 min., VHS and 16mm, B/W, Multi-Focus, Inc.). Five women discuss their hopes and fears about childbirth. Shows births at home, the hospital, and a cesarean section.

"Here in My Arms" (1991, 20 min., VHS, Fanlight Productions). Documents a couple's private adoption of a baby boy from Mexico. (This film received an honorable mention in the 1991 National Council on Family Relations Media Competition.)

"High Risk Pregnancy" (19 min., VHS, Films for the Humanities and Sciences, Inc.). Smoking, alcohol, and drug use are among the issues discussed in this film as contributors to risky pregnancy.

"Infertility" (28 min., VHS, Fanlight). This video provides an explanation of the causes of infertility, along with an overview of possible treatments. Couples discuss medical solutions and the decision to adopt a child. From "The Doctor Is In" series, Dartmouth-Hitchcock Medical Center.

"Influences: Innocence Betrayed" (1992, 24 min., VHS, Kent State University). Follows children as they attempt to cope with learning and behavior difficulties resulting from prenatal drug use.

"It's Our Baby: Parents Talk About Certified Nurse-Midwife Birth Care" (1992, 25 min., VHS, The Cinema Guild). Examines nurse-midwifery as an increasingly popular alternative to traditional hospital childbirth methods. (This film was a winner in the 1992 National Council on Family Relations Media Competition.)

"The Miracle of Life" (1983, 57 min., VHS and 16mm, University of Minnesota Film and Video). Documents human reproduction through color micro-photography inside living human beings.

"Not All Parents Are Straight" (1987, 58 min., VHS, University of Minnesota Film and Video). This program examines the dynamics of the parent-child relationship within several different households where children are being raised by gay and lesbian parents.

"Pregnancy, Alcohol, and Tobacco Don't Mix" (20 min., VHS, Altschul). Viewers meet three young mothers and learn their reasons for choosing a healthy lifestyle. The effects of Fetal Alcohol Syndrome are explained, and tips for becoming tobacco-free are provided. Throughout the program it is stressed that avoiding harmful substances during pregnancy can mean only one outcome: a healthy baby and a healthy mother.

"Pregnancy: Caring for Your Unborn Baby" (20 min., VHS, AIMS). Parents make many of their most important choices affecting their child's health during the first 9 months—before birth. This film reveals the lifelong impairment caused by poor nutrition, smoking, drugs, and alcohol.

"Project Future: Teenage Pregnancy, Childbirth, and Parenting" (1992, 145 min., VHS, Vida Health Communications). Follows 12 young men and women from the third trimester through the third month postpartum. (This film was a winner in the 1992 National Council on Family Relations Media Competition.)

"Sexuality After Childbirth" (1988, 14 min., VHS, Indiana University Audio Visual Center). Addresses parents' concerns following childbirth about when they can resume their sex life and what changes will need to be made. Suggests a couple's social and sexual lives will undergo a period of reconstruction following the birth.

"The Twelve-Month Pregnancy" (19 min., VHS, Films for Humanities). Much of the fetus's critical development occurs before a woman knows she is pregnant. This program encourages a preconception exam, teaches specifics about planning a successful pregnancy, cautions against the risks of the mother's use of alcohol, and describes the possible effect of drugs.

Bibliography

The books and articles listed below may be helpful for instructors wishing additional background or information on some of the topics covered in this chapter. In addition, the books listed in this chapter's "Suggested Reading" in the textbook may also be useful.

American Fertility Society. "In Vitro Fertilization-Embryo Transfer (IVF-ET) in the United States: 1990 Results from the IVF-ET Registry." *Fertility and Sterility,* Jan. 1992, 57(1), 15–24.

Armstrong, P., and S. Feldman. *A Wise Birth.* New York: William Morrow and Co., 1990.

Boles, A. J., and H. Curtis-Boles. "Black Couples and the Transition to Parenthood." *American Journal of Social Psychiatry,* Dec. 1986, 6(1), 27–31.

Bozett, F. W. (ed.). *Gay and Lesbian Parents.* New York: Praeger, 1987.

Cowan, C. P., and P. A. Cowan. "Who Does What When Partners Become Parents: Implications for Men, Women, and Marriage." *Marriage and Family Review,* 1988, 12(3–4), 105–131.

Cramer, D. "Gay Parents and Their Children: A Review of Research and Practical Implications." *Journal of Counseling and Development,* 1986, 64, 504–507.

Forrest, J. D., and S. Singh. "The Sexual and Reproductive Behavior of American Women, 1982–1988." *Family Planning Perspectives*, Sept. 1990, 22(5), 206–214.

Harper, B. Gentle Birth Choices. Rochester, VT: Healing Arts Press, 1995.

Hetherington, S. E. "A Controlled Study of the Effect of Prepared Childbirth Classes on Obstetric Outcomes." *Birth,* June 1990, 17(2), 86–90.

Jones, C. *Mind Over Labor*. New York: Penguin, 1988.

Kitzinger, S. *The Complete Book of Pregnancy and Childbirth*. New York: Knopf, 1996.

Leifer, M. *Psychological Effects of Motherhood: A Study of First Pregnancy*. New York: Praeger, 1990.

Louv, R. *Fatherlove*. New York: Pocket Books, 1993.

Marieb, E. N. *Human Anatomy and Physiology*. Redwood City, CA: Benjamin/Cummings, 1992.

Marsiglio, W. "Male Procreative Consciousness and Responsibility: A Conceptual Analysis and Research Agenda." *Journal of Family Issues,* 1991, 12, 268–290.

Menning, B. E. *Infertility: A Guide for Childless Couples*. (2d ed). New York: Prentice Hall, 1988.

Panuthos, C., and C. Romeo. *Ended Beginnings: Healing Childbearing Losses*. New York: Warner Books, 1984.

Pruett, K. *The Nurturing Father: Journey Toward Complete Man*. New York: Warner Books, 1987.

Reamy, K., and S. White. "Sexuality in the Puerperium: A Review." *Archives of Sexual Behavior,* 1987, 16(2), 165–187.

Romberg, R. *Circumcision: The Painful Dilemma*. South Hadley, MA: Bergin and Garvey, 1985.

Waterson, E. J., and I. M. Murray-Lyon. "Preventing Alcohol Related Birth Damage: A Review." *Social Science and Medicine,* 1990, 30(3), 349–364.

Zoldbrod, A. *Men, Women, and Infertility*. New York: Lexington Books, 1993.

WORKSHEET 27

The fetus in uterus and cross section of placenta

Label the parts of this uterus and cross section of placenta in pregnancy.

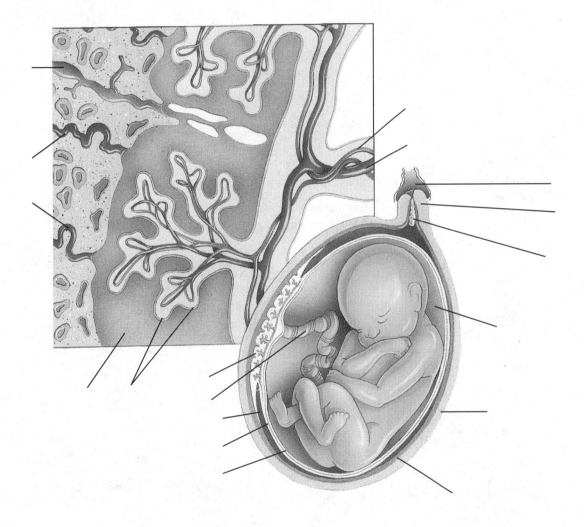

Source: P. Insel and T. Roth. 1998. *Core Concepts in Health* (8th ed.). Mountain View, CA: Mayfield Publishing Co.

Strong/DeVault/Sayad, *Human Sexuality,* 3rd ed. © 1999 Mayfield Publishing Company. Chapter 12

Name _____ Section _____ Date _____

WORKSHEET 28

Assessing your readiness to become a parent

Many factors have to be taken into account when you are considering parenthood. The following are some questions you should ask yourself and some issues you should consider when making this decision. Some issues are relevant to both men and women; others apply only to women. There are no "right" answers—you must decide for yourself what your answers reveal about your aptitude for parenthood.

Yes   No

Physical Health

____ ____ 1. Are you in reasonably good health?

____ ____ 2. Do you have any behaviors or conditions that could be of special concern?

- ____ Obesity
- ____ Smoking
- ____ Drug use
- ____ Hypertension
- ____ Previous problems with pregnancy or delivery
- ____ Anemia
- ____ Diabetes
- ____ Sexually transmitted diseases
- ____ Epilepsy
- ____ Prenatal exposure to DES

____ ____ 3. Are you under 20 or over 35 years of age?

____ ____ 4. Do you or your partner have a family history of a genetic problem that a baby might inherit?

- ____ Hemophilia
- ____ Sickle cell anemia
- ____ Down's syndrome
- ____ Tay-Sachs disease
- ____ Phenylketonuria (PKU)
- ____ Cystic fibrosis
- ____ Thalassemia
- ____ Other

Financial Circumstances

____ ____ 1. Will your health insurance cover the costs of pregnancy, prenatal tests, delivery, and medical attention for the mother and baby before and after the birth?

____ ____ 2. Can you afford the supplies for the baby: diapers, bedding, crib, stroller, car seat, clothing, food, and medical supplies?

____ ____ 3. Will one parent leave his or her job to care for the baby?

____ ____ 4. If so, can the decrease in family income be worked into the family budget?

____ ____ 5. If both parents will continue to work, has affordable child care been set up?

____ ____ 6. The first few years of raising a baby can cost $10,000; can you save and/or provide the necessary money?

Education, Career, and Child Care Plans

____ ____ 1. Have you completed as much of your education as you want?

____ ____ 2. Have you sufficiently established yourself in a career, if that is important to you?

____ ____ 3. Have you investigated parental leave and company-sponsored child care?

____ ____ 4. Do both spouses agree on child care arrangements?

Strong/DeVault/Sayad, *Human Sexuality*, 3rd ed. © 1999 Mayfield Publishing Company. Chapter 12

Yes   No

Lifestyle and Social Support

_____ _____ 1. Would you be willing to give up the freedom to do what you want to do when you want to do it?

_____ _____ 2. Would you be willing to restrict your social life, to give up leisure time and privacy?

_____ _____ 3. Would you and your partner be prepared to spend more time at home? Would you have enough time to spend with a child?

_____ _____ 4. Are you prepared to be a single parent if your partner leaves or dies?

_____ _____ 5. Do you have a network of family and friends who will help you with the baby? Are there community resources you can call on for additional assistance?

Readiness

_____ _____ 1. Are you prepared to have a helpless being completely dependent on you 24 hours a day?

_____ _____ 2. Do you like children? Have you enough experiences with babies, toddlers, and teenagers?

_____ _____ 3. Do you think time spent with children is time well spent?

_____ _____ 4. Do you communicate easily with others?

_____ _____ 5. Do you have enough love to give a child? Can you express affection easily?

_____ _____ 6. Do you feel good enough about yourself to respect and nurture others?

_____ _____ 7. Do you have safe ways of handling anger, frustration, and impatience?

_____ _____ 8. Would you be willing to devote a great part of your life, at least 18 years, to being responsible for a child?

Relationship with Partner

_____ _____ 1. Does your partner want to have a child? Is he or she willing to ask these same questions of himself or herself?

_____ _____ 2. Have you adequately discussed your reasons for wanting a child?

_____ _____ 3. Does either of you have philosophical objections to adding to the world's population?

_____ _____ 4. Have you and your partner discussed each other's feelings about religion, work, family, and child raising? Are your feelings compatible and conducive to good parenting?

_____ _____ 5. Would both you and your partner contribute in raising the child?

_____ _____ 6. Is your relationship stable? Could you provide a child with a really good home environment?

_____ _____ 7. After having a child, would your partner and you be able to separate if you should have unsolvable problems? Would you feel obligated to remain together for the sake of the child?

Name _____ Section _____ Date _____

WORKSHEET 29

Facts about pregnancy and childbirth

Review your knowledge of pregnancy and childbirth by answering the questions below. Refer to your textbook if necessary.

Conception

1. Tract the journey of the egg in a woman's body:

   _____

   (fertilized)

   ___ovary___   _____   _____

   _____

   How long does the egg's journey take? _____   (unfertilized)

2. Trace the journey of sperm cells from ejaculation to conception:

   ___penis___   _____   _____   _____   _____

   How does a sperm cell penetrate an egg? _____

3. List three possible reasons for infertility in women.

   a. _____

   b. _____

   c. _____

   List two possible reasons for infertility in men.

   a. _____

   b. _____

4. List and define four treatments for infertility.

   a. _____

   b. _____

   c. _____

   d. _____

Pregnancy

1. List three early signs and symptoms of pregnancy.

   a. _____

   b. _____

   c. _____

2. List specific changes that occur in the following during pregnancy.

uterus _____

breasts _____

muscles and ligaments _____

pelvic joints _____

circulatory system _____

kidneys _____

body weight _____

emotions _____

3. What are Braxton Hicks contractions? When do they occur and why?

_____

_____

4. List three characteristics of the fetus during each trimester. What systems have developed? How large is the fetus?

1st trimester	2nd trimester	3rd trimester
_____	_____	_____
_____	_____	_____
_____	_____	_____

5. List six important components of good prenatal care.

a. _____   d. _____

b. _____   e. _____

c. _____   f. _____

Childbirth

What occurs during each of the three stages of labor? How long does each stage last?

1st stage: _____

2nd stage: _____

3rd stage: _____

38 Fertilization and Early Development of the Embryo

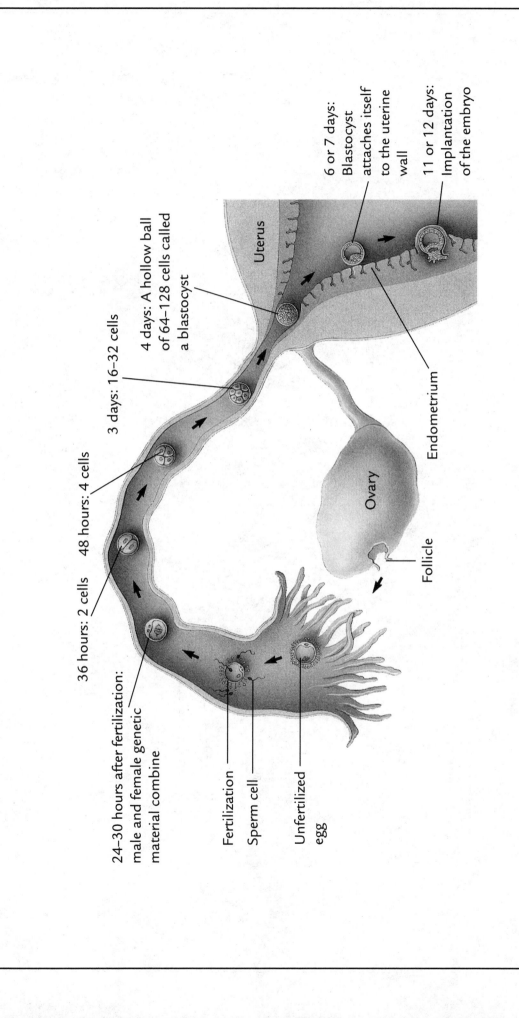

36 hours: 2 cells

48 hours: 4 cells

3 days: 16–32 cells

4 days: A hollow ball of 64–128 cells called a blastocyst

24–30 hours after fertilization: male and female genetic material combine

Fertilization

Sperm cell

Unfertilized egg

Uterus

6 or 7 days: Blastocyst attaches itself to the uterine wall

11 or 12 days: Implantation of the embryo

Endometrium

Ovary

Follicle

Strong/DeVault/Sayad, Human Sexuality, 3rd ed. © 1999 Mayfield Publishing Company

The Fetus in Uterus and Cross Section of Placenta

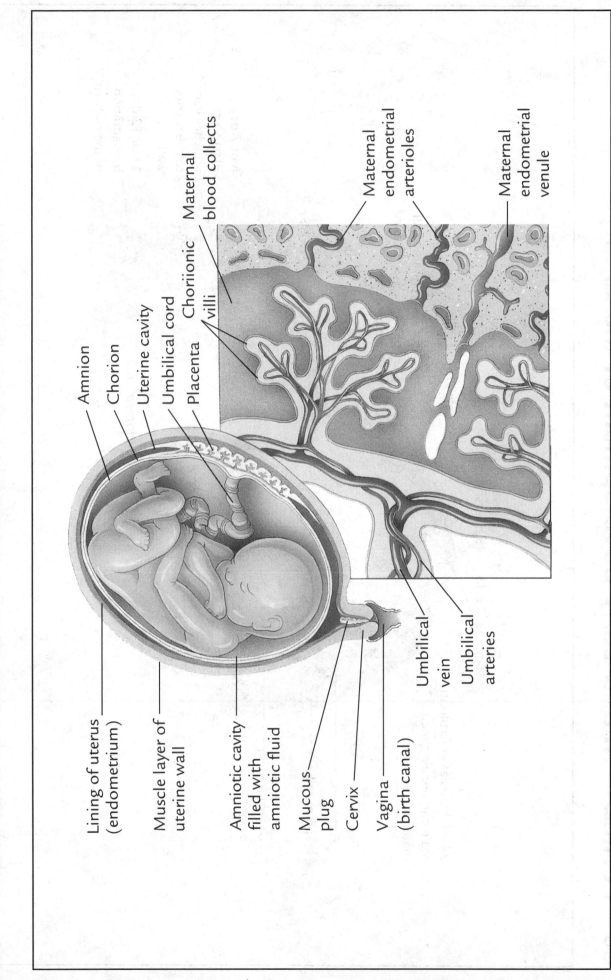

Amnion

Chorion

Uterine cavity

Umbilical cord

Placenta

Chorionic villi

Maternal blood collects

Maternal endometrial arterioles

Maternal endometrial venule

Lining of uterus (endometrium)

Muscle layer of uterine wall

Amniotic cavity filled with amniotic fluid

Mucous plug

Cervix

Vagina (birth canal)

Umbilical vein

Umbilical arteries

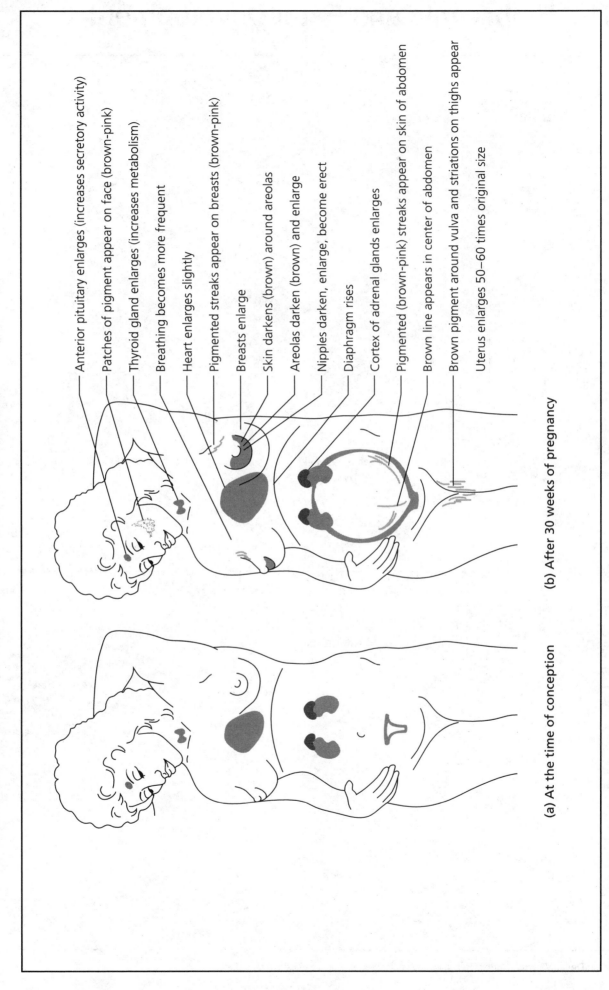

Anterior pituitary enlarges (increases secretory activity)

Patches of pigment appear on face (brown-pink)

Thyroid gland enlarges (increases metabolism)

Breathing becomes more frequent

Heart enlarges slightly

Pigmented streaks appear on breasts (brown-pink)

Breasts enlarge

Skin darkens (brown) around areolas

Areolas darken (brown) and enlarge

Nipples darken, enlarge, become erect

Diaphragm rises

Cortex of adrenal glands enlarges

Pigmented (brown-pink) streaks appear on skin of abdomen

Brown line appears in center of abdomen

Brown pigment around vulva and striations on thighs appear

Uterus enlarges 50–60 times original size

(a) At the time of conception

(b) After 30 weeks of pregnancy

Strong/DeVault/Sayad, *Human Sexuality*, 3rd ed. © 1999 Mayfield Publishing Company

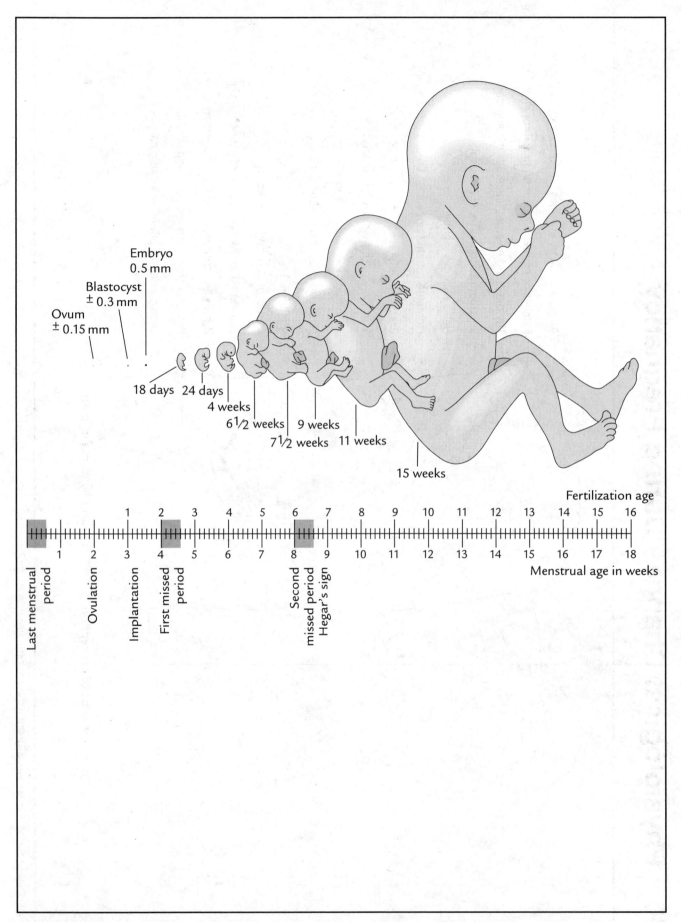

Ovum
± 0.15 mm

Blastocyst
± 0.3 mm

Embryo
0.5 mm

18 days 24 days

4 weeks

6½ weeks

7½ weeks

9 weeks

11 weeks

15 weeks

Fertilization age

1 2 3 4 5 6 7 8 9 10 11 12 13 14 15 16

1 2 3 4 5 6 7 8 9 10 11 12 13 14 15 16 17 18

Menstrual age in weeks

Last menstrual period

Ovulation

Implantation

First missed period

Second missed period

Hegar's sign

Strong/DeVault/Sayad, *Human Sexuality*, 3rd ed. © 1999 Mayfield Publishing Company

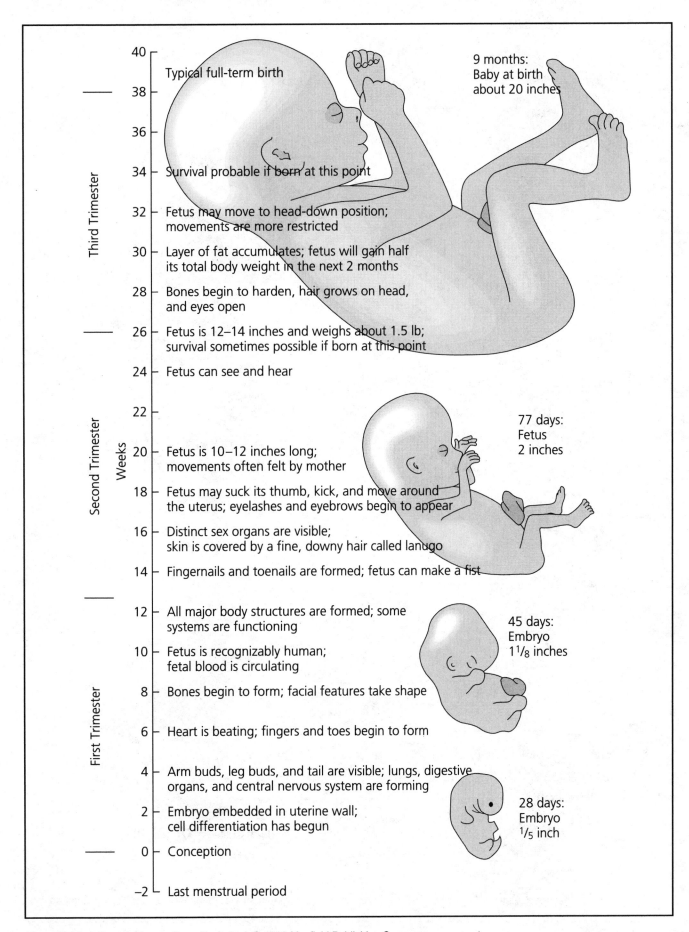

40 — Typical full-term birth

9 months:
Baby at birth
about 20 inches

38 —

Third Trimester

36 —

34 — Survival probable if born at this point

32 — Fetus may move to head-down position; movements are more restricted

30 — Layer of fat accumulates; fetus will gain half its total body weight in the next 2 months

28 — Bones begin to harden, hair grows on head, and eyes open

26 — Fetus is 12–14 inches and weighs about 1.5 lb; survival sometimes possible if born at this point

24 — Fetus can see and hear

22 —

Second Trimester

77 days:
Fetus
2 inches

20 — Fetus is 10–12 inches long; movements often felt by mother

Weeks

18 — Fetus may suck its thumb, kick, and move around the uterus; eyelashes and eyebrows begin to appear

16 — Distinct sex organs are visible; skin is covered by a fine, downy hair called lanugo

14 — Fingernails and toenails are formed; fetus can make a fist

12 — All major body structures are formed; some systems are functioning

45 days:
Embryo
1 1/8 inches

First Trimester

10 — Fetus is recognizably human; fetal blood is circulating

8 — Bones begin to form; facial features take shape

6 — Heart is beating; fingers and toes begin to form

4 — Arm buds, leg buds, and tail are visible; lungs, digestive organs, and central nervous system are forming

2 — Embryo embedded in uterine wall; cell differentiation has begun

28 days:
Embryo
1/5 inch

0 — Conception

–2 — Last menstrual period

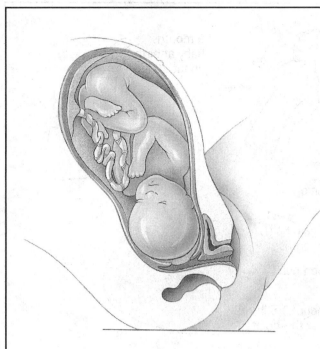

(a) early stages of labor;
cervix begins to dilate

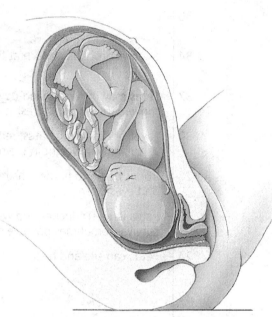

(b) second stage of labor;
cervix completely dilated

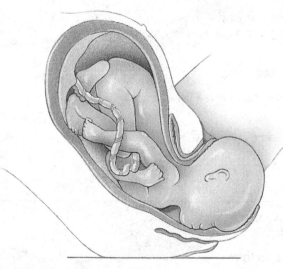

(c) late stage of labor;
baby's head is completely turned;
head begins to emerge

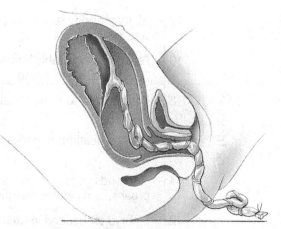

(d) final stage of labor;
delivery of the placenta

Source: P. Insel and T. Roth. 1998. *Core Concepts in Health* (8th ed.). Mountain View, CA: Mayfield Publishing Company.

Strong/DeVault/Sayad, *Human Sexuality,* 3rd ed. © 1999 Mayfield Publishing Company

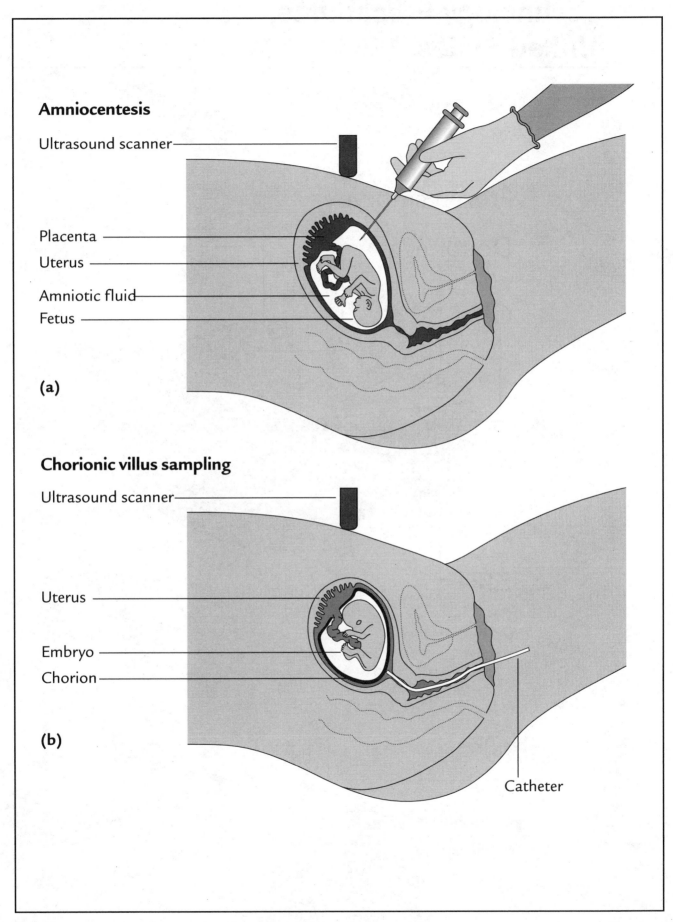

Amniocentesis

Ultrasound scanner

Placenta

Uterus

Amniotic fluid

Fetus

(a)

Chorionic villus sampling

Ultrasound scanner

Uterus

Embryo

Chorion

(b)

Catheter

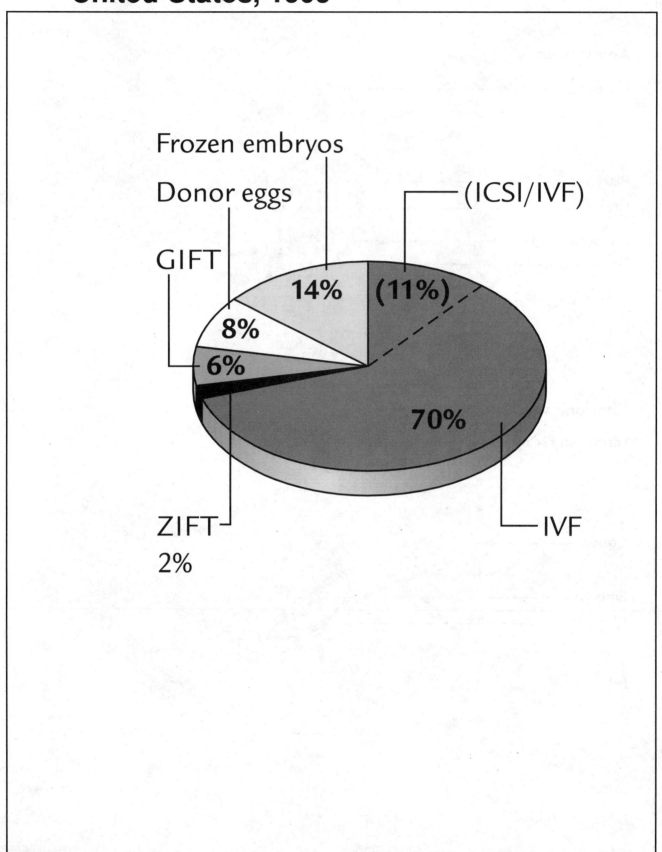

Frozen embryos

Donor eggs

GIFT

(ICSI/IVF)

14%   (11%)

8%

6%

70%

ZIFT

2%

IVF

Strong/DeVault/Sayad, *Human Sexuality*, 3rd ed. © 1999 Mayfield Publishing Company

CHAPTER 13

THE SEXUAL BODY IN HEALTH AND ILLNESS

CHAPTER OUTLINE

Living in Our Bodies: The Quest for Physical Perfection
    Eating Disorders
    Retreating from Sexuality

Alcohol, Drugs, and Sexuality
    Alcohol Use and Sexuality
    Drug Use and Sexuality
    Think About It: Anabolic Steroids: Not All They're Pumped Up to Be

Sexuality and Aging
    Women's Issues
    Men's Issues

Sexuality and Disability
    Physical Limitations
    Vision and Hearing Impairment
    Chronic Illness
    Developmental Disabilities
    The Sexual Rights of People with Disabilities

Sexuality and Cancer
    Women and Cancer
    Think About It: Assessing Medical Risk
    Men and Cancer

Other Sexual Health Issues
    Toxic Shock Syndrome
    Endometriosis
    Think About It: The Unkindest Cut? Female Circumcision
    Lesbian Health Issues
    Prostatitis
    DES Sons and Daughters

LEARNING OBJECTIVES

At the conclusion of Chapter 13, students should be able to:

1. Define and describe the principal eating disorders, their origin, relationship to sexuality, prevention, and treatment.
2. Describe the effects of alcohol and drugs on sexuality, including their use as disinhibitors, effects, and relationship to sexual risk taking.
3. Discuss issues of sexuality and aging, especially menopause for women and slower sexual responses for men.
4. Discuss issues of sexuality and disability with reference to the special needs of those with physical limitations, chronic illnesses, and developmental disabilities.

5. Discuss issues of sexuality and cancer for women, including its detection, treatment, and psychological impact.

6. Discuss issues of sexuality and cancer for men, including its detection, treatment, and psychological impact.

7. Discuss women's sexual health issues, including toxic shock syndrome, endometriosis, and lesbian health issues.

8. Discuss the practice of female circumcision, including the process, prevalence, effects, and cultural issues.

9. Discuss prostatitis, its detection, treatment, and psychological impact.

10. Discuss the impact of DES on the daughters and sons of women who took it.

11. Recognize and define key terms introduced in the chapter.

DISCUSSION QUESTIONS

Breast Cancer. Discuss the impact of breast cancer on self-image and relationships.

Prostate and Testicular Cancer. Discuss the sexual issues men have around male reproductive cancers, such as erectile dysfunctions and changes in body image.

Alcohol. In small groups, discuss the role of alcohol in personal relationships. How is it used to initiate sexual encounters? Does it enhance sexuality?

Sexual Rights of People with Disabilities. Discuss the sexual rights of those with disabilities as described in the text.

Female Circumcision. Some African women believe that female circumcision is a legitimate part of their cultural tradition. They believe that Western opposition to it reflects cultural imperialism. Do you agree? Why?

Lesbians and Health Care. What special needs or concerns do lesbians have regarding health care?

ACTIVITIES

Alcohol: Have students conduct informal interviews with friends or acquaintances about the role of alcohol in their social lives. What are its functions? What are its consequences? What are the pressures to use or not use it?

Assessing Body Image. Ask students to complete Worksheet 30 (Body Image). Discuss their scores, drawings, and comments. How do they think gender affects their responses? (Note that this worksheet is also found in the *Study Guide.*)

Personal Drinking Guide. Ask students to evaluate their reasons for drinking using Worksheet 31. Discuss the results. (You may wish to have referral suggestions should any students express concern over their level of drinking.)

SEX AND POPULAR CULTURE

Discussion: Have students look at old magazines, TV shows, and movies, and discuss how the "ideal" female figure changes with fashion—the boyish flapper of the 1920s, the full-figured woman of the 1950s (exemplified by Marilyn Monroe), thin women in the 1960s, and so on. What is the ideal female body type today? Does it differ by gender and orientation?

Discussion: Looking at magazines, TV shows, and movies from the past and present, have students discuss the "ideal" male body as it changes with fashion, noting chest and facial hair, pecs and biceps, and buttocks. What is the ideal male body type today? Does it differ by gender and orientation?

Discussion: How are men and women with physical and developmental limitations or disabilities treated on TV or in the movies? Are they sexual? Although people with disabilities are generally invisible in the media, examples may be found in the movies "Coming Home" and "Scent of a Woman."

Discussion: Menopause is a frequent topic in women's magazines. Is it treated as an illness or as a normal part of aging? What attitudes are expressed toward it? How can you evaluate the validity of journalistic stories on menopause?

Discussion: What images do alcohol commercials convey about sexuality? What are the health consequences of drinking? The sexual consequences?

Activity: Have students report on six titles of stories and articles on sexual health issues from magazines and newspapers. What images or attitudes do the titles convey?

HEALTH CONSIDERATIONS

Discussion: Read the World Health Organization's definition of sexual health: "The integration of the physical, emotional, intellectual, and social aspects of sexual being, in ways that are positively enriching and that enhance personality, communication and love." Discuss the different elements of the definition.

Discussion: If you were counseling individuals with chronic illnesses, such as diabetes, cardiovascular disease, and arthritis, what would you tell them about sexuality? Their partners?

Activity: Create a collage of female models advertising youth-oriented products. Are these images related to eating disorders, or are eating disorders independent of such outside influences?

Activity: Role-play the breast reconstruction decision: health-care professional, woman with breast cancer, her partner (may be male or female). Scenario: Woman is about to have mastectomy and is seeking counseling about breast reconstruction; both she and her partner are ambivalent about her "disfigurement."

Activity: Role-play post-hysterectomy counseling: health-care professional, woman, and her partner. Role-play discussion of sexual concerns of the woman and her partner.

Activity: Have students evaluate a news story or magazine article about a medical risk associated with sexual health. Use criteria found in the box titled "Assessing Medical Risk."

Activity: Ask students to survey patient information about the impact of cancer, chronic diseases, and physical disabilities. What information is made available about their impact on sexuality? What information should be included?

GUEST SPEAKERS/PANELS

Invite a health professional who works with people with physical or developmental limitations to discuss sexuality.

Invite a health care professional who works with gay men and lesbians to discuss their health needs.

Form a student panel to discuss alcohol and sexuality.

Invite a speaker to share his or her story about an eating disorder.

SUPPORT MATERIAL

Films and Videos

"Breast Cancer: Adjusting to It" (1983, 20 min., VHS, Multi-Focus, Inc.). Nine women talk candidly about breast cancer and their surgery.

"Breast Cancer: Alternatives to Mastectomy" (1983, 28 min., VHS, Multi-Focus, Inc.). Two women discuss their decision to select alternative treatments to mastectomy.

"Breast Cancer: Breast Reconstruction" (1983, 13 min., VHS, Multi-Focus, Inc.). Three women discuss their breast reconstruction surgeries. The discussion focuses on problems with prosthesis, clothing fit, attitudes of medical professionals, emotional support, and self-image.

"Breast Cancer: Chemotherapy" (1983, 13 min., VHS, Multi-Focus, Inc.). Six women talk about their physical and emotional reactions to undergoing chemotherapy and how it impacts their families and new relationships.

"The Choice Is Yours: The Effect of Alcohol and Drugs on the Decision-Making Process" (24 min., VHS, Media Guild). "The Choice Is Yours" is both the title and the theme of this video. The effect of peer pressure, alcohol, and drugs on the decision-making ability of teens and young adults is vividly portrayed. This award-winning video realistically depicts the dilemmas faced by young people in a social setting. Characters make decisions about sex, drugs, and alcohol. The issues of safe sex, abstinence, sexual orientation, sexually transmitted diseases, unplanned pregnancy, and AIDS are dealt with frankly.

"Coping with Serious Illness" (1980, 28 min., 16mm, PCR: Films and Video in the Behavioral Sciences). A documentary of the last two years of a woman with cancer. Documents coping with sexuality and loving during times of illness.

"Infertility: Nature's Heartache" (28 min., VHS, Films for the Humanities and Sciences, Inc.). This video looks at the causes and treatments for infertility.

"Influences: Innocence Betrayed" (1992, 24 min., VHS, Kent State University). Follows children as they attempt to cope with learning and behavior difficulties resulting from prenatal drug use.

"Just What Can You Do?" (1972, 23 min., VHS and 16mm, Multi-Focus, Inc.). A discussion with two male paraplegics and their wives, a male quadriplegic and his wife, and a female paraplegic. They frankly share their adventures, fears, and attitudes toward life and sexuality.

"No Less a Woman" (1981, 23 min., VHS and 16mm, Multi-Focus, Inc.). This film takes a look at the problems of single and married women who are attempting to recover from the far-reaching effects of a mastectomy.

"Notes for My Daughter: Breast Cancer and Its Effects on the Family" (1994, 60 min., VHS, Films for the Humanities and Sciences). Drama about a mother who hides a diagnosis of breast cancer from her daughter.

"PMS and Endometriosis" (19 min., VHS, Films for the Humanities and Sciences, Inc.). Looks at PMS and endometriosis—origins, impact, and treatments.

"Self Health" (1974, 23 min., VHS and 16mm, Multi-Focus, Inc.). Women share their experiences and learn explicitly how to do self-examinations of the breasts and vagina and the bimanual examination.

"Sex and the Handicapped" (no date, 15 min., 16mm, PCR: Films and Video in the Behavioral Sciences). Discusses the problems of handicapped people in regard to sexuality and the ways in which human services professionals can be of help. Focuses on contact problems of the blind and deaf and sexual techniques and technical aids for individuals who use wheelchairs.

Bibliography

The books and articles listed below may be helpful for instructors wishing additional background or information on some of the topics covered in this chapter. In addition, the books listed in this chapter's "Suggested Reading" in the textbook may also be useful.

Abbey, A. "Acquaintance Rape and Alcohol Consumption on College Campuses: How Are They Linked?" *Journal of the American College Health,* Jan. 1991, 39(4), 165–169.

Beck, M. "Menopause." *Newsweek,* May 25, 1992, 71–79.

Beckmann, C. R., M. Gittler, B. M. Barzansky, and C. A. Beckmann. "Gynecologic Health Care of Women with Disabilities." *Obstetrics and Gynecology,* July 1989, 74(1), 75–79.

Bills, S. A., and Duncan, D. F. "Drugs and Sex: A Survey of College Students' Beliefs." *Perceptual and Motor Skills,* 1991, 72, 1293–1294.

Boston Women's Health Book Collective. *The New Our Bodies, Ourselves for the New Century.* New York: Touchstone, 1998.

Bullard, D., and S. Knight (eds.). *Sexuality and Disability: Personal Perspectives.* St. Louis, MO: C. V. Mosby, 1981.

Finger, Anne. "Deemed Sexless." *Utne Reader,* 1993, 56, 107–108.

Flanigan, B. J. "The Social Context of Alcohol Consumption Prior to Female Sexual Intercourse." *Journal of Alcohol and Drug Education*, Sept. 1990, 36(1), 97–113.

Greenwood, S. *Menopause Naturally: Preparing for the Second Half of Life.* Volcano, CA: Volcano Press, 1989.

Judelson, D., and D. Vell. *The Women's Complete Wellness Book.* New York: Golden Books, 1998.

Kaplan, H. S. "A Neglected Issue: The Sexual Side Effects of Current Treatment for Breast Cancer." *Journal of Sex and Marital Therapy,* Mar. 1992, 18(1), 3–19.

Kolodny, R., W. Masters, and V. Johnson. *Textbook of Sexual Medicine.* Boston: Little, Brown, 1979.

Kroll, K., and E. Klein. *Enabling Romance.* Bethesda, MD: Woodbine House, 1995.

Leiblum, S. R. "Sexuality and the Midlife Woman. Special Issue: Women at Midlife and Beyond." *Psychology of Women Quarterly,* Dec. 1990, 14(4), 495–508.

Levine, M. P. "The Role of Culture in Eating Disorders." D. N. Suggs and A. W. Miracle (eds.). *Culture and Human Sexuality.* Pacific Grove, CA: Brooks/Cole, 1993.

Mulligan, T., and C. R. Moss. "Sexuality and Aging in Male Veterans: A Cross-Sectional Study of Interest, Ability, and Activity." *Archives of Sexual Behavior,* Feb. 1991, 20(1), 17–25.

Robertson, M. M. "Lesbians as an Invisible Minority in the Health Services Arena." *Health Care for Women*

WORKSHEET 30

Body image

International, April 1992, 13(2), 155–163.
Schover, L. *Sexuality and Fertility After Cancer.* New York: Wiley, 1997.

Assessing Your Body Image

	Never	**Sometimes**	**Often**	**Always**
1. I dislike seeing myself in mirrors.	0	1	2	3
2. When I shop for clothing I am more aware of my weight problem, and consequently I find shopping for clothes somewhat unpleasant.	0	1	2	3
3. I'm ashamed to be seen in public.	0	1	2	3
4. I prefer to avoid engaging in sports or public exercise because of my appearance.	0	1	2	3
5. I feel somewhat embarrassed by my body in the presence of someone of the other sex.	0	1	2	3
6. I think my body is ugly.	0	1	2	3
7. I feel that other people must think my body is unattractive.	0	1	2	3
8. I feel that my family or friends may be embarrassed to be seen with me.	0	1	2	3
9. I find myself comparing myself with other people to see if they are heavier than I am.	0	1	2	3
10. I find it difficult to enjoy activities because I am self-conscious about my physical appearance.	0	1	2	3
11. Feeling guilty about my weight problem preoccupies most of my thinking.	0	1	2	3
12. My thoughts about my body and physical appearance are negative and self-critical.	0	1	2	3

Now, add up the number of points you have circled in each
column: _____   0 + _____ + _____ + _____

Score Interpretation

The lowest possible score is 0 and this indicates a positive body image. The highest possible score is 36 and this indicates an unhealthy body image. A score higher than 14 suggests a need to develop a healthier body image.

In the space provided, draw (1) your body and (2) your perception of an ideal body of a person of your gender.

(1) My body   (2) My idea of the ideal body

What differences do you see between your drawing of your own body and that of your ideal?

Where do your ideas about an ideal body come from?

List five positive things about your body.

1. _____

2. _____

3. _____

4. _____

5. _____

WORKSHEET 31

Personal drinking guide

Questionnaire used with permission. J. D. Nash. 1986. *Maximize Your Body Potential*. Palo Alto, CA: Bull Publishing.

Evaluate Your Reasons for Drinking

Be honest with yourself. It is necessary for you to know why you drink in order to control your alcohol-related behavior. Put a check next to the statements that are true for you.

I drink to tune myself in—to

_____   enhance enjoyment of people, activities, special occasions

_____   promote social ease by relaxing inhibitions, aiding ability to talk and relate to others

_____   complement and add to enjoyment of food

_____   relax after a period of hard work and/or tension

_____   allow myself to be sexual

I drink to tune myself out—to

_____   escape problems

_____   mask fears when courage and self-confidence are lacking

_____   block out painful loneliness, self-doubt, feelings of inadequacy

_____   substitute for close relationships, challenging activity

_____   mask a sense of guilt about drinking

_____   forget about sexual anxieties/problems

Alcohol Content

Drinks differ in the amount of pure alcohol they contain; therefore, a "drink" means different amounts of liquid depending on the type of drink. A proof value indicates concentration of alcohol in a particular drink; the proof value is equal to twice the percentage of alcohol in a drink. To calculate the number of ounces of pure alcohol in a drink, multiply the size of the drink by the percentage of alcohol it contains (one-half proof value). For example, a 12 oz. beer (10 proof) has 0.6 oz. of pure alcohol (10 proof = 5% alcohol concentration; 0.05×12 oz. = 0.6 oz.).

Calculate the number of ounces of pure alcohol in each of the following drinks.

Drink	Size (oz.)	Proof value	Oz. of pure alcohol
beer	12	10	_____
wine	6	24	_____
sherry	4	40	_____
liquor	1.5	80	_____

Try the calculations on different size drinks and drinks of different alcohol content.

_____   _____   _____   _____

_____   _____   _____   _____

Maintenance Rate (or how long to sip a drink)

Remember that the effects of alcohol will be greater when your blood alcohol content (BAC) is rising than when you keep it stable or allow it to fall. BAC is directly proportional to the rate of ethyl alcohol intake. Assuming a general maintenance rate (rate at which the body rids itself of alcohol) of 0.1 oz. of pure alcohol per hour per 50 pounds of body weight, you can calculate the approximate length of time it takes you to metabolize a given drink by applying the following formula:

$$\frac{2.5 \times \text{proof of drink} \times \text{volume ((size in oz.) of drink}}{\text{body weight)}} = \text{time in hours per drink}$$

For example, to calculate how long it should take to drink one can (12 oz.) of 10 proof beer for a person weighing 150 pounds:

$$\frac{2.5 \times 10 \times 12}{150} = 2 \text{ hours}$$

So, it takes this 150-pound individual 2 hours to completely metabolize one 12 oz. can of 10 proof beer.

Choose your favorite three drinks (or choose three of the examples from the previous page) and use this formula to calculate your maintenance rate for each drink.

1. $\dfrac{(\quad\ ) \times (\quad\ ) \times (\quad\ )}{(\quad\ )} = $ _____ hours/drink

1. $\dfrac{(\quad\ ) \times (\quad\ ) \times (\quad\ )}{(\quad\ )} = $ _____ hours/drink

1. $\dfrac{(\quad\ ) \times (\quad\ ) \times (\quad\ )}{(\quad\ )} = $ _____ hours/drink

In Case of Excess

To sober up, the only remedy that works is to stop drinking and allow time. For any given type of drink, the amount of time would be the number of drinks you have consumed multiplied by your maintenance rate for that drink. For the example given above, if the 150-pound individual had consumed three 12 oz. cans of 10 proof beer, he or she would have to wait 6 hours before the alcohol would be metabolized. Calculate the amount of time that would have to elapse for you to metabolize all the alcohol if you had consumed three of one of the types of drinks you calculated a maintenance rate for above:

$3 \times (\quad\ ) = $ _____ hours

Given this consumption level, your answer here indicates the number of hours you should wait before driving.

CHAPTER 14
SEXUAL ENHANCEMENT AND THERAPY

CHAPTER OUTLINE

Sexual Enhancement
    Self-Awareness
    Intensifying Erotic Pleasure

Sexual Disorders and Dysfunctions
    Sexual Disorders
    Male Sexual Dysfunctions
    Female Sexual Dysfunctions

Physical Causes of Sexual Dysfunctions
    Physical Causes in Men
    Physical Causes in Women
    Treatment of Physical Problems

Psychological Causes of Sexual Dysfunctions
    Immediate Causes
    Conflict Within the Self
    Think About It: Sexual Abuse, Assault, and Dysfunctions
    Relationship Causes

Treating Sexual Problems
    Masters and Johnson: A Cognitive-Behavioral Approach
    Think About It: Cultural/Ethnic Differences and Sex Therapy
    Helen Singer Kaplan: Psychosexual Therapy
    Other Therapeutic Approaches
    Gay and Lesbian Sex Therapy
    Seeking Professional Assistance

LEARNING OBJECTIVES

At the conclusion of Chapter 14, students should be able to:

1. Discuss the basis of sexual enhancement programs and the role of self-awareness, including conditions for "good" sex and "homework" exercises.

2. Describe ways of intensifying erotic pleasure, including the role of arousal and replacing coitus with erotic activities.

3. List the phases of Kaplan's tri-phasic sexual response model and identify the disorders or dysfunctions associated with each phase.

4. Identify sexual disorders and describe hypoactive sexual desire and sexual aversion.

5. Describe the major male sexual dysfunctions, including erectile dysfunctions and inhibited, delayed, or premature ejaculation.

6. Describe the major female sexual dysfunctions, including vaginismus, dyspareunia, and anorgasmia.

7. Discuss the physical causes and treatments of sexual dysfunctions for women and men, including devices for men with erectile difficulties.

8. Discuss with examples the psychological causes of sexual disorders and dysfunctions, including immediate causes, conflicts with oneself, and relationship causes.

9. Describe the treatment of sexual difficulties through cognitive-behavioral, psychosexual, PLISSIT, and self-help and group therapy approaches.

10. Identify considerations in choosing a sex therapist, including unique considerations for gay men and lesbians.

11. Recognize and define key terms introduced in this chapter.

DISCUSSION QUESTIONS

Disorders/Dysfunctions. Discuss the difference between disorders and dysfunctions. Ask when lack of erection or orgasm becomes defined as a sexual dysfunction. What are the criteria for defining difficulties as disorders or dysfunctions? Is the decision culturally relative?

Hypoactive Sexual Desire Versus Sexual Aversion. Define and differentiate between hypoactive sexual desire and sexual aversion.

Factors That Contribute to Sexual Dysfunction. Review the list of physical and psychological causes of sexual dysfunction. Ask students which would be most difficult to deal with. Why? Ask students to privately identify those which they have or feel they could potentially have as a result of their learning experiences or beliefs. (This list may go into the student's gender and sexual identity paper.)

Treating Sexual Problems. Based on the overview of approaches to treating sexual problems provided in the text, discuss the pros and cons of each. Ask students which, if any, would be most acceptable to them.

ACTIVITIES

Conditions for Good Sex. In small groups, ask each student to list what she or he believes are conditions for good sex, and discuss. The group should then jointly compile a list of conditions for good sex and report them to the class. Discuss.

What You Wish Your Lover Would Do. Ask students to anonymously write on 3 x 5 cards what they wish their partner would do to increase their erotic pleasure. Randomly distribute the cards to small groups for discussion. Ask each group to find a consensus and describe the results to the class. Ask if these wishes apply equally to heterosexual and gay/lesbian relationships.

Reducing Ineffective Sexual Behavior. Role-play a couple in which one partner is unable to fulfill his or her erotic potential because of ineffective behavior by the partner. In one role-playing session, the woman needs clitoral stimulation to have an orgasm; in the other, the man is insufficiently aroused by his partner.

SEX AND POPULAR CULTURE

Popular Culture Response Paper (Worksheet 32): Sexual Problems. Ask students to read a magazine or newspaper article about sexual problems. What kinds of advice does the article give? What are the male/female dynamics in resolving the problem?

Discussion: Utilizing Zilbergeld's six requirements for "great sex," ask students to identify media characters or relationships that meet all (or most or some) of those requirements. Which requirements are most frequently met? Not met? Do media images promote "great sex"?

Discussion: What are popular stereotypes of men and women with sexual dysfunctions, such as "impotent," "frigid," and so on? The man who "can't get it up" is often the source of comedy. Is there a comparable comic treatment for women who are nonorgasmic or are they seen as more problematic, "frigid," for example?

HEALTH CONSIDERATIONS

Discussion: What special considerations are necessary for a therapist when conducting sex therapy with individuals and couples from non-Western cultures?

Discussion: Discuss how the PLISSIT model is used in a therapy situation.

Discussion: What kinds of information does a therapist need to know when taking a sexual history? What particular health, psychological, or relationship factors are important? What does a therapist need to know about sexuality and ethnicity when dealing with an African American, Latino, Asian American, or other ethnic client?

Activity: Role-play a therapist working with a gay couple. One member complains about inability to have erections with his partner. Next, role-play a therapist working with a lesbian couple in which sex has ceased between the two women. What are the special issues that may arise for gay men or lesbians in therapy? What special considerations, if any, must the therapist make when working with gay or lesbian individuals or couples?

Activity: Role-playing homework exercises. Therapist/counselor and client. The scenario: The therapist advises a shy female client to engage in sexual homework exercises. Replay a second time with the client a male.

GUEST SPEAKERS/PANELS

Invite a therapist involved in relationship enhancement work. Ask him or her to discuss how to enhance relationships and sexuality.

Invite a sex therapist or marriage counselor to discuss how to deal with sexual difficulties or problems in relationships.

Invite a urologist to discuss treatment of physical problems in men, including implants and pumps.

SUPPORT MATERIAL

Films and Videos

"Sex and Marriage" (1991, 42 min., VHS, The Glendon Association). This documentary traces the roots of diminished sexual desire from early experiences to social attitudes. (This film received an honorable mention in the 1991 National Council on Family Relations Media Competition.)

"Sexual Disorders" (1992, 60 min., VHS, Kent State University). Discusses a variety of sexual dysfunctions and sexual disorders focusing on pedophilia, rape, gender dysphoria and desire, and arousal disorders.

"When Sex Was Good, It Was Very Good. When It Was Bad—" (1985, 28 min., VHS, Kent State University). A frank presentation of sexual dysfunctions and their treatment with several specialists. Puppets are used for some of the dramatizations.

"You Can Last Longer" (1992, 10 min., VHS, Multi-Focus, Inc.). This video narrated by Maggi Rubenstein deals with male premature ejaculation and discusses ways to improve a man's ability to sustain an erection during lovemaking.

"You Can Last Longer: Ejaculatory Control" (38 min., VHS, Focus International). This film received outstanding reviews at the 1995 Western Psychological Association Film Festival.

Bibliography

The books and articles listed below may be helpful for instructors wishing additional background or information on some of the topics covered in this chapter. In addition, the books listed in this chapter's "Suggested Reading" in the textbook may also be useful.

Annon, J. *The Behavioral Treatment of Sexual Problems*. Honolulu, HI: Enabling Systems, 1974.

Barbach, L. *For Each Other: Sharing Sexual Intimacy*. Garden City, NY: Doubleday, 1982.

Cooper, A. "Sexual Enhancement Programs: An Examination of Their Current Status and Directions for Future Research." *Archives of Sexual Behavior,* Nov. 1985, 21(4), 387–404.

Darling, C., and J. K. Davidson. "Enhancing Relationships: Understanding the Feminine Mystique of Pretending Orgasm." *Journal of Sex and Marital Therapy,* 1986, 12, 182–196.

Espín, O. M. "Cultural and Historical Influences on Sexuality in Hispanic/Latin Women: Implications for Psychotherapy." C. Vance (ed.). *Pleasure and Danger: Exploring Female Sexuality.* Boston: Routledge and Kegan Paul, 1984.

Heiman, J., et al. "Historical and Current Factors Discriminating Sexually Functional from Sexually Dysfunctional Married Couples." *Journal of Marital and Family Therapy*, April 1986, 12(2), 163–174.

Heiman, J., and LoPiccolo, J. *Becoming Orgasmic: A Sexual Growth Program for Women.* Englewood Cliffs, NJ: Prentice-Hall, 1988.

Kaplan, H. S. *Disorders of Desire.* New York: Bruner/Mazel, 1979.

Klein, Marty. *Ask Me Anything: A Sex Therapist Answers the Most Important Questions for the '90s.* New York: Simon & Schuster, 1992.

Lavee, Y. "Western and Non-Western Human Sexuality: Implications for Clinical Practice." *Journal of Sex and Marital Therapy*, Sept. 1991, 17(5), 203–213.

Lieblum, S., and R. Rosen. *Sexual Desire Disorders.* New York: Guilford Press, 1988.

LoPiccolo, J. "Counseling and Therapy for Sexual Problems in the Elderly." *Clinics in Geriatric Medicine,* 1991, 7, 161–179.

Nichols, M. "Bisexuality in Women: Myths, Realities, and Implications for Therapy. Special Issue: Women and Sex Therapy." *Women and Therapy,* 1988, 7, 235–252.

Ogden, G. *Women Who Love Sex.* New York: Pocket Books, 1994.

Reece, R. "Special Issues in the Etiologies and Treatments of Sexual Problems Among Gay Men." *Journal of Homosexuality,* 1988, 15, 43–57.

Renshaw, D. *Seven Weeks to Better Sex.* New York: Random House, 1995.

Spector, I. P., and M. P. Carey. "Incidence and Prevalence of the Sexual Dysfunctions: Critical Review of the Empirical Literature. *Archives of Sexual Behavior,* Aug. 1990, 19(4), 389–408.

Tavris, C. *The Mismeasure of Women.* New York: Norton, 1992.

Torgovnick, M. *Primitive Passions: Men, Women, and the Quest for Ecstasy.* New York: Random House, 1996.

Zilbergeld, B. *The New Male Sexuality: A Guide to Sexual Fulfillment.* New York: Bantam Books, 1992.

WORKSHEET 32

Popular culture response paper: Sexual Problems

Name of article:

Description of content:

What advice or message about sexual problems did the article present?

What are the male/female dynamics in resolving the problem?

Comments:

Strong/DeVault/Sayad, *Human Sexuality,* 3rd ed. © 1999 Mayfield Publishing Company. Chapter 14

46 Sexual Dysfunctions in Nonclinical Sample

Strong/DeVault/Sayad, *Human Sexuality*, 3rd ed. © 1999 Mayfield Publishing Company

47 Male Sexual Dysfunctions by Ethnicity

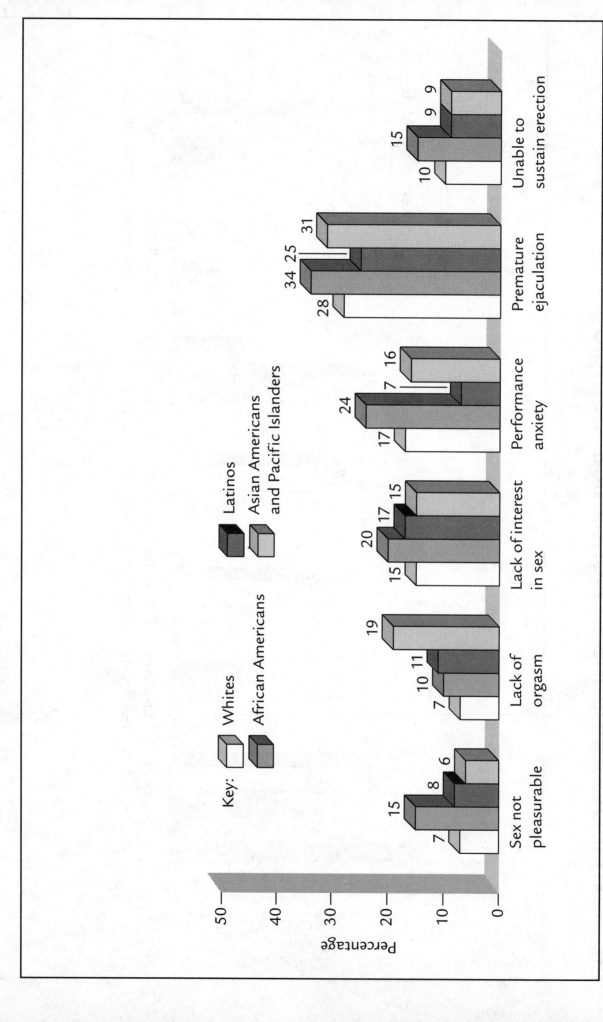

Strong/DeVault/Sayad, *Human Sexuality*, 3rd ed. © 1999 Mayfield Publishing Company

Female Sexual Dysfunctions by Ethnicity

Key:
- Whites
- African Americans
- Latinas

Pain during sex
- 15
- 13
- 14

Sex not pleasurable
- 20
- 30
- 20

Lack of orgasm
- 23
- 29
- 20

Lack of interest in sex
- 31
- 45
- 35

Performance anxiety
- 11
- 15
- 12

Climax too early
- 8
- 20
- 18

Difficulty lubricating
- 21
- 13
- 12

Percentage

Data on Asian Americans and Pacific Islanders not available.

Strong/DeVault/Sayad, *Human Sexuality*, 3rd ed. © 1999 Mayfield Publishing Company

49 Treatments Available for Erectile Dysfunction

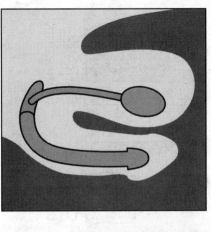

(a) Suppository

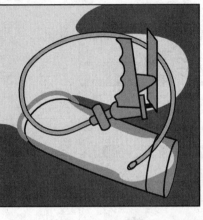

(b) Injection

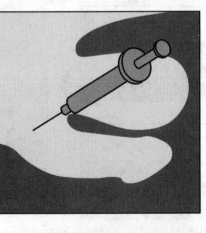

(c) Vacuum pump

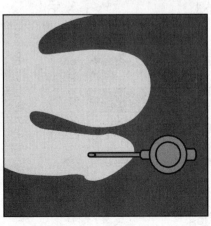

(d) Implant

Source: From *Newsweek*, November 17, 1997. Copyright 1997, Newsweek, Inc. All rights reserved. Reprinted by permission.

CHAPTER 15

SEXUALLY TRANSMITTED DISEASES

CHAPTER OUTLINE

X-Rated Diseases: The Psychological Impact of STDs
    Practically Speaking: STD Attitude Scale

The STD Epidemic
    Social Factors
    Biological Factors

Principal STDs
    Chlamydia
    Gonorrhea
    Urinary Tract Infections
    Syphilis
    Think About It: The Tuskegee Syphilis Study: "A Tragedy of Race and Medicine"
    Genital Warts
    Genital Herpes
    Hepatitis
    Vaginal Infections
    Other STDs
    Parasites

STDs and Women
    Biological Sexism
    Pelvic Inflammatory Disease (PID)
    Cystitis

Preventing STDs
    Risk Taking
    Abstinence
    Think About It: The Health Belief Model
    Good Health, Safer Sex
    Practically Speaking: Safer and Unsafe Sex Practices

LEARNING OBJECTIVES

At the conclusion of Chapter 15, students should be able to:

1. Discuss societal ambivalence concerning STDs.

2. List and describe the social and biological factors contributing to the increase in the incidence of STDs.

3. List and describe the principle STDs (chlamydia, gonorrhea, genital warts, genital herpes, syphilis, hepatitis, urinary tract and vaginal infections, and parasitic infestations), including incidence, symptoms, and treatment.

4. Discuss the Tuskegee syphilis study and its impact on contemporary attitudes of African Americans toward public health agencies.

5. Discuss the impact of STDs on women, including "biological sexism," pelvic inflammatory disease (PID), and cystitis.

6. Discuss factors involved in STD prevention, including risk taking, abstinence, and safer sex.

7. Describe the components of the health belief model and give examples of each.

8. Recognize and define key terms introduced in the chapter.

DISCUSSION QUESTIONS

Chicken Pox as a Moral Problem. Ask how many students in your class have had chicken pox and how it affected them psychologically; ask whom they have told. Then point out that chicken pox is caused by a herpes virus that is very similar to the one that causes genital herpes. But those with genital herpes are stigmatized, whereas those who have chicken pox are not. Why? Because genital herpes is sexually transmitted and therefore has "moral" connotations connected with it. Ask what would be the health consequences—delayed treatment, failure to contact others who may be exposed, shame, stigmatization, and so on—of identifying chicken pox as a moral problem rather than as a medical one.

Medicine and Morals. Ask the class to discuss if STDs are primarily a medical or a moral question or both. Why are individuals reluctant to reveal they are or have been infected? What kind of stigma is involved?

Biological Sexism. Discuss the biological reasons why women are at greater risk than men for many STDs.

ACTIVITIES

Activity: On 3 x 5 cards, have students anonymously list any STD they have had or currently have, how they felt about it, and what impact it had on their relationship. Randomly distribute cards to small groups for discussion. How do you get your partner to practice safer sex? Yourself?

Activity: Ask students to anonymously list on 3 x 5 cards what practices they consider "safer sex," "possibly safe," and "unsafe." Randomly distribute in small groups for discussion. Do participants know which practices are safer, possibly safe, and unsafe? What do they need to do to practice safer sex?

Activity: Many people don't like to use condoms. Ask students to list 3–5 common reasons people give for not using condoms. Discuss how appropriate the responses are.

Activity: Role-play in which you tell your partner you have an STD. Each scenario requires two people. Scenario 1: You are about to begin a sexual relationship and you want to tell your partner you have an STD. Scenario 2: You have been involved with several people on a casual, open basis and have discovered you have a STD and must tell each partner. Scenario 3: You have been married for 4 years and you have contracted an STD as the result of an extramarital affair.

Activity: Role-play your pregnant partner discovering she has been infected with an STD by you. Your partner has been monogamous and believed that you had been as well. Note the manifold consequences of having an STD in a presumably monogamous relationship.

Facts About Sexually Transmitted Diseases. Have students complete Worksheet 33 if they need to review this subject. (This worksheet is also found in the *Study Guide.*)

Do Your Attitudes and Behaviors Put You at Risk for STDs? Distribute Worksheet 34 for students to complete and discuss. Are they familiar with all of the risk factors? Do they plan to make any changes in their behaviors and attitudes?

Talking About STDs and Prevention. Have students complete Worksheet 35 and discuss their responses. Students may want to discuss pros and cons of various answers. (This worksheet is also found in the *Study Guide.*)

SEX AND POPULAR CULTURE

Popular Culture Response Paper (Worksheet 36): STDs. Ask students to find a newspaper or magazine article about STDs. (They may need to look in *Newspaper Index, Reader's Guide to Periodicals,* or use the Internet.) What kind of attitudes or information is presented about STDs? Is it moralistic? Is it primarily statistical? Does it deal with the psychological or relationship factors?

Discussion: With all the sex that occurs in the media, why doesn't anyone on the soaps or in movies get an STD? (Similarly, no one gets pregnant unless it's a made-for-TV movie on the subject.) What message does that convey about STDs and risk taking?

Discussion: In the 1980s, before the advent of HIV/AIDS, there was what was called "herpes hysteria." (Some called herpes the "media disease.") It was called an "incurable" disease; those with herpes were identified as herpes "sufferers" and were stigmatized; it was called the result of "promiscuity." Since then, herpes hysteria has vanished. Why? What do you think were the underlying causes of this "hysteria"? What were the consequences of herpes hysteria for those infected by herpes?

HEALTH CONSIDERATIONS

Self-Assessment: STD Attitude Scale. Ask students to complete the box titled "STD Attitude Scale". What is their likelihood of getting an STD? What can be done to reduce the risks? Discuss in small groups.

Discussion: Social and cultural factors have had a significant impact on the increase of STDs. What can be done to alter the situation?

Discussion: Discuss health belief model (using transparency). Break students into small groups and ask them to identify each factor in their own lives that is relevant to their taking or not taking action to avoid STDs.

Discussion: Read the box titled "The Tuskegee Syphilis Study: 'A Tragedy of Race and Medicine.'" If you were a White health-care worker in the African American community, what would you tell clients who distrusted you because of the Tuskegee experiment?

Activity: Role-play a couple discussing STDs. Scenario: Imagine a couple is about to become sexually involved. How would they ask about each other's health status?

Activity: Arrange a visit individually or as a class to an STD clinic.

Activity: Role-play condom use. Scenario: Imagine a man doesn't want to use a condom. What do you do? Role-play a heterosexual couple and a gay couple.

Activity: Role-play a visit to an STD clinic. One student plays the health-care worker and the other the client. Begin with the signing-in process. Afterwards, ask students how they would feel about going to an STD clinic. What additional information do they need about what happens in a clinic?

GUEST SPEAKERS/PANELS

Invite a health-care worker or physician involved in STD prevention or treatment. College/university health-care professional may discuss STDs on campus.

SUPPORT MATERIAL

Films and Videos

"ABCs of STDs" (20 min., VHS, Polymorph). This film provides the basic information on STDs in a nonthreatening manner and in simple language—what the most common STDs are, how they are transmitted, what the symptoms are, and what to do if you think you may have one. The video also deals with communicating with sexual partners.

"A Million Teenagers" (1992, 25 min., VHS, Churchill Media). Two peer counselors discuss STDs—gonorrhea, chlamydia, herpes, syphilis, and AIDS—with a class. (This film was a winner in the 1992 National Council on Family Relations Media Competition.)

"Bad Blood: The Tuskegee Syphilis Experiment" (1992, 60 min., VHS, PBS). A moving documentary tracing history of the syphilis experiment that used African American men as guinea pigs; contains interviews with survivors and excerpts from the play.

"How to Use a Condom: Condom & Lubricant" (1988, 15 min., VHS, Multi-Focus, Inc.). Using an acrylic model of a penis, Dr. Clark Taylor demonstrates the correct and incorrect ways to put condoms on and take them off. This video is also available in Spanish.

"Let's Talk About STD: Testing for Young Women & Testing for Young Men" (1992, 2 videos, 12 min. each, VHS, ETR Associates). Without preaching, hip-hop characters break through common fears and social stigmas, convincing viewers that STD testing is vital for reproductive health.

"No Rewind: Teenagers Speak Out on HIV and AIDS Awareness" (1992, 22 min., VHS, ETR Associates). HIV-positive teenagers inform their peers that teens are the fastest growing group at risk for HIV. Communication, transmission, and the role of alcohol and drugs are discussed.

"Sexually Transmitted Diseases: Straight Talk" (15 min., VHS, Altschul). This program covers six STDs: chlamydia, gonorrhea, syphilis, genital warts, genital herpes, and AIDS. All facets of these diseases are covered, including their causes, symptoms, and potential effects if left untreated. It is stressed that the only way to cure or treat STDs is to get proper medical attention.

"STD Blues" (33 min., VHS, Phoenix/BFA) The personal stories of three teenage couples, each taking a different route in their sexual choices, are explored in depth.

Bibliography

The books and articles listed below may be helpful for instructors wishing additional background or information on some of the topics covered in this chapter. In addition, the books listed in this chapter's "Suggested Reading" in the textbook may also be useful.

Aral, S., and K. K. Holmes. "Epidemiology of Sexual Behavior and Sexually Transmissible Diseases." K. K. Holmes et al. (eds.). *Sexually Transmitted Diseases* (3d ed.). New York: McGraw-Hill, 1998.

Balshem, N., G. Oxman, D. Van Rooven, and K. Girod. "Syphilis, Sex and Crack Cocaine: Images of Risk and Morality." *Social Science and Medicine,* July 1992, 35(2), 147–160.

Brandt, A. M. *No Magic Bullet: A Social History of Venereal Disease in the United States Since 1880.* New York: Oxford University Press, 1987.

Cates, W. J., and K. M. Stone. "Family Planning, Sexually Transmissible Diseases and Contraceptive Choices: A Literature Update. Part I." *Family Planning Perspectives,* Mar. 1992, 24(2), 75–84.

Darrow, W. W., and K. Siegel. "Preventive Health Behavior and STD." K. K. Holmes et al. (eds.). *Sexually Transmitted Diseases* (3d ed.). New York: McGraw-Hill, 1998.

Fullilove, R. E., M. T. Fullilove, B. P. Bowser, and S. Gross. "Risk of Sexually Transmissible Disease Among Black Adolescent Crack Users in Oakland and San Francisco, Calif." *JAMA: Journal of the American Medical Association,* Feb. 9, 1990, 263(6), 851–855.

Gershman, K. A., and R. T. Rolfs. "Diverging Gonorrhea and Syphilis Trends in the 1980s: Are They Real?" *American Journal of Public Health*, Oct. 1991, 81(10), 1263–1267.

Greenberg, J., L. Magder, and S. Aral. "Age at First Coitus: A Marker for Risky Sexual Behavior in Women." *Sexually Transmissible Diseases,* Nov. 1992, 19(6), 331–334.

Hatcher, R., et al. *Contraceptive Technology: 1990–1992.* New York: Irvington Publishers, 1993.

Holmes, K. K., et al. (eds.). *Sexually Transmitted Diseases* (3d ed.). New York: McGraw-Hill, 1998.

Joffe, G. P., et al. "Multiple Partners and Partner Choice as Risk Factors for Sexually Transmissible Disease Among Female College Students." *Sexually Transmissible Diseases,* Sept. 1992, 19(5), 272–278.

Maccato, M. L., and R. H. Kaufman. "Herpes Genitalis." *Dermatologic Clinics,* April 1992, 10(2), 415–422.

McNeely, J. S. G. "Pelvic Inflammatory Disease." *Current Opinion in Obstetrics and Gynecology,* Oct. 1992, 4(5), 682–684.

Mertz, G. J., J. Benedetti, R. Ashley, S. A. Selke, and L. Corey. "Risk Factors for the Sexual Transmission of Genital Herpes." *Annals of Internal Medicine,* Feb. 1, 1992, 116(3), 197–202.

Moran, J. S., et al. "The Impact of Sexually Transmissible Diseases on Minority Populations." *Public Health Reports,* Nov. 1989, 104(6), 560–564.

Nilsson Schonnesson, L. "Educational Requirements of Human Sexuality in the Counseling for and Prevention of Sexually Transmissible Diseases." *Seminars in Dermatology,* June 1990, 9(2), 185–189.

Rice, R. J., P. L. Roberts, H. H. Handsfield, and K. K. Holmes. "Sociodemographic Distribution of Gonorrhea Incidence: Implications for Prevention and Behavioral Research." *American Journal of Public Health,* Oct. 1991, 81(10), 1252–1258.

Rosenberg, M. J., A. J. Davidson, J. H. Chen, F. N. Judson, and J. M. Douglas. "Barrier Contraceptives and Sexually Transmissible Diseases in Women: A Comparison of Female-Dependent Methods and Condoms." *American Journal of Public Health,* May 1992, 82(5), 669–674.

Rothenberg, R. B. "These Other STDs." *American Journal of Public Health,* 1991, 81, 1250–1251.

Thomas, S. B., and S. C. Quinn. "The Tuskegee Syphilis Study, 1932 to 1972: Implications for HIV Education and AIDS Risk Education Programs in the Black Community." *American Journal of Public Health,* Nov. 1991, 81(11), 1498–1504.

Name _____ Section _____ Date _____

WORKSHEET 33

Facts about sexually transmitted diseases

Familiarize yourself with different types of sexually transmitted diseases by completing the chart below.

	Early signs and symptoms (in men and women)	Effects of long-term or untreated infection	Diagnosis and treatment
HIV infection			
Hepatitis B			
Syphilis			
Chlamydia			
Gonorrhea			

Strong/DeVault/Sayad, *Human Sexuality,* 3rd ed. © 1999 Mayfield Publishing Company. Chapter 15

	Early signs and symptoms (in men and women)	Effects of long-term or untreated infection	Diagnosis and treatment
Pelvic inflammatory disease			
Genital warts			
Herpes			
Trichomoniasis			
Candida albicans (yeast infection)			
Pubic lice			
Scabies			

WORKSHEET 34

Do your attitudes and behaviors put you at risk for STDs?

All sexually transmitted diseases are preventable. You have control over the behaviors and attitudes that place you at risk for contracting STDs and for increasing their negative effects on your health. To identify your risk factors for STDs, read the following list of statements and identify whether they're true or false for you.

T or F

_____ 1. I have never been sexually active. (If false, continue. If true, you are not at risk; respond to the remaining statements based on how you realistically believe you would act.)

_____ 2. I am in a mutually faithful relationship with an uninfected partner or am not currently sexually active. (If false, continue. If true, you are at minimal risk now; respond to the remaining statements according to your attitudes and past behaviors.)

_____ 3. I have only one sexual partner.

_____ 4. I always use a latex condom for each act of intercourse.

_____ 5. I use a lubricant containing the spermicide nonoxynol-9.

_____ 6. I discuss STDs and prevention with new partners before having sex.

_____ 7. I do not use alcohol or another mood-altering drug in sexual situations.

_____ 8. I would tell my partner if I thought I had been exposed to an STD.

_____ 9. I am familiar with the signs and symptoms of STDs.

_____ 10. I regularly perform genital self-examination.

_____ 11. When I notice any sign or symptom of any STD, I consult my physician immediately.

_____ 12. When diagnosed with an STD, I inform all recent partners.

_____ 13. When I have a sign or symptom of an STD that goes away on its own, I still consult my physician.

_____ 14. I do not use drugs prescribed for friends or sexual partners or left over from other illnesses to treat STDs.

_____ 15. I do not share syringes or needles to inject drugs.

False answers indicate attitudes and behaviors that may put you at risk for contracting STDs or for suffering serious medical consequences from them.

Strong/DeVault/Sayad, *Human Sexuality,* 3rd ed. © 1999 Mayfield Publishing Company. Chapter 15

WORKSHEET 35

Talking about STDs and prevention

The time to think about prevention of STDs is before you have sex. Caring about yourself and your partner means asking questions and being aware of signs and symptoms.

1. List three ways to bring up the subject of STDs with a new partner. How would you ask whether or not he or she has been exposed to any STDs or engaged in any risky behaviors? (Remember that since many STDs can be asymptomatic it is important to know about past behaviors even if no STD was diagnosed.)

   a. _____

   _____

   b. _____

   _____

   c. _____

   _____

2. List three ways to bring up the subject of condom use with your partner. How might you convince someone who does not want to use a condom?

   a. _____

   _____

   b. _____

   _____

   c. _____

   _____

3. If you had had an STD in the past that you might possibly still pass on (e.g., herpes), how would you tell your partner(s)?

   a. _____

   _____

   b. _____

   _____

   c. _____

   _____

Strong/DeVault/Sayad, *Human Sexuality,* 3rd ed. © 1999 Mayfield Publishing Company. Chapter 15

4. If you were diagnosed with an STD that you believe was given to you by your current partner, how would you begin a discussion of STDs with him or her?

_____

_____

_____

_____

_____

_____

Talking about STDs may be a bit awkward, but the temporary embarrassment of asking intimate questions is a small price to pay to avoid contracting or spreading disease.

WORKSHEET 36

Popular culture response paper: STDs

Name of article:

Description of content:

What underlying message or stereotype about STDs did the article present?

Did it deal with psychological or relationship factors?

Comments:

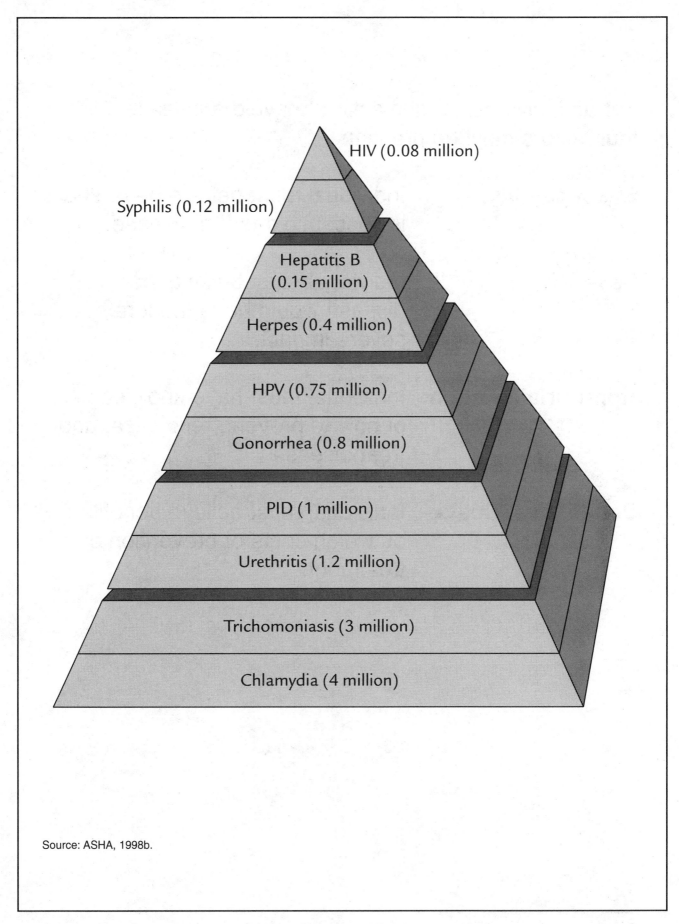

HIV (0.08 million)

Syphilis (0.12 million)

Hepatitis B
(0.15 million)

Herpes (0.4 million)

HPV (0.75 million)

Gonorrhea (0.8 million)

PID (1 million)

Urethritis (1.2 million)

Trichomoniasis (3 million)

Chlamydia (4 million)

Source: ASHA, 1998b.

For an individual to take action to avoid a disease, four factors must be present:

Susceptibility: Individual must believe he or she is susceptible to the disease.

Severity: Individual must believe the disease would have moderate to severe impact.

Appropriate Action: Individual must have knowledge of how to prevent, recognize, and treat disease.

Benefits vs. Costs: Individual must believe benefits outweigh costs of prevention or treatment.

CHAPTER 16

HIV AND AIDS

CHAPTER OUTLINE

LEARNING OBJECTIVES

At the conclusion of Chapter 16, students should be able to:

1. List and describe the conditions and symptoms associated with HIV or AIDS.

2. Describe the principal components and functions of the immune system, the characteristics of the human immunodeficiency virus, and the process and progress of HIV infection.

3. Explain how HIV can and cannot be transmitted and discuss behaviors that put one at risk.

4. Discuss the effects of the AIDS epidemic on the gay community, including social, political, and psychological factors.

5. Discuss HIV/AIDS issues as they relate to women, children, adolescents, and older adults.

6. Discuss the AIDS epidemic in relation to socioeconomic status and ethnicity.

7. Explain how to protect oneself against HIV infection and describe the principal types of HIV tests.

8. Discuss the issues surrounding HIV/AIDS education and prevention programs.

9. Describe the basic medical treatments for HIV and AIDS.

10. Discuss issues surrounding living with AIDS and caring for someone with AIDS, including discrimination and individual needs.

11. Recognize and define key terms introduced in the chapter.

DISCUSSION QUESTIONS

HIV/AIDS Myths. Ask students to identify myths about HIV/AIDS. What do these myths reflect? Lack of knowledge? Fear? Prejudice?

HIV and AIDS. Discuss the difference between HIV and AIDS, a frequent source of confusion for students.

Impact of HIV/AIDS on Sexual Attitudes and Behavior. Ask students how HIV/AIDS has affected sexual attitudes and behavior. Have they actually changed their behavior or are they only more anxious about being infected by HIV?

Friends/Relatives/Acquaintances HIV-positive or with AIDS. Ask students to indicate by a show of hands how many know people who are HIV-positive or who have AIDS. How has this knowledge affected their attitudes about these people?

Structure of HIV. Discuss the structure of HIV. Use the transparency master titled "The Structure of HIV" for illustration.

Religious Conservatives and HIV/AIDS Epidemic. What impact have the beliefs and ideas of religious conservatives had on public health and public education measures to curb the HIV/AIDS epidemic?

Condom Availability and the Schools. As adolescents are among the fastest growing segments of the population testing HIV-positive, should condoms be made available to high school students to curb HIV transmission? What are the pros and cons?

Safer Sex Versus Abstinence. Which should be emphasized in public health measures? From a public health perspective, what are the advantages and disadvantages of each?

Ethnicity and HIV/AIDS. African Americans and Latinos are disproportionately infected with HIV. What factors account for this disparity?

ACTIVITIES

Self-Assessment: Have students complete the box titled "HIV-Prevention Attitude Scale." How vulnerable is each person to HIV? In small groups, discuss the various items on the scale.

Myths of Transmission. Ask students to name the different modes of HIV transmission of which they have heard. (It doesn't matter whether they are accurate.) List them on the blackboard. Review which are correct and which are incorrect. For incorrect modes, indicate why they are erroneous. Ask why such modes may be believed.

Sexual Transmission. Have students anonymously rank on 3 x 5 cards the most likely modes of sexual transmission of HIV. Discuss. Note that transmission occurs because of mode of behavior, not because a person is gay. Both heterosexuals and gay men, for example, engage in anal intercourse, the most risky form of sexual behavior.

SEX AND POPULAR CULTURE

Discussion: Compare HIV/AIDS to STDs in regard to coverage in the media. How are they covered differently? Why?

Discussion: How has reluctance to use sexual terminology, such as "semen," "anal intercourse," and "condoms," on television and radio affected public education efforts to curtail the HIV/AIDS epidemic? Compare this reluctance with the ever-present sex scenes and sexual innuendos present in the broadcast media. Why the contrast?

HEALTH CONSIDERATIONS

Discussion: Discuss safer sex practices. It is important to emphasize to students that using condoms sometimes or most of the time is not practicing safer sex.

Discussion: What impact has anti-gay prejudice had on attempts to curb the HIV/AIDS epidemic?

Discussion: Discuss what happens with HIV testing and how to get it in your community or college, giving addresses, telephone numbers, and times of testing.

Discussion: Some believe that HIV/AIDS are divine retribution for violating religious prescriptions against premarital sex and homosexuality. As such, they are a moral problem, not a medical one. How would you respond?

Activity: Ask students to find out what resources are available in their community or college for HIV/AIDS testing, counseling, and support. How adequate are they for meeting current and projected needs? Report results to class.

Activity: Find representative pamphlets/booklets on HIV/AIDS for high school students. How effective are they in educating students about safer sex and HIV/AIDS prevention? Are they realistic for adolescents?

Activity: Role-play a health-care worker and client. The health-care worker is trying to determine the path of the HIV infection. The first client identifies as a heterosexual male; the next as a lesbian. (Both have had sex with men.) Scenario 1: Heterosexual male tests positive for HIV. Scenario 2: Lesbian tests positive for HIV.

GUEST SPEAKERS/PANELS

Invite a public health official or college health-care professional to discuss HIV/AIDS in your community or college.

Invite a person(s) who is HIV-positive or living with AIDS to discuss what the infection has meant to them. Such speakers have a very powerful effect on students.

Form a student panel to discuss what can be done to encourage safer sex practices among students.

SUPPORT MATERIAL

Films and Videos

"Absolutely Positive" (87 min., VHS, 16mm, Frameline). In spite of immense media coverage of AIDS, there has been little exploration of the people with HIV. This video is the story of how 11 men and women are coping with testing positive for HIV.

"AIDS and Your World" (25 min., VHS, Fanlight). The teens and twenty-somethings who speak candidly in this film offer a compassionate, honest, and empowering lesson of prevention. Having personally confronted the AIDS epidemic, they convincingly urge viewers to make healthy choices.

"AIDS at Issue: Coping with an Epidemic" (22 min., VHS, Filmakers Library). This program gives voice to the many moral, legal, ethical, and economic concerns that AIDS raises, such as education in the schools, needle-exchange programs, mandatory testing, the rights of people with AIDS, and condom advertising on television.

"AIDS/HIV Antibody Test Counseling" (1987, 19 min., VHS, Multi-Focus, Inc.). Three role-plays show a counselor discussing the benefits and advantages of taking an HIV test, a counselor explaining what a negative test result means, and a counselor explaining what a positive test result means.

"AIDS, Allie's Story" (1989, 14 min., VHS, Kent State University). From an ABC News "20/20" report, this is the story of Allie Gertz, a popular artist who contracted HIV from a boyfriend she had known for years.

"AIDS in Rural America" (1989, 27 min., VHS, University of Minnesota Film and Video). Focuses on the social and psychological aspects of addressing AIDS in the rural communities of America.

"AIDS: What Everyone Needs to Know" (20 min., VHS, 16mm, SVE/Churchill). This extensive second revision of the top-rated AIDS teaching film furnishes up-to-date information and interviews with particular relevance for the 1990s. Animation and live action explain how the HIV virus works, risky and safe behaviors, and the latest advances in the diagnosis and management of AIDS. Reflects the changing profile of the at-risk community through all-new interviews with infected teens, women, heterosexuals, and minorities. Includes new coverage of the AIDS antibody test, who should take it, and when. Stresses the absolute necessity of avoiding infection. Available in Spanish.

"AIDS-Wise" (22 min., VHS, New Day). Ten young people whose lives are affected by AIDS reveal thoughts, feelings, and experiences in their own words from their own environments. Deeply moving, not sentimental, their stories break through the youthful sense of being invulnerable, ultimately leaving viewers feeling empowered, knowing they have choice and control over contracting AIDS. Study guide available.

"All of Us and AIDS" (30 min., VHS, New Day). A film about how not to get AIDS.

"College Students and AIDS" (26 min., VHS, University of California). This video helps students identify and overcome the social and psychological barriers that prevent them from lowering their risks of becoming infected with HIV. It features undergraduate students discussing a variety of issues related to their at-risk activities. The students include both men and women and represent many ethnic groups. Accompanying facilitator's guide.

"Common Threads: Stories from The Quilt" (1989, 79 min., VHS, HBO Video). A heavily awarded, made-for-cable-TV documentary about the AIDS quilt and the people it memorializes. Winner of the 1989 Academy Award for Best Feature Documentary.

"Condoms: More Than Birth Control" (11 min., VHS, Polymorph). This video focuses on condom use: why it is important to use condoms, how they should be used, how to minimize the risk of failure. The video presents women with a number of ways they can persuade reluctant partners to participate in using a condom for mutual protection.

"Craig's Story" (23 min., VHS, Media Guild). A high school student discovers he is HIV-positive in this drama to educate viewers about HIV transmission and prevention. The fact that Craig is a non–drug-using heterosexual male dramatically illustrates that anyone can get AIDS. Craig's health teacher lectures about the symptoms, transmission, and prevention of the AIDS virus. Young viewers will realize AIDS can happen to anyone and will understand the importance of abstinence and safer sex.

"The Immune Response" (22 min., VHS, CRM). Time-lapse microphotography and an animated sequence illustrate the complex human defense system.

"Immune Response and Immunization" (16 min., 16mm, Benchmark). This film clarifies the role of immunization in the control or virtual eradication of some diseases and explains the nature, preparation, and effects of the several vaccines that provide passive or active immunity.

"Immunodeficiency: A Disease of Life (19 min., VHS, CRM). An up-to-date examination of cell biology focusing on the types of conditions that weaken the body and act as catalysts in a general suppression of the immune system.

"The Invisible Protector" (27 min., VHS, Altschul). In this introductory program, the functioning of the immune system is compared to the teamwork that takes place in a football game. Bright computer graphics depict the role of antibodies and other parts of defense of the immune system in easy-to-understand terms. Noted professionals in the fields of pharmacology and immunology discuss the components that make up the immune system and how it may react to transplants, allergies, and diseases it cannot control.

"Mending Hearts" (57 min., VHS, Baxley). This video documents two years in the lives of four people with HIV who are struggling to come to terms with reality and change their lives to accommodate their diagnosis. Interwoven with the stories are interviews with friends, health professionals, and street soldiers in the battle against AIDS. Leader's guide available.

"Meridith: A Young Mother with AIDS" (1988, 19 min., VHS, Multi-Focus, Inc.). Meridith discovers that her boyfriend had AIDS. She describes how women can decrease their chances of getting the virus and shares the painful deterioration she is suffering.

"No Rewind: Teenagers Speak out on HIV and AIDS Awareness" (22 min., VHS, ETR Associates). HIV-positive teenagers inform their peers that teens are the fastest growing group at risk for HIV. Communication, transmission, and the role of alcohol and drugs are discussed.

"Sex, Love, & AIDS," Part 1 & 2 (1986, 20 min. each, VHS, Multi-Focus, Inc.). Frank conversations between nine HIV-positive men. Two of the men appear in part two and discuss possible options for safer sex.

"Sexual Roulette" (1988, 15 min., VHS, Multi-Focus, Inc.). A drama about the need for honesty in relationships in the age of AIDS. The characters face the possibility of HIV infection when one of them reveals his HIV infection.

"Teen AIDS in Focus" (17 min., VHS, ETR Associates). Two HIV-positive men talk to a class of high school students, answering questions and delivering a strong prevention message.

"The Hidden Epidemic: Homophobia and AIDS" (1991, 30 min., VHS, Multi-Focus, Inc.). Interviews with persons from various backgrounds that address the issue of homophobia and how it affects HIV risk reduction efforts. Homophobia is one of the factors that prevents people from changing their attitudes and behaviors about AIDS.

"Too Close for Comfort" (27 min., VHS, ETR Associates). A drama about a young man who experiences homophobia and job discrimination after testing positive for HIV. Includes an eight-lesson discussion guide that expands upon the themes of the film.

Bibliography

The books and articles listed below may be helpful for instructors wishing additional background or information on some of the topics covered in this chapter. In addition, the books listed in this chapter's "Suggested Reading" in the textbook may also be useful.

Aboukler, J. P., and A. M. Swart. "Preliminary Analysis of the Concorde Trial." *Lancet,* April 3, 1993, 341(8849), 889–890.

Butcher, A. H., D. T. Manning, and E. C. O'Neal. "HIV-Related Sexual Behaviors of College Students." *Journal of American College Health,* Nov. 1991, 40(3), 115–118.

Catania, J. A., et al. "Prevalence of AIDS-Related Risk Factors and Condom Use in the United States." *Science,* 1992, 258(1101).

Centers for Disease Control and Prevention. "Facts about Condoms and Their Use in Preventing HIV Infection and Other STDs." *HIV/AIDS Prevention,* July 30, 1993, 1–3.

Centers for Disease Control and Prevention. "HIV/AIDS Surveillance Report," December 1997, 9(2), 1–43.

Centers for Disease Control and Prevention. "Update: Barrier Protection Against HIV Infection and Other Sexually Transmitted Diseases." *Morbidity and Mortality Weekly Report,* Aug. 6, 1993, 42(30), 589–596.

Channing L. Bete Co., Inc. *What Do You Know About HIV?* South Deerfield, MA: Channing L. Bete Co., Inc., 1995.

Chu, S. Y., T. A. Peterman, L. S. Doll, J. W. Buehler, and J. W. Curran. "AIDS in Bisexual Men in the United States: Epidemiology and Transmission to Women." *American Journal of Public Health,* Feb. 1992, 82(2), 220–224.

Department of Health and Human Services: *Surgeon General's Report to the American Public on HIV Infection and AIDS.* Washington, DC: U.S. Public Health Service, 1993.

Essex, M., and P. J. Kanki. "The Origins of the AIDS Virus." *Scientific American,* Oct. 1988, 65–71.

Jemmott, J. B. I., L. S. Jemmott, and G. T. Fong. "Reductions in HIV Risk-Associated Sexual Behaviors among Black Male Adolescents: Effects of an AIDS Prevention Intervention." *American Journal of Public Health,* Mar. 1992, 82(3), 372–377.

Kantrowitz, B. "Teenagers and AIDS." *Newsweek,* Aug. 3, 1992, 44–49.

Minkoff, H. L., and J. A. DeHovitz. "Care of Women Infected with the Human Immunodeficiency Virus." *JAMA: Journal of the American Medical Association,* Oct. 23, 1991, 266(16), 2253–2258.

Padian, N. S., S. C. Shiboski, and N. P. Jewell. "Female to Male Transmission of Human Immunodeficiency Virus." *JAMA: Journal of the American Medical Association,* Sept. 25, 1991, 266(12), 1664–1667.

Roper, W. L., H. B. Petersen, and J. W. Curran. "Commentary: Condoms and HIV/STD Prevention—Clarifying the Message." *American Journal of Public Health,* April 1993, 83(4), 501–503.

San Francisco AIDS Foundation. *AIDS Medical Guide,* 5th ed. San Francisco: Impact AIDS, 1998.

Senechek, D. *Placing AIDS and HIV in Remission: A Guide to Aggressive Medical Therapy for People with HIV Infection.* San Francisco: Senyczak Publications, 1998.

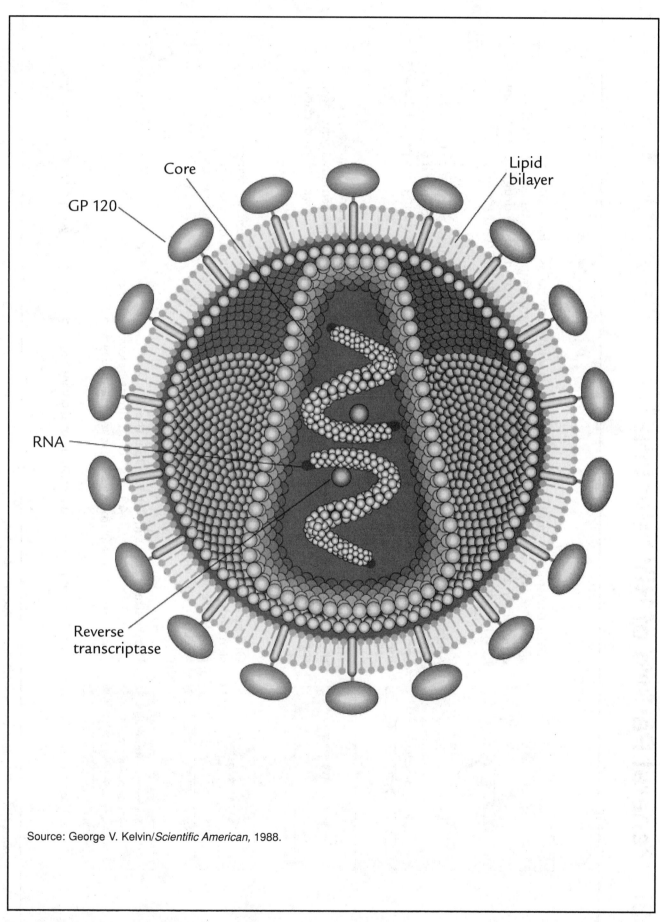

GP 120

Core

Lipid bilayer

RNA

Reverse transcriptase

Source: George V. Kelvin/*Scientific American,* 1988.

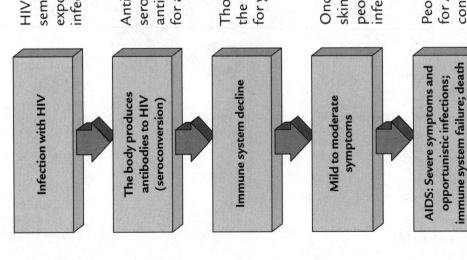

Infection with HIV

HIV is transmitted through intimate contact with body fluids: blood, blood products, semen, or vaginal secretions. The primary means of transmission are sexual contact, direct exposure to blood through transfusions (prior to 1985) or injection drug use, and from an infected mother to her child during pregnancy, childbirth, or breast-feeding.

The body produces antibodies to HIV (seroconversion)

Antibodies usually appear within 6 months of the initial infection, a process known as seroconversion. Once antibodies appear, an infected person tests positive if given an HIV antibody test. About 30% of people experience flulike symptoms during this period, lasting for a few days to a few weeks.

Immune system decline

Though the individual may have no symptoms, the virus is infecting and destroying cells of the immune system, unless blocked by drug therapies. Many people remain asymptomatic for years. New drug therapies are extending the lives of many people with HIV infection.

Mild to moderate symptoms

Once the immune system is damaged, many people begin to experience symptoms such as skin rashes, fatigue, weight loss, night sweats, and so on. When the damage is more severe, people are vulnerable to opportunistic infections. Treatments may allow recovery, but infections often recur.

AIDS: Severe symptoms and opportunistic infections; immune system failure; death

People are diagnosed with AIDS if they develop one of the conditions defined as a marker for AIDS or if their CD4 T-cell count drops below $200/mm^3$. Chronic or recurrent illnesses continue until the immune system fails, and death results.

Note: The pattern of HIV infection is different for every patient, and not everyone infected with HIV will go through all these stages.

Strong/DeVault/Sayad, *Human Sexuality*, 3rd ed. © 1999 Mayfield Publishing Company

54 Transmission Routes of HIV Among Adults

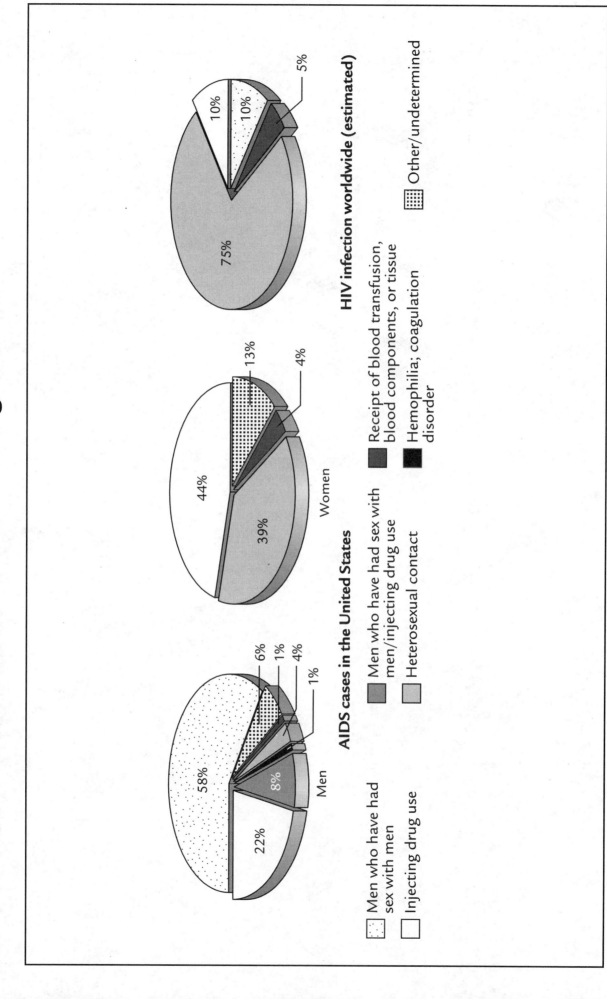

AIDS cases in the United States

Men
- 58%
- 22%
- 6%
- 1%
- 4%
- 8%
- 1%

Women
- 44%
- 39%
- 13%
- 4%

HIV infection worldwide (estimated)
- 75%
- 10%
- 10%
- 5%

Legend:
- Men who have had sex with men
- Injecting drug use
- Men who have had sex with men/injecting drug use
- Heterosexual contact
- Receipt of blood transfusion, blood components, or tissue
- Hemophilia; coagulation disorder
- Other/undetermined

Strong/DeVault/Sayad, *Human Sexuality*, 3rd ed. © 1999 Mayfield Publishing Company

CHAPTER 17

SEXUAL COERCION: HARASSMENT, AGGRESSION, AND ABUSE

CHAPTER OUTLINE

LEARNING OBJECTIVES

At the conclusion of Chapter 17, students should be able to:

1. Discuss the issues surrounding the definition of sexual harassment, including the difference between flirtation and harassment.

2. Describe the different ways sexual harassment takes place in schools, colleges, and the workplace.

3. Discuss heterosexual bias and identify sources of anti-gay prejudice, including religion, and how to decrease discrimination and violence against gays/lesbians.

4. Compare and contrast motivations and the different forms of sexual aggression, including acquaintance, stranger, marital, and gang rape.

5. Explain the impact of rape on its survivors, including rape trauma syndrome.

6. Describe means of preventing sexual assault.

7. Identify the preconditions and forms of child sexual abuse, including characteristics of children at risk.

8. Describe initial and long-term effects of sexual abuse and sexual abuse trauma.

9. Discuss the principles involved in child sexual abuse prevention programs and obstacles to implementation.

10. Discuss the debate over recovered (repressed) memories versus false memories as it applies to sexual abuse.

11. Recognize and define key terms introduced in the chapter.

DISCUSSION QUESTIONS

Politically Correct/Sexist. Much of the debate about date rape and sexual harassment centers around labeling responses as "politically correct" or "sexist." Ask the class to define these terms. Who tends to use them? Are these terms useful in clarifying issues or are they a form of name calling? Discuss banning the use of those terms in class and using descriptive phrases and arguments in their place.

Flirting or Harassing. Ask students how to distinguish between flirtation and sexual harassment. Ask them to give examples of each and discuss. Are there gender differences? Does it make a difference whether one is superior to the other? A peer? Dating? Has concern about sexual harassment changed people's behavior?

Sexual Harassment in Elementary and High School. Ask students to discuss sexual harassment in public schools. How was it generally treated by the administration? Peers? What impact did it have on self-esteem and the ability to learn? How did harassment at various ages differ?

Sexual Harassment in College/University. Discuss sexual harassment in college. What are the policies in college? What can students do if they are being harassed? Have there been well-known incidents in your college or community? If so, analyze.

Impact of Anti-Gay Prejudice on Heterosexuals. What impact does anti-gay prejudice have on heterosexuals? Examples may include alienation from family members, inability to express affection for members of the same sex, and so on.

Gay Rights. Ask students to distinguish between equal protection, antidiscrimination laws, affirmative action, and quota programs in relationship to homosexuality. Why are equal protection and anti-discrimination laws confused with affirmative action and quota programs? Should gay men and lesbians be granted equal protection and rights for employment? Military service? Marriage? Parenting, child custody, and adoption?

Religion and Homosexuality. Ask students what their religious teachings say about homosexuality. Is their faith debating or reevaluating teachings regarding homosexuality? Do their churches or synagogues permit gay/lesbian ministers? Do they believe homosexuality or homosexual behavior is a sin? What role should religion play in determining gay/lesbian civil rights? An excerpt from the Evangelical Lutheran Church titled "Homosexuality and the Christian Faith" is provided as a Student Handout for this chapter. This Student Handout can be distributed and discussed in light of the preceding questions.

Sexual Aggression. To clarify discussions, ask students to distinguish among sexual aggression, sexual coercion, sexual assault, sexual pressure, and rape. People often use the terms interchangeably, resulting in considerable confusion, as people may be arguing about different things.

Rape Myths. Ask students to identify rape myths. What function do these myths have?

Stranger Rape Versus Date or Acquaintance Rape. Ask students to distinguish between the two. Ask why stranger rape is more "believable" than date rape.

Characteristics of Sexually Coercive Men. Discuss general characteristics of sexually coercive men. Why do these characteristics contribute to the likelihood of sexual coercion? Note that these characteristics do not "cause" sexual coercion; "sensitive" men may also be coercive.

Student/Faculty Involvement. Some universities and colleges ban romantic interactions between instructors and students at any time; others restrict such bans to when students are taking a class from the instructor only. Some include TAs or graduate students in the ban. Do you believe student/faculty bans are reasonable? Why? Can they be enforced?

Discussion of Sexual Abuse with Your Child. Considering how much sexual abuse takes place within the family (parent, sibling, uncle or aunt, grandparent), ask the class how one educates or protects one's child from intrafamilial abuse without making him or her distrusting of his or her own family members.

ACTIVITIES

Sexual Harassment Role-Playing. Scenario 1: Exertion of power. A woman's boss is sexually harassing her, threatening her with job loss if she does not sleep with him. Have woman respond in order to stop it. Scenario 2: Hostile learning environment. A male student continuously makes obscene remarks and gestures to a female student in class. Have woman respond in order to stop it.

Gender Differences in Identifying Sexual Harassment. Ask students to discuss whether the following behaviors are sexually harassing:

> Gender-stereotyped jokes or depictions
>
> Teasing sexual remarks
>
> Unwanted suggestive looks or gestures
>
> Unwanted letters or telephone calls
>
> Unwanted leaning or cornering
>
> Unwanted pressure for dates
>
> Unwanted touching
>
> Unwanted pressure for sexual activity

Discuss whether there are gender differences in perception. Why?

When No Is No. Role-play interaction in which a woman indicates she does not want to have sex with an insistent date. Play different levels of intensity at which she can indicate no. Ask which level is least ambiguous.

Possible Sexual Abuse. To explore the complexities of dealing with child sexual abuse, ask students to act out three scenarios. Scenario 1 (with parent/child): Your child tells you that his or her favorite uncle (your brother with whom you are very close) is acting "weird" to him or her. Elicit more information from the child. Scenario 2 (with parent/ his or her brother): You talk with your brother about your concerns; he denies abuse. Scenario 3 (with mother/father): Decide what to do next: Believe child or uncle, call police, deal with problem within family, ignore it.

SEX AND POPULAR CULTURE

Discussion: Sexual harassment and date rape are becoming an increasingly controversial issue in the media. What are some of the issues raised in the media? Do they accurately portray the problem? Compare media coverage to research discussed in the textbook and lectures.

Discussion: Have the class listen to or watch Rush Limbaugh or Howard Stern. What is their point of view regarding sexual harassment, date rape, or other relevant sexual issues. How do they support their positions?

Discussion: Child sexual abuse is a popular topic of daytime talk shows. What kind of information is given in such shows? Is there intellectual content as well as emotional content? From the talk shows, what would you infer about the nature of child sexual abuse (such as prevalence, consequences)? Does what you learn from talk shows complement or contradict research findings? Comment.

Discussion: What rape myths are perpetuated by the media? What is the motivation of rapists on TV and in the movies? What type of women get raped? Does the media reflect the research findings? Some critics suggest that on TV and in the movies, nontraditional women get raped more often than traditional women as a means of putting nontraditional women "in their place." Is there evidence to support or refute this argument?

Activity: Find newspaper or magazine articles or commentaries in which the terms "politically correct" and "sexist" are used in relationship to sexual or gender issues. (For example, see the *Newsweek* cover story, "Sexual Correctness," October 25, 1993, 52–64.) Circulate them in class or in small groups. What common themes emerge? What is the impact of using these labels? What is their context? What are the points of view of people using them?

HEALTH CONSIDERATIONS

Discussion: What impact does sexual harassment have on young girls' and adolescents' self-esteem and well-being? Should sexual harassment be considered a mental health issue?

Discussion: Imagine you are a health worker in an elementary school. A teacher says he believes one of his students is being sexually abused. What would you do?

Activity: Role-playing sexual assault crisis counselor and survivor. Scenario 1: Female rape victim comes to rape crisis counselor the afternoon following her rape. Scenario 2: Male sexual assault victim comes to rape crisis counselor the afternoon following his rape. How do dynamics change depending on the sex of the sexual assault survivor?

GUEST SPEAKERS/PANELS

Invite a college spokesperson to discuss sexual harassment policies at your college/university. Help students clarify what constitutes sexual harassment.

Invite a rape educator or a rape crisis worker to address the class on rape issues. Discuss rape in your community and resources available to rape survivors.

Invite a therapist working with sexually abused children to discuss sexual abuse and therapy.

Form a panel of female and male students to discuss sexual harassment on campus, including their own experiences, understanding of what constitutes harassment, problems in communication, and so on.

Form a male/female student panel to discuss when "no" means no. Discuss various ways refusal is indicated and which are most realistic in actual dating situations.

SUPPORT MATERIAL

Films and Videos

"Campus Rape" (1991, 21 min., VHS, Rape Treatment Center). Examines the problem of campus rape through interviews with four victims and other college students. (This film was a winner of the 1991 National Council on Family Relations Media Competition.)

"Dating, Sex, and Trouble: Acquaintance Rape" (24 min., VHS, Sunburst). This video describes the wide range of behaviors that may constitute sexual assault. It interviews survivors of rape and portrays the concept of rape as an act of violence, not passion. Narrated by a psychologist.

"Domestic Violence: Voices from Within" (27 min., VHS, Baxley). Battering is the major cause of injury to women— more frequent than auto crashes, muggings, and rapes combined, and half of all couples will experience at least one instance of abuse. The video explores the relationships that support domestic violence through interviews with an abuser and two abuse survivors.

"Four Men Speak Out on Surviving Childhood Sexual Abuse (1992, 30 min., VHS, Varied Directions International). Presents actual survivors of childhood sexual abuse who discuss how it affected their lives and the steps they are taking toward recovery. (This film received an honorable mention in the 1992 National Council on Family Relations Media Competition.)

"Heart on a Chain: The Truth About Date Violence" (1991, 15 min., VHS, Indiana University). Three dramatized case studies look at the various ways in which date violence occurs.

"How Far Is Too Far?" (1988, 18 min., VHS, University of Minnesota Film and Video). An ABC "20/20" episode documents what sexual harassment means for real people in real-life work situations. A reporter interviews women who have won court cases against their harassers.

"Incest" (28 min., VHS, Films for Humanities). What are the rights and responsibilities of incest survivors long after the crime? How do they overcome years of denial and guilt to confront their parents and accept the facts of their victimization? This specially adapted Phil Donahue program investigates these and related issues.

"Just Because of Who We Are" (1986, 28 min., VHS, University of Minnesota Film and Video). This program focuses on the issue of violence against lesbians. The women in this documentary tell personal stories of family rejection, arrests, and attempts at institutional "cures."

"Linda Fairstein for the Prosecution" (1991, 23 min., VHS, Kent State University). Prosecutor Linda Fairstein, chief of the Manhattan DA's sex crimes unit, discusses some of her cases and her views of the legal system.

"No Easy Answer" (32 min., VHS, ETR). This program discusses sexual abuse prevention, emphasizing decision making, assertive communication, nurturing rather than abusiveness, incest, rape, acquaintance rape, attitudes about rape, and how to help a survivor.

"No Means No: Understanding Acquaintance Rape" (1992, 33 min., VHS, Human Relations Media). Features an acquaintance rape mock trial and discussions of how to know when "no" means "no." (This was a winner in the 1992 National Council on Family Relations Media Competition.)

"Prisoners of Incest" (1984, 54 min., VHS, PCR: Films and Video in the Behavioral Sciences). A documentary that examines the impact of incest on a family—the secrecy, guilt, fear, and lack of communication.

"Rape: An Act of Hate" (30 min., VHS, Films for Humanities). FBI statistics show that a woman is raped every 7 minutes in the United States. This program seeks to determine why people rape and to help people protect themselves against this crime. It examines the history and mythology of rape and explains who are its most likely targets. The program contains interviews with experts from the media, law enforcement, and sociology.

"Rape: Face to Face" (1982, 55 min., VHS, University of Minnesota Film and Video). Examines the causes and consequences of rape. Includes an emotional confrontation between rapists and victims of rape.

"Rape: Not Always a Stranger" (1988, 25 min., VHS, University of Minnesota Film and Video). A rape counselor and law enforcement officer discuss strategies for avoiding rape.

"Sexual Abuse of Children: America's Secret Shame" (1980, 28 min., 16mm, Indiana University Audio Visual Center). Provides an in-depth look at the extent of child sexual abuse in America and examines what can be done about it.

"Sexual Harassment: Serious Business" (1993, 25 min., VHS, Insight Media). A series of vignettes (implied, verbal, and physical) demonstrates the effects of harassment in the workplace.

"Surviving Rape, a Journey Through Grief" (1992, 30 min., VHS, Kent State University). Explains the five stages of the grieving process that rape victims encounter: denial, anger, depression, bargaining, and acceptance.

"Violence: Myth vs. Reality" (13 min., VHS, Altschul). This program explores six myths commonly believed by young people that can lead to violence. Some of the myths highlighted include needing a weapon for protection or joining a gang, and the impact of drugs and alcohol on violence.

"The Wrong Idea: A Cross-Cultural Training Program About Sexual Harassment" (1988, 20 min., VHS, University of Minnesota Film and Video). Nine vignettes portray campus sexual harassment incidents using a culturally diverse cast.

"Young Adults and Domestic Violence" (20 min., VHS, Altschul). This program looks at the components of dating violence, from physical attacks to mental and emotional abuse. Also examined are key causes of youth dating violence, from pervasive media messages to behavior patterns learned at home.

Bibliography

The books and articles listed below may be helpful for instructors wishing additional background or information on some of the topics covered in this chapter. In addition, the books listed in this chapter's "Suggested Reading" in the textbook may also be useful.

Beitchman, J. H., et al. "A Review of the Long-Term Effects of Child Sexual Abuse." *Child Abuse and Neglect,* Jan. 1992, 16(1), 101–119.

Benson, D., et al. "Acquaintance Rape on Campus: A Literature Review." *Journal of American College Health,* Jan. 1992, 40(4), 157–165.

Finkelhor, D. *Child Sexual Abuse: New Theory and Research.* New York: Free Press, 1984.

Fontes, L. A. (Ed.). *Sexual Abuse in Nine North American Cultures: Treatment and Prevention.* Thousand Oaks, CA: Sage Publications, 1995.

Herek, G. M., D. C. Kimmel, H. Amaro, and G. B. Melton. "Avoiding Heterosexist Bias in Psychological Research." *American Psychologist,* Sept. 1991, 46(9), 957–963.

Johnson, C. B., M. S. Stockdale, and F. E. Saal. "Persistence of Men's Misperceptions of Friendly Cues Across a Variety of Interpersonal Encounters." *Psychology of Women Quarterly*, Sept. 1991, 15(3), 463–475.

Malz, Wendy. *The Sexual Healing Journey.* New York: HarperCollins, 1991.

Nugent, R., and J. Gramick. "Homosexuality: Protestant, Catholic, and Jewish Issues: A Fishbone Tale." *Journal of Homosexuality,* 1989, 18, 7–46.

Priest, R. "Child Sexual Abuse Histories Among African-American College Students: A Preliminary Study." *American Journal of Orthopsychiatry,* July 1992, 62(3), 475–476.

Russell, D. E. H. *Rape in Marriage.* Bloomington, IN: Indiana University Press, 1990.

Sigelman, C. K., et al. "Courtesy Stigma: The Social Implications of Associating with a Gay Person." *Journal of Social Psychology,* 1991, 131, 45–56.

Sorenson, S. B., and J. M. Siegel. "Gender, Ethnicity, and Sexual Assault: Findings from a Los Angeles Study." *Journal of Social Issues,* March 1992, 48(1), 93–104.

Williams, K. B., and R. R. Cyr. "Escalating Commitment to a Relationship: The Sexual Harassment Trap." *Sex Roles,* 1992, 27(1/2), 47–72.

Wyatt, G. E. "The Sociocultural Context of African American and White American Women's Rape." *Journal of Social Issues*, March 1992, 48(1), 77–91.

HOMOSEXUALITY AND THE CHRISTIAN FAITH

Excerpt from Evangelical Lutheran Church. Department for Studies of the Division for Church in Society. "Human Sexuality and the Christian Faith: A Study of the Church's Reflection and Deliberation." Copyright © November 1991. Evangelical Lutheran Church of America.

Prohibition Against Sexual Activity Between Males

Two passages are often seen as explicitly condemning sexual activity between males—Leviticus 18:22 and 20:13. These are part of the Holiness Code, which instructed the Israelites as to how they should live in ways set apart and distinct from those of other people.

> The literary context for the prohibition against lying "with a male as with a woman" (18:22) is a collection of precepts dealing with sexual relations. The first set of prohibitions (vs. 6–18) deals with sexual acts within the extended family, that is, between relatives and spouses of relatives living in tents or houses in the circle of the grandparents. The laws are intended to guard against all forms of promiscuity within this circle. The set of laws in verses 19–23 includes a potpourri of forbidden practices: intercourse with a woman in her menstrual uncleanness, adultery, child sacrifice (said to be a Canaanite practice), male-to-male intercourse, and bestiality.
>
> Most of the same content is repeated in chapter 20, where either the death penalty, or exclusion from the community, or a specific curse is added for certain offenses.... The death penalty is [prescribed] for cursing one's parents (vs. 9), adultery (v. 10), incest (vs. 12), male-to-male intercourse (vs. 13), intercourse with one's mother-in-law (vs. 14), and bestiality (vss. 16–17).

Those who compiled this material in Leviticus viewed sexual activity between two males as a serious offense.

Although there is little to determine if sexual activity between males was condemned or condoned among Israel's neighbors, there is evidence to suggest that this was used as a means of imposing power and punishment by one man on another. Because of this, these verses may refer to the imposition of sex by one man on another, that is, same-sex activity that is abusive.

Only males are mentioned in these Leviticus verses. This could have been because of the belief that to waste semen was to waste life. It also could have been because of the need to provide offspring, so that the community scorned any form of sexual activity in which there was no possibility of producing children. It could also have been that the priestly compilers of this material viewed sexual activity between males as contrary to God's designs at creation, as indicated particularly in the creation story in Genesis 1.

Implications of the Biblical Witness for
Lesbian and Gay Relationships Today

People evaluate data regarding sexual orientation in different ways. Often their evaluations reinforce the position they already hold on this issue. They also draw different implications for how lesbian or gay persons should be treated. Here are three voices:

> We may need to accept that homosexual orientation is a given, but only as part of the falseness or distortion of creation. Such people should refrain from practicing their homosexuality. They can choose to refrain from such sinful behavior.

> Homosexuality is sin no matter what current data says. Sin must be condemned by the church. We should accept sinners, but must insist that they repent and change their ways and live according to God's heterosexual intent for all people.

> Homosexuality seems to be a part of God's creation. It should be affirmed and lived out according to the same moral standards as heterosexuality. It is not inherently sinful, although it is capable of being corrupted by sin in the same ways as heterosexuality.

A Lutheran framework for sexual ethics must consider the witness of Scripture and the church's tradition, including their judgments regarding sexual activity between those of the same sex. We also must be open to the implications of new discoveries and experiences of God's creation. These help us understand the meaning of the biblical witness for our own day. We need to ask what will be most faithful and effective for the church's contemporary mission and ministry in the world.

On the one hand, we have heard that homosexual behavior is sin. On the other hand, some confessing Christians testify to the signs of God's gracious love in the lives of gay and lesbian persons. How do we deal with these conflicting messages?

We need to examine assumptions about the Bible's rejection of homosexual behavior, in light of new understandings of homosexuality:

(1) The concept of sexual *orientation* was unknown to the biblical authors. None of the relevant passages refer specifically to homosexual *orientation*. Biblical passages that prohibit or condemn particular same-sex behaviors presumed that all persons are heterosexual by nature.

If we understand that some persons are sexually oriented toward persons of the same sex, is it appropriate to insist that they refrain from expressing their sexuality in ways that are "natural" to them? On what basis should they be discouraged or encouraged to be sexually active? Is it appropriate to suggest that they seek to become and live as if they were heterosexual? Why or why not? What is God's will for us as sexual beings? Does this vary if we are gay or lesbian?

(2) In the ancient Middle East and the Roman world, much of the same-sex activity was exploitative and abusive. That reality affected the biblical view of such activity.

Is it appropriate to draw moral judgments from these passages and apply them to gay or lesbian relationships that are mutually loving? Why or why not? Ought we to make the same judgments about all sexual acts between persons of the same sex? Can the qualities of a committed sexual relationship be present when partners are of the same sex?

(3) Procreation has been viewed as a central purpose of sexuality (e.g., Gen. 1:28—"be fruitful and multiply"), even though other purposes for sexuality are cited in Scripture (e.g., Gen. 2 and Song of Solomon). The inability of a lesbian or gay couple to procreate on their own has been viewed by many as a basis for rejecting their sexual expression. Many churches in this century, including Lutheran, have moved away from viewing the purpose of sexuality primarily in terms of procreation. The church blesses many heterosexual marriages today in which procreation is not intended or possible.

How essential is procreation to the meaning of sexuality? Is the mandate to procreate a sufficient basis for opposing gay and lesbian activity today?

(4) Purity or holiness concerns also have undergirded judgments against same-sex behavior. Impure acts such as sexual activity between persons of the same sex (in Leviticus and Romans) were considered to be repellent in and of themselves. Purity concerns were put in perspective and transformed in the New Testament. Jesus and Paul sought to break down the barriers that purity rules erected between people and between communities.

Are purity concerns sufficient grounds for Christians to reject homosexual relationships today? How should the church respond to those for whom purity concerns continue to operate?

(5) Male-female physical complementarity has been seen as essential for acts of sexual intercourse, for "completing one another," and for becoming "one flesh." The biblical creation stories have been used to reinforce this view based on their assumption that all human beings are by nature heterosexual. However, these stories emphasize the common humanity as well as the differences of male and female. The biblical witness is that we are sexual, relational beings who need one another.

Can God's intention for life together be lived out in female-female and male-male as well as in male-female relationships of sexual intimacy? Why or why not? Can persons of the same sex become "one flesh"? Is there a danger of either ignoring or basing too much on physiological differences?

(6) Sex-role stereotypes that presume a dominant male and a passive female also make it difficult for many people to accept lesbian or gay couples. Biblical passages are sometimes used to reinforce these stereotypes. Two women together may violate our notion that a woman needs a man to complete and to lead her. Two men being intimate and loving may unnerve us because we assume that men compete with rather than complete each other. Many stereotypes about gay men and lesbian women are based on the mistaken notion that same-sex relationships only mimic the traditional sex roles of heterosexual relationships—one partner playing the "masculine" and the other the "feminine" role.

How do your notions of what it means to be male and female relate to your reactions to gay and lesbian relationships? As traditional gender roles change, how might this affect judgments about gay or lesbian relationships?

(7) Although the Gospels nowhere record Jesus speaking on the matter of same-sex relationships, through his words and his actions he communicated a lot about how we should relate to one another.

> What are some of the values and principles which Jesus proposed for ordering our relationships in general? How do these apply to how we should view or live out sexual relationships today?

As we wrestle with the biblical witness, we must distinguish between moral judgments regarding same-sex activity in biblical times and in our own time. In light of the biblical witness we realize we live in the interim where no absolutistic judgments can be drawn. Sexual activity between those of the same sex tended to be linked in the Bible to matters of purity, idolatry, and abuse. The few biblical passages that refer to same-sex activity (with a much different social meaning than today) do not settle the issue. We must turn to the whole biblical witness, centered in Jesus Christ who alone justifies us before God. It is in turning to this focus in the next section that we discover an evangelical basis for addressing this concern today.

Sin, the New Creation, and Gay and Lesbian Relationships

Lutherans have a high regard for what is considered "natural" according to God's law. However, our moral judgments begin with the biblical understanding that we are "naturally inclined" to turn away from God and to sin. No matter what our sexual orientation, we all are afflicted with sin ("all have sinned and fallen short..."). Sin is revealed in our acts and in our attitudes, particularly toward those who are different from us. Lutherans know well the anxiety, insecurity, and fear that plague human beings. We also know how hard we may strive to appear "good" and "righteous," especially out of disdain for those who, from our perspective, clearly fall short. Not only can we mistake society's judgment—or approval—for God's, but we resist God's judgment on our attempts to be righteous. We sometimes misuse God's law or judgment against others as a cover for our own fears and anxieties. When rightly used, however, God's law exposes all the ways we fall short of trusting in God. We all are in need of daily repentence. Jesus Christ challenges our sinful tendencies to rank or judge who is more sinful. The Bible emphasizes that Christ is the one who saves us all from sin.

Through baptism we enter the struggle between the old and the new creation. The law given by Christ—to love God and our neighbor as ourself—guides our lives in the interim. We focus on the suffering and the needs of our neighbors. The marks of the church are not only the word and sacraments but also the witness to the suffering cross of Christ. Those who are most despised become the focus of our care and justice-seeking. As the body of Christ we stand with all who are victims of sin and injustice.

In the midst of the suffering and oppression, we may also find signs of love, hope, and commitment. Some gay men and some lesbian women testify to the loving, life-enhancing character of their committed relationships with one another. Such testimony may challenge some of our past assumptions and understandings.

Is it possible that some committed lesbian or gay relationships might be signs of the transforming love of God's new creation in Christ, a love that is continually crossing old boundaries? Or are they violations of God's intention?

We also know that love and compassion require structure and order. Without order the possibilities for promiscuity and abuse have freer reign. Promiscuity is present in the gay community. It is difficult for faithful love between two people to be sustained over the long-term without social supports and structures, that is, without the ordering function that Lutherans associate with the law. Gay and lesbian relationships have generally lacked such social and legal support. Still, some gay or lesbian couples have enjoyed long-term committed relationships, often in the face of passive if not active opposition.

How might the lack of social protection and recognition for gay relationships encourage promiscuity or short-term commitments among gay people? How should the church respond to gay or lesbian couples who desire the recognition and blessing of their union? Why? How should we respond to those who are sexually active in committed but not monogamous relationships? Should homosexual relationships be judged by any different standards than heterosexual relationships?

Many people will continue to react to homosexuality as simply wrong or repulsive. We often cannot account for why certain behaviors or thoughts attract or repel us. Ongoing study, reflection, and significant conversation with gay and lesbian people are needed. Our feelings, no matter how deep and negative, should not be translated into words or actions that violate the dignity of others. We are accountable for what we say and do.

Does personal disagreement with the lifestyle of a group of people justify discriminatory policies against them? Why or why not? For what public policies affecting gay and lesbian people in society should the church advocate?

For the Faith Community's Consideration

What does it mean for the church to respond to those in our midst who are gay and lesbian? The church should do so not out of fear but out of our central identity in Christ and the new creation that is initiated through him. Because we are the body of Christ, we are called to conform our words and deeds to his boundary-crossing love and inclusive justice. What will best serve God's mission in the world today needs to be a central concern.

Members of this church may not be able to agree on many aspects of homosexuality, but serious consideration should be given to the following:

(1) Lesbian women and gay men are already present in our congregations, schools, workplaces, and neighborhoods. Most of us do not know who they are. If we make comments about homosexuality that condemn all lesbian and gay people as immoral, we may be deeply offending and alienating the person next to us, implying that one's sexual orientation is determinative of one's character.

How should we respond instead?

(2) "Gay-bashing" of all kinds must be resisted and challenged. Name-calling and stereotypes are hurtful. Interpersonal violence is never acceptable. If someone reveals that he or she is gay or lesbian, they have entrusted you with an intimate and vulnerable part of their being.

How would you honor this disclosure if it were shared with you?

(3) Gay and lesbian people, like heterosexual people, are children of God who need the means of race and the community of faith. Our baptism makes us children of God. God does not revoke our baptism when we discover our sexual orientation. A congregation that does not welcome persons whatever their sexual orientation needs to wrestle with basic questions about what it means to be the church.

Are gay men and lesbian women truly welcome in your congregation? Are their gifts recognized and used? Are they encouraged to participate in all the activities of the church in the same ways as heterosexual people? Why or why not?

(4) We all are sinners in need of God's grace. Neither homosexual nor heterosexual people are justified by their sexual orientation but only by the gracious self-giving love of God. We also need to realize that what we personally find repulsive is not necessarily sinful.

In light of the above discussions and the biblical study of chapter two, should homosexuality as we know it today continue to be viewed as sin in ways that heterosexuality is not? Why or why not?

(5) Our sexuality is God's good gift intended to be lived out in loving relationships with others. For some, this may not include a genital relationship with another person. For most, however, this includes a partner of the opposite sex. For those who are homosexual in orientation, this may involve a partner of the same sex.

Should sexual orientation be seen as a gift of God? Why or why not? How should homosexual or heterosexual orientation be viewed theologically? How should homosexual or heterosexual activity be evaluated ethically?

(6) A life of celibacy can be an important witness to the coming reign of God. Yet both St. Paul and the Lutheran Confessions recognized that this gift of the Spirit cannot be required of all.

Is it appropriate to expect all who are homosexual to remain celibate? Why or why not?

(7) This study has emphasized that the fullness of sexuality is to be lived out in stable, committed relationships of love and fidelity. New historical evidence suggests that some same-sex relationships may have been blessed by the church in the past. The church may need to re-examine its position on this matter today.

Is it consistent to hold up the central value of commitment and at the same time deny committed gay and lesbian couples the church's recognition and blessing? Why or why not?

As we deliberate on these and other questions, we need to pray for the guidance of God's Spirit, talk with lesbian and gay persons, and continue to study and discuss.

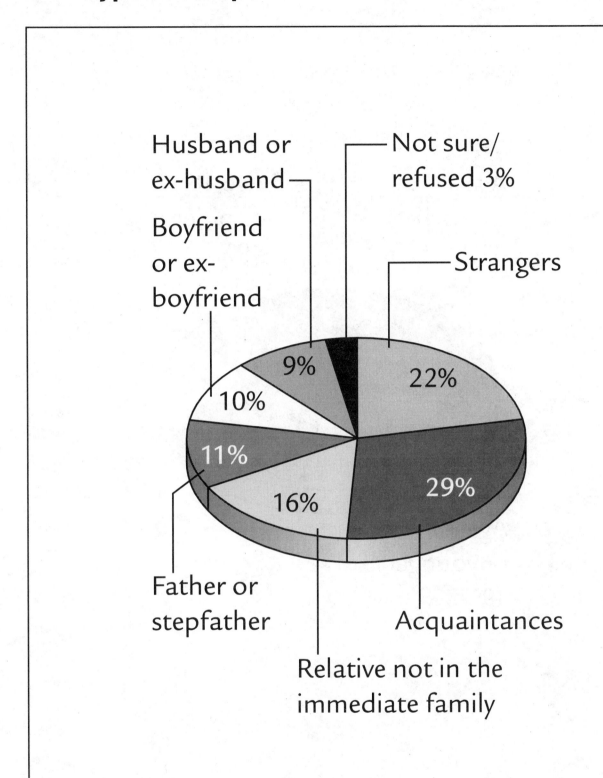

Husband or ex-husband

Boyfriend or ex-boyfriend

Not sure/ refused 3%

Strangers

9%

10%

11%

22%

29%

16%

Father or stepfather

Relative not in the immediate family

Acquaintances

Source: Data from National Victim Center, 1992

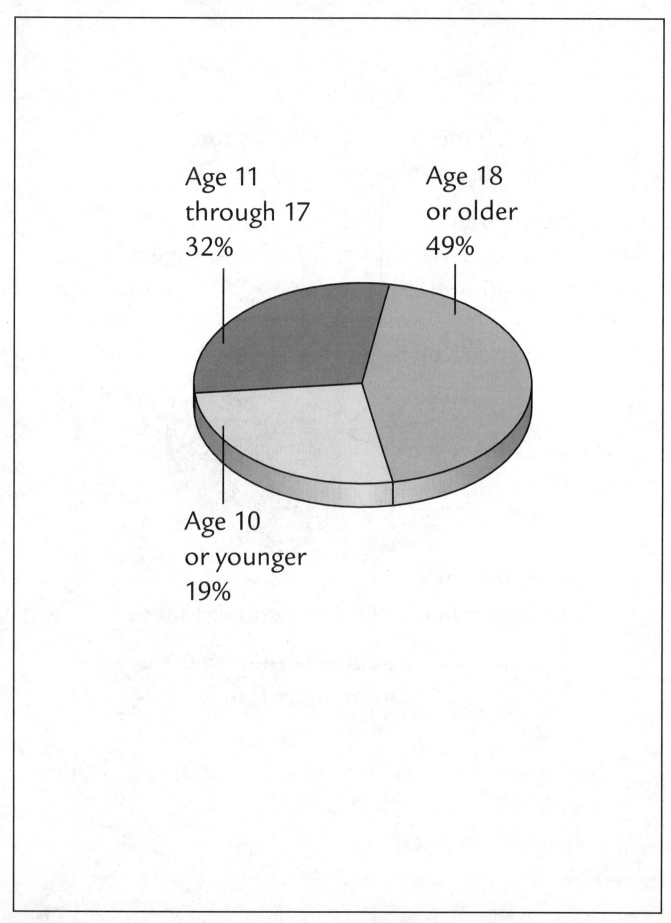

Age 11
through 17
32%

Age 18
or older
49%

Age 10
or younger
19%

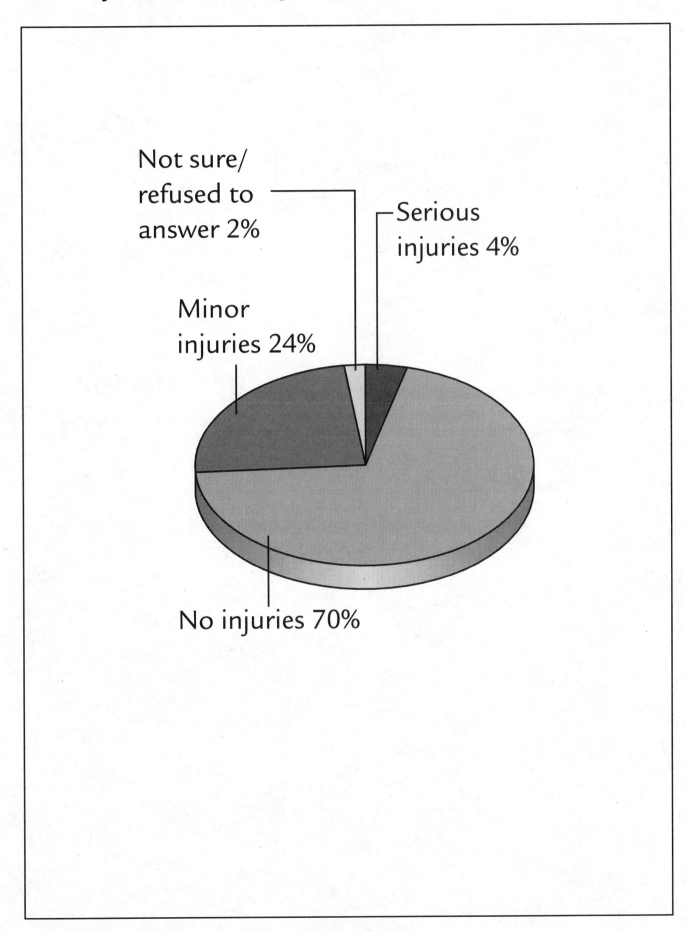

Not sure/refused to answer 2%

Serious injuries 4%

Minor injuries 24%

No injuries 70%

Strong/DeVault/Sayad, *Human Sexuality,* 3rd ed. © 1999 Mayfield Publishing Company

CHAPTER 18

COMMERCIAL SEX: SEXUALLY ORIENTED MATERIAL AND PROSTITUTION

CHAPTER OUTLINE

Sexually Oriented Material in Contemporary America
    Is It Pornography or Erotica? Is It Obscene?
    Sexually Oriented Material and Popular Culture
    The Effects of Sexually Oriented Material
    Censorship, Sexually Oriented Material, and the Law
    Think About It: Rock, Rap, and Righteousness: Censorship and Popular Music

Prostitution
    Females Working in Prostitution
    Males Working in Prostitution
    Prostitution and the Law
    The Impact of HIV/AIDS

LEARNING OBJECTIVES

At the conclusion of Chapter 18, students should be able to:

1. Distinguish the differences in meanings between sexually oriented material, pornography, and erotica.

2. Discuss changing perspectives about pornography, including the role of deviance and moral outrage and the significance of personal response.

3. Discuss the reasons people use sexually oriented material.

4. Evaluate arguments concerning the impact of sexually oriented material on behavior, especially aggression against women and gender discrimination.

5. Discuss child pornography, including its impact on children, laws against it, and debate about its extent.

6. Evaluate the arguments concerning the censorship of sexually oriented material, including legal issues revolving around obscenity as well as popular music.

7. Discuss female prostitution, including motivation and types of prostitution.

8. Discuss male prostitution, including differences between delinquent and gay male prostitutes.

9. Discuss prostitution and the law, including decriminalization, regulation, and the HIV/AIDS epidemic.

10. Recognize and define key terms introduced in the chapter.

DISCUSSION QUESTIONS

Interest in Sexually Oriented Material. Discuss the reasons people read or view sexually oriented material or activities.

Sexual Aggression and Sexually Oriented Material. What evidence is there to link sexual aggression with sexually oriented material? Evaluate and critique the evidence.

Feminism and Censorship. Discuss whether sexually explicit material tends to liberate or subordinate women.

Sexual Objectification. What is sexual objectification? Do women sexually objectify men? Does objectification perform a benign erotic function?

Prostitution. What are the reasons women and men become prostitutes? Is it less stigmatizing to refer to someone as a "sex worker" than as a "prostitute"? Discuss whether prostitution should be decriminalized/regulated.

ACTIVITIES

Defining Pornography and Erotica. On 3 x 5 cards, ask students to anonymously define pornography and erotica. Distribute the cards randomly in small groups for discussion. Ask the group to arrive at a common consensus for each term and report to the class.

Experiences with Sexually Oriented Material. Ask students to anonymously describe their experiences (whether positive, negative, or both) with sexually oriented material. Distribute answers randomly in small groups for discussion. Ask groups to report positive and negative experiences associated with sexually oriented material; write them on the blackboard.

SEX AND POPULAR CULTURE

Activity: Play music or show music videos with sexually explicit, vulgar, or obscene lyrics (there is usually at least one song causing controversy at any particular time). Discuss why some like it and others are offended by it. Discuss whether it should be censored. Discuss larger legal and constitutional issues involved in censorship.

Activity: Ask students to gather material that has been deemed "obscene" in the past and create a table display. It might include "French postcards" from the 1900s, birth control information from the 1920s, and classic nineteenth-century nude paintings.

Discussion: What is the image of prostitutes in Hollywood films? Discuss "Pretty Woman." Many actresses complain about limits of women's roles in the movies, indicating that playing a prostitute is one of the major roles available to them. Why the limited roles? What prominent actresses have played prostitutes? (They include Shirley MacLaine, Jodie Foster, and Julia Roberts.)

Discussion: There is generally less violence in sexually oriented material than in mainstream movies and TV crime shows. Why are censorship efforts directed more toward sexually oriented nonviolent material than toward nonsexual violent material?

Popular Culture Summary Paper. Have students review the popular culture response papers completed during the course, then complete the summary paper (Worksheet 37). Encourage students to share their observations with the class.

Discussion: While censorship of heterosexual sexual activities is diminishing, it continues to be strong regarding gay and lesbian themes and sexual activities. The text presents an illustration from *Daddy's Roommate,* a children's book about a gay man whose son visits him and his partner. It is one of the most censored books in America because some people argue that it violates "traditional family values." Do you think children's books that portray loving gay/lesbian families should be prohibited from schools and libraries?

Discussion: Assuming you were the curator for an art museum, what criteria would you use to select art? Is there any type you would refuse to display? (You may wish to use Robert Mapplethorpe's photography as an example of censoring material for its "homoeroticism.")

HEALTH CONSIDERATIONS

Discussion: Some argue that sexually explicit gay videos and magazines are a valuable form of safe sex for gay men. They are seen as a means for gay men to reaffirm their sexuality in the face of fear and loss due to HIV/AIDS. Do you agree? Why or why not?

Discussion: Discuss the role of male prostitutes and their bisexual/heterosexual clients in transmitting HIV to women.

Discussion: Should prostitution be decriminalized or regulated as a public health measure to encourage STD/HIV testing? Debate pros and cons.

Activity: Role-playing: A health-care worker tries to convince a prostitute to use condoms to prevent STDs and HIV. In both scenarios, the prostitute is resistant. Scenario 1: Health-care worker and female prostitute. Scenario 2: Health-care worker and male prostitute.

GUEST SPEAKERS/PANELS

Invite a sex worker to discuss his or her work and experiences.

Form a student panel to discuss the pros and cons of censorship of sexually oriented material.

SUPPORT MATERIAL

Films and Videos

"History of the Blue Movie" (1984, 75 min., VHS, The Sexuality Library). Chronicles the evolution of the "dirty movie" from the 1920s to the present. Includes scenes from old stag movies, amateur videos, and current films. Explicit.

"Hookers" (1975, 25 min., VHS and 16mm, Multi-Focus, Inc.). A documentary on prostitution. Interviews with several women are interspersed with episodes of their meetings with male clients. Filmed in collaboration with COYOTE, an organization dedicated to changing the economic, political, and legal status of prostitutes.

"Pornography: The Double Message" (1985, 28 min., VHS, Indiana University Audio Visual Center). Deals with how viewers of hard-core pornography perceive women and sex. Uses graphic film clips of violent pornography to demonstrate the nature of the genre.

Bibliography

The books and articles listed below may be helpful for instructors wishing additional background or information on some of the topics covered in this chapter. In addition, the books listed in this chapter's "Suggested Reading" in the textbook may also be useful.

Barry, K. *The Prostitution of Sexuality: The Global Exploitation of Women*. New York: New York University Press, 1995.

Bryant, J., and D. Brown. "Uses of Pornography." In Z. Dolf and B. Jennings (eds.). *Pornography: Research Advances and Policy Considerations*. Hillsdale, NJ: Lawrence Earlbaum Associates, 1989.

Byrne, D., W. A. Fisher, J. Lambreth, and H. E. Mitchell. "Evaluations of Erotica: Facts or Feelings." *Journal of Personality and Social Psychology*, 1974, 29, 111–116.

Davis, M. S. *Smut: Erotic Reality/Obscene Ideology*. Chicago: University of Chicago Press, 1985.

Delacoste, F., and P. Alexander (Eds.). *Sex Work: Writings by Women in the Sex Industry*. Pittsburgh, PA: Cleis Press, 1991.

Dimen, M. "Politically Correct? Politically Incorrect?" In C. S. Vance (ed.). *Pleasure and Danger: Exploring Female Sexuality*. New York: Routledge & Kegan Paul, 1984.

Duncan, D. F., and J. W. Donnelly. "Pornography as a Source of Sex Information for Students at a Private Northeastern University." *Psychological Reports,* June 1991, 68(3, Pt. 1), 782.

Garcia, L. T., and L. Milano. "A Content Analysis of Erotic Videos." *Journal of Psychology and Human Sexuality,* 1990, 3(2), 95–103.

Reiss, I. *An End to Shame: Shaping Our Next Sexual Revolution.* Buffalo, NY: Prometheus Books, 1990.

Rio, L. M. "Psychological and Sociological Research and the Decriminalization or Legalization of Prostitution." *Archives of Sexual Behavior,* April 1991, 20(2), 205–218.

Savitz, L., and L. Rosen. "The Sexuality of Prostitutes: Sexual Enjoyment Reported by 'Streetwalkers'." *Journal of Sex Research,* 1988, 24, 200–208.

Senn, C., and H. L. Radtke. "Women's Evaluations of and Affective Reactions to Mainstream Violent Pornography, Nonviolent Pornography, and Erotica." *Violence and Victims,* Sept. 1990, 5(3), 143–155.

Wallace, J., and M. Mangan. *Sex, Laws, and Cyberspace.* New York: Henry Holt, 1996.

Weisberg, D. K. *Children of the Night.* New York: Free Press, 1990.

WORKSHEET 37

Popular Culture Summary Paper

Looking back on the various popular culture response papers that you have completed, pick one type of media from which you have done the majority of reporting and respond to the following:

Type of media selected (music, film, television, etc.):

Generalized themes you observed:

Your feelings about these themes:

What impact (if any) does this type of media have on your attitudes, values, and behaviors? (Respond to this question as honestly as you can.)

Attitudes:

Values:

Beliefs:

What have you learned as a result of your observations?

Strong/DeVault/Sayad, *Human Sexuality,* 3rd ed. © 1999 Mayfield Publishing Company. Chapter 18